NOAH'S ARK IS STRANDED

NOAH'S ARK IS STRANDED

by
Björn Berglund

Photographs by
Ingemar Berling

Translated from the Swedish by
Sheila La Farge

A Merloyd Lawrence Book
DELACORTE PRESS/SEYMOUR LAWRENCE

The photographs, including the cover, were taken by Ingemar Berling except for the following by Jan Rietz, pages 4, 5, 22,23,39, 44–45, 55, 77, 120, 121, 124, upper picture, 133, 136–37, 164, 165, 166, 173, 175, 176–77, 181, 182, 189, 190–91, 197, 198, 200, and Stig A. Nilsson, pages 62–63.

First published in Swedish by Forum Publishers, Stockholm, under the title *Noaks ark har strandat i gräset*. Copyright © 1973 by Björn Berglund

English translation copyright © 1976 by Dell Publishing Co., Inc.

All rights reserved. No part of this book may be reproduced in any form or by any means without the prior written permission of the Publisher, excepting brief quotes used in connection with reviews written specifically for inclusion in a magazine or newspaper.

Manufactured in the United States of America
First American printing

Book designed by Elaine Golt Gongora

Library of Congress Cataloging in Publication Data

Berglund, Björn E
  Noah's ark is stranded.

  Translation of Noaks ark har strandat i gräset.
  "A Merloyd Lawrence book."
  1. Ecology—Africa. 2. Nature conservation—Africa. I. Title.
QH194.B4713 1976   333.9′5′09676   76–18212
ISBN 0–440–06434–1

Ecology teaches
the dependence of
the living organism
upon the environment
and their
harmonious interaction.

CONTENTS

A Green Prologue
x

The Humility in a Giraffe's Eyes
1

The Rhinoceros and the Minister for the Environment
17

A Single Blade of Grass
37

Shade Is the Tree's Thanks for Help
57

Lions Have a Hard Time
75

Perhaps My Favorite Animal
96

A Very Big Problem
117

Two Gulps of Water a Year
137

A Jungle Utopia
169

The Example of Lake Nakuru
187

Bibliography
207

Index
209

This book is based primarily on impressions from visits to a number of East African national parks. The best known are located on this map.

KENYA
1. Nairobi National Park. *Nairobi is the capitol of Kenya and the center of East Africa. The United Nations' Environmental Secretariat is there. From its multistory building in the city center, one can see wild giraffes, antelopes and ostriches in Nairobi National Park. There are also lions, cheetahs and occasionally leopards, zebras, gnus, water buffaloes, impalas, Thomson's gazelles, Grant's gazelles and many other animals.*
2. Amboseli National Park. *Borders on Tanzania. Kilimanjaro, Africa's highest mountain, rises against the sky with its snow-covered peak in the distance. Here one encounters elephants, buffaloes, giraffes and some of the few rhinos still surviving. The animals are used to humans. They let us approach them.*
3. Tsavo National Park. *Two parks, East and West Tsavo. East Tsavo is wilder: one can meet the fantastic long-necked gerenuk (giraffe gazelle) and perhaps the shy lesser kudu. West Tsavo's landscape is more pleasant. Tsavo is above all the land of the elephant and the rhino.*
4. Lake Nakuru National Park. *An astonishing bird sanctuary.*

TANZANIA
5. Serengeti National Park. *Paradise may not have looked like the Serengeti. All the same, the Serengeti is paradise. Its savanna is varied and beautiful and most of Africa's large animals are very common here.*
6. Ngorongoro National Park. *A volcanic crater full of wild creatures.*
7. Lake Manyara National Park. *At noon in this game reserve by the lake, lions like to lie and rest in the trees.*

UGANDA
8. Ruwenzori National Park. *Formerly called Queen Elizabeth Park, this extends along Lake Edward and the border of Zaire and the rain forests. Here the hippo is more common than elsewhere.*
9. Kabalega National Park. *Formerly called Murchison Park. Famous for its white rhinos. The kob antelope and the incredibly beautiful oribi are also common. The banks of the Victoria Nile teem with crocodiles and hippos.*

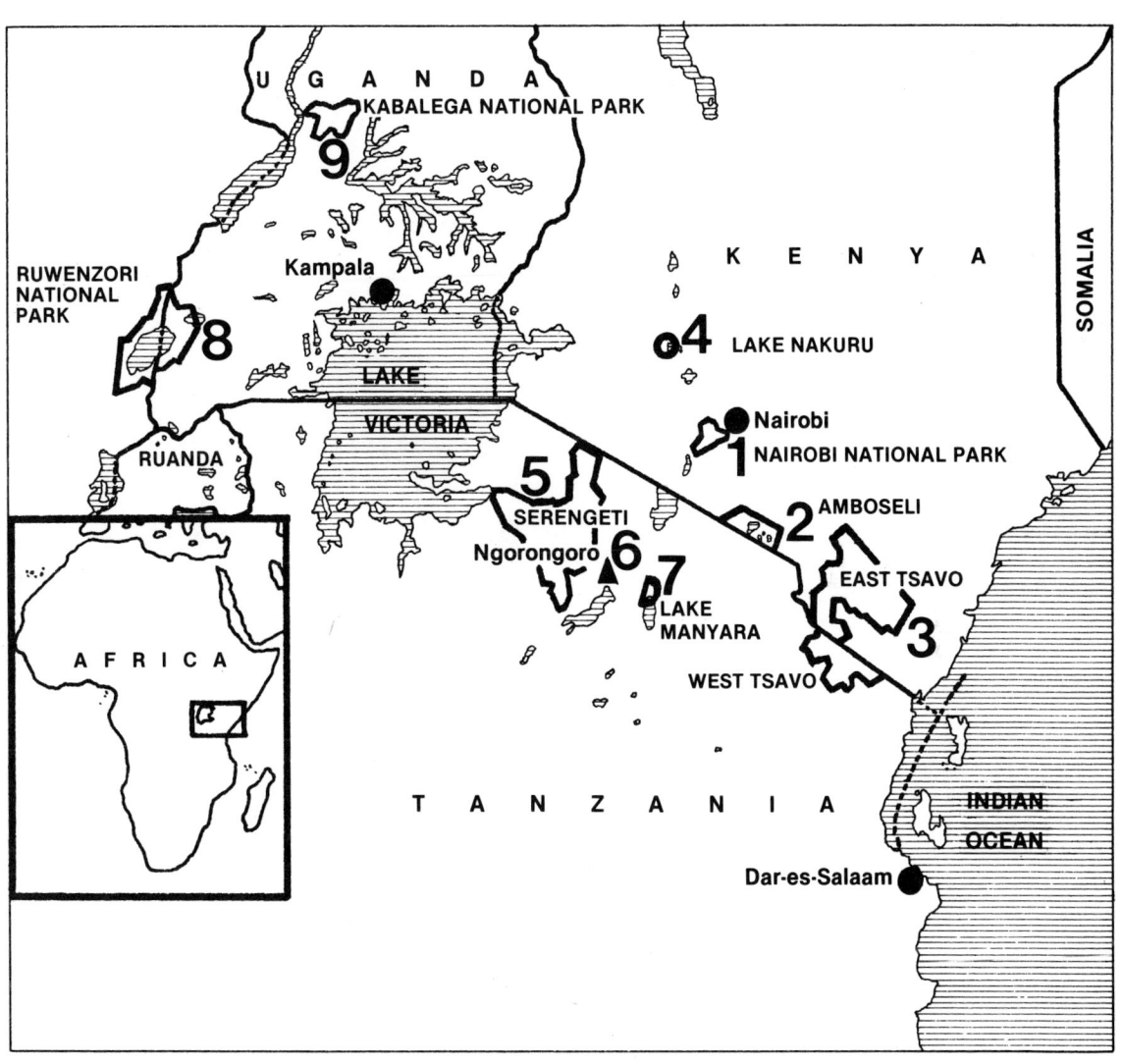

A GREEN PROLOGUE

Evolution is going haywire. Humanity is being driven or driving itself to destruction. So they say. Are they right, these "prophets of doom"? (Brave men and women strong enough not to be taken in by the dream of the good life.)

They have sowed their abstract visions that jingle with megawatts and increased production percentages. Their grim visions weep without tears, bleed without blood; and yet they may be true—for that very reason.

The United Nations' World Conference on the Human Environment confirmed that on solemn occasions even people in high political positions allow plenty of scope for idealism.

That's not bad. Perhaps it's something to pin our hopes on. It may well be all we have left.

Otherwise, the world conference gave no clear indication whether those attending had hidden resources of strong feeling to support their idealism. They were all apparently practical people with know-how. But practical reasoning is not enough if we are to save our world.

We also have to be able to look deep in the eye of a meadow flower and understand the cells in a blade of grass as they speak to us through a gazelle.

We are waiting for a prophet to come along with flowers in his hair who will tell us how to live! ("We will live like the rhinoceros. Our future society will resemble the rain forest.")

The great, famous, storybook creatures—elephants, giraffes, zebras, antelope—established themselves comfortably in the savanna grasslands after they were let out of the ark. In their midst, we will find that answers are in fact given to some of the desperate questions about the future of the good life on earth.

It is easy to learn from this and change the world. Out there in the green grass, Noah's ark is still waiting to be launched again.

THE HUMILITY IN A GIRAFFE'S EYES

And God blessed Noah and his sons, and said unto them, Be fruitful, and multiply, and replenish the earth. And the fear of you and the dread of you shall be upon every beast of the earth, and upon every fowl of the air, upon all that moveth upon the earth, and upon all the fishes of the sea; into your hand are they delivered.

Genesis 9:1–2

The humility in a giraffe's large eyes, always looking down at us, can stir our conscience. Our conscience is bad. Humans and giraffes evolved together on the savanna. The giraffe acquired a long neck and excellent vision. Humans instead evolved a large thinking brain and the ability to walk on two legs. The giraffe's good vision is no longer enough to insure its survival. It is dependent upon humans using their special abilities in the right way.

When we least expect it, a giraffe appears among the trees in the savanna. It looks down at us with a haughty and reproachful expression in its shiny dark eyes. We doff our safari hats and apologize. What is the giraffe thinking? Could we have hurt it?

Some data on giraffes:
· Height: five–six meters. Tallest of all animals.
· Body length: two meters. Shortest of all mammals in proportion to its height.
· Weight of the male: 1–1.5 tons.
· Frequency of heartbeat: 150 beats a minute (170 when running), compared with the cow's heart that pounds a pitiful 17 times a minute.
· Gives birth standing. At birth, the baby weighs 80 kilos and tumbles into the world with a thud from a height of 1.5 meters.
· Galloping speed: 50 kilometers an hour, when it is in a hurry.
· Walking pace: 15 kilometers an hour.
· Eats most of the time (six–eight hours out of every twelve). Eighty-five percent of its food consists of small leaves (150 kilos a week).
· Sleeps uneasily, five minutes at a time, a total of perhaps two hours out of twenty-four (but it also dozes while standing).
· The giraffe's best friend is the oxpecker, a bird that climbs like a woodpecker up its back, over its face and ears and everywhere, picking off parasites with its bloodred beak. With these birds along, the giraffe dares to sleep at noon. When danger threatens, the oxpecker's shrill whistlings wake it up.

We're in the Serengeti, the fantastic national

park in Tanzania. We are among the tourists who travel to East Africa in ever-increasing numbers these days, mainly to meet the giraffes and other storybook creatures. Even before the age of three, every child learns what an elephant, a rhinoceros, a hippo, a zebra and a giraffe look like.

We learn to identify our own behavior, habits and values in their characteristics. We don't learn to recognize real elephants in the storybook world, but rather a human elephant wearing trousers and suspenders, who drives around in a white sports car and is called Babar. Once in the wild, we've never had any trouble disregarding those human qualities that we've added to animals in fiction. On the African savanna, giraffes and elephants became soulless, dangerous beasts that were "put down" by European and American intruders for pleasure and profit.

Those humans forgot nursery-tale happiness. Between 1880 and 1910, more than

To the human male, all giraffes look like beautiful females. The shapely males need to compete with each other constantly to demonstrate their ranking order in the herd and to vie for the females' favors. But the battle between males for leadership has evolved into a lovely ritual and one rarely sees a violent fight. A head equipped with horns is a dangerous instrument. Often, however, as in these pictures, two males would rather caress each other than fight. Tenderness between males often leads to a pure sort of homosexuality. In fact, among giraffes love between males appears more common than between males and females.

two million elephants were shot to death in Africa, mostly for the ivory—this was before plastic—and that slaughter secured the colonialists' place on the Africans' land.

All the same, the elephant still exists, and so does the giraffe. Neither species is threatened by extinction. Not yet. They can be saved for the future if we humans learn to understand the conditions under which we and they live, what the threat to them and to us is like, why it arose and how it can be avoided.

But how can you make contact with a giraffe?

Two males come alongside each other, stand still, cheek to cheek, but that's not an expression of tenderness. They wiggle their ears. Then suddenly one of them delivers an uppercut with its skull.

Its skull weighs 13 kilos.

They use their heads like hammers on the long shafts of their necks. Usually this is a mild, bloodless sport. The giraffes' horns are imbedded in soft skin for safety's sake. But this boxing can be very violent. One of the world's few giraffe experts, Anne Christine Innis, reports a battle that ended when one male fell to the ground unconscious and lay there like a wreck for 20 minutes, after which time it rose on trembling legs and presumably hobbled off groggily among the trees.

With luck, a tourist will see this head-boxing on his safari in the Serengeti. In a way, I think that experiences like this increase our respect for giraffes and help bridge the tragic gap of misunderstanding that humans put between themselves and other animals. Head-boxing is the male giraffe's way of winning and demonstrating leadership in a herd. It is also a gauge of strength in the competition for females—rather the way human males show off for girls' favors with modern variants today.

Now we're lying on the edge of the swimming pool at Lobo Wildlife Lodge, a luxury hotel on the highest peak (2,156 meters) in the highlands that form the Serengeti. Tasteful, exciting architecture blends the modern buildings unobtrusively into the side of the mountaintop. Far beneath us, zebras, buffaloes and a few giraffes wander about. Group tours from travel agencies all around the world often stop here. We're lucky; it's a wonderful place. Today most of the guests at Lobo Wildlife Lodge are Germans.

A short distance away, just outside the national park, lie the ruins of Fort Ikoma—today a stylish hotel. From its walls tourists practiced sharpshooting at the "dumb and ill-tempered Negroes" during the time Tanganyika was known as German East Africa, when scattered groups of nomads and hunters struggled to maintain their existence in what is now the Serengeti.

Now the Serengeti belongs to the wild animals. Economically, this national park, like most of the others in East Africa, serves to draw foreign currency into the state's treasury from the tourists of rich countries.

In 1958, 14,000 people from the outside world spent two- or three-week holidays in East Africa. In 1970, the number had increased to more than 100,000. The Serengeti had 60,000 visitors in 1972. Here money can be made from unspoiled nature, and it is a fact that today, even if only the animals of the Serengeti earn any income and pay for themselves, the national park can be saved. The park is slightly larger than the state of Connecticut, and planters press against the western border of the game reserve with legitimate demands for more land as their population increases.

I am served a beer beside the pool at Lobo Wildlife Lodge and enjoy it immensely, as though I were not in Africa but rather in Germany or Sweden or America.

Fourteen million people live in Tanzania, about 95 inhabitants per square kilometer. Ninety-five percent live in the country, but two-thirds of that land is dry, underdeveloped bush, most of it infected with tsetse flies which spread sleeping sickness, making it unfit for either livestock or humans. The population increases 2.7 percent annually. In proportion to its present level of development, Tanzania is overpopulated. Seventy-five percent of the adults can neither read nor write. The daily protein consumption is 60 grams per person, the bare minimum for survival, and this is only a mean average, veiling whole regions of severe malnutrition. The average life span is 40 years.

This average Tanzanian is hungry. He is one of those spawned by the continuing population explosion. He takes a plot of earth.

He is poor. He cannot afford to fertilize the land. He doesn't have time to let the earth rest. He destroys his soil.

He does not know why this happens. He can neither read nor write. He has yet to be given the opportunity of learning agricultural science, never mind ecology.

He cannot understand that giraffes must live too. He is hungry, and besides, he may never have seen a giraffe.

He must be freed from the burden of injustices.

We expect him to understand that future life must also be assured. We insist that he understand that living conditions for his grandchildren on earth are determined by what is done today. None of which he is allowed to decide. Instead, it is all negotiated by the rich, by the people in power, that small handful. Poor people are always the victims. Every human who has enough to eat does so at the expense of at least two who are starving. The distribution of the world's resources is that unjust.

But does this have anything to do with giraffes?

The German tourists and I loll there on the mountaintop in our bathing suits, looking at the giraffes through our binoculars. We tell each other how fantastic this is, a real paradise. How fortunate the world is to possess such riches! How can we prevent the extinction of the rhinoceros? What can we do to make sure that in the future the enormous herds of gnus will be able to wander

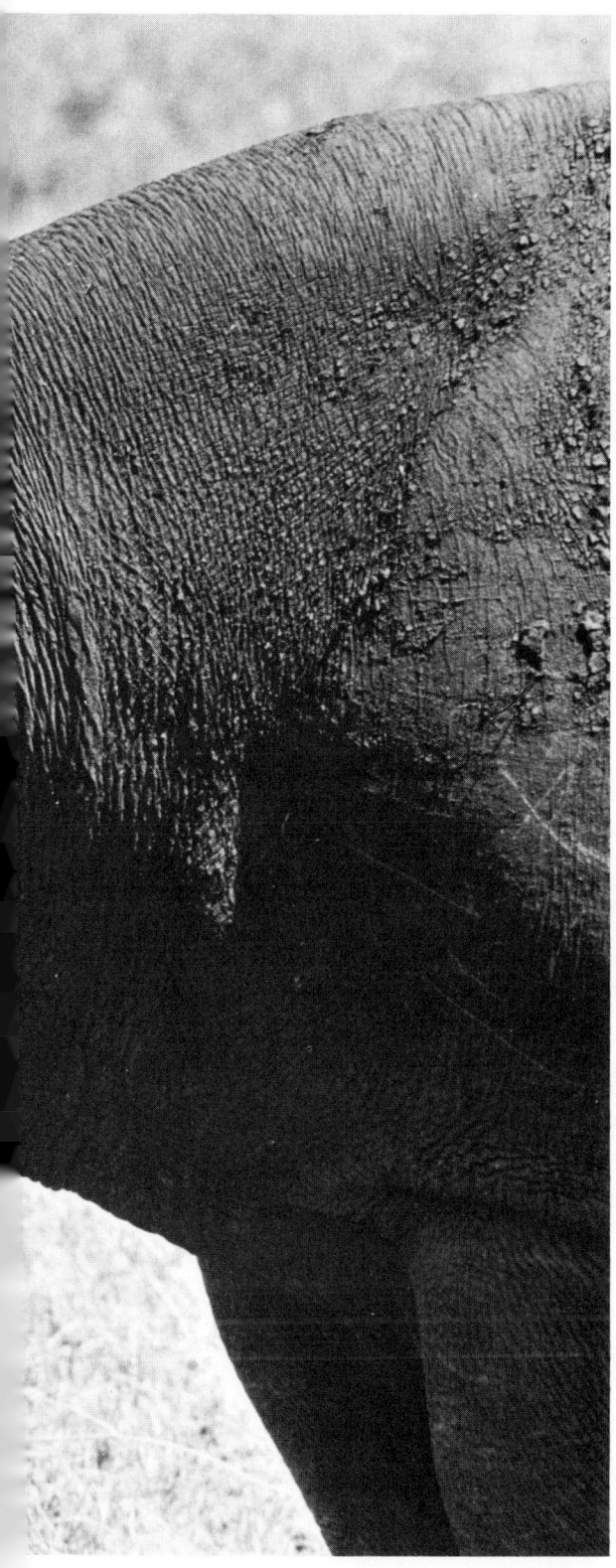

freely over the sufficiently large ecological area that their subsistence requires?

We say it's a disgrace ("eine Schändlichkeit," the Germans say) to the world that poachers break into the Serengeti game reserve at night and kill zebra and buffalo. The Germans hope that the penalties will be severe for the almost 200 people who land in jail every year.

And I take out the U.N.'s environmental declaration, thinking that perhaps a solution is sketched in Principle 19, which states that:

> education in environmental matters, for the younger generation as well as adults, giving due consideration to the underprivileged, is essential in order to broaden the basis for an enlightened opinion and responsible conduct . . . in protecting and improving the environment in its full human dimension.

Then I found Principle 8 which reads that "economic and social development is essential . . . for creating conditions on earth that are necessary for the improvement of the quality of life."

That's enough. I feel sure that I've heard

Very often when a rhino is speared to death in Amboseli National Park, its horn is removed. A rhino's horn sells for a high sum. Why? Look at its shape! Phallic worship combined with old legends about the rhino's fabulous sexual powers—their mounting can actually last for 40 minutes—has lead to the false notion that powdered rhinoceros horn increases sexual potency.

it all before. Of course, this also involves the relationship between humans and giraffes. Similarly, it involves condemning the methods of a small rich minority in an affluent area who ruthlessly grab ever more of the common resources (calling this "economic development"). Meanwhile, if they have time, they hypocritically debate a possible distribution of a portion of humanity's resources in a more equitable way—while the beer gets warm on the terrace of Lobo Wildlife Lodge.

How can we even consider whether the animals in the developing countries can be saved, when not even human survival can be guaranteed?

Human beings dominate the earth and determine its future, and the animals are inescapably in our hands. They will give in to our demands; their territories will be destroyed. No fencing of land, no national park rules, can save those animals we think we

---

The preceding picture was of a black (hooklipped) rhino. This white (square-lipped) rhino and her calf are an endangered species. Patiently and without appreciably changing, the white rhino has borne its unique body over the African savannas for perhaps 5,000,000 years. It has managed to escape the expanding, changing demands of humans and the environment for a long time. Of the large mammal species that evolved with the rhino long before humans, roughly half gradually became extinct during the first 10,000 years following man's appearance in the community.

love, until we have learned to love human beings too.

Giraffes run the risk of being left mutilated and bleeding beside the road down which we're rattling on our way to destruction. But they're not the only victims. The sacrifice of human beings will be much larger.

Our dominion has its disadvantages. We have the power to destroy ourselves as well as our living environment. This power of ours is unparalleled. But can we also save our world?

Humans and animals keep pace; human poverty creates poverty for animals. There is only one way to insure prosperous wildlife for the future. That is to create prosperity for human beings.

In the districts of the Amboseli National Park in Kenya, the nomadic population increases by 3 percent a year. This results in a reduction of the relative yield of milk produced by the nomads' cattle. In order to guarantee their health and survival at the end of the dry season, when the grass is poor and the milk yield consequently low, the people are obliged to buy the nourishment they lack. Since their entire capital is bound up in their livestock, this necessitates selling some of their animals. But this would reduce their secure means of support. So instead, they steal into the Amboseli game reserve and kill a few rhinos with spears, cut off the horns and sell them illegally.

Fifteen rhinos were killed in Amboseli between 1967 and 1970. The hunting still goes on, since the nomads still have to worry about providing for themselves. If the killing continues at this same rate, the last rhino will have disappeared from Amboseli by 1977. Whatever happens, it has already gone too far. There's no longer any possibility of saving the rhino in Amboseli.

Now attempts are being made to improve the nomads' situation. This example shows that it is necessary to improve human living conditions if you want to save animals from extinction. Fencing in is not enough. No game and poaching supervision, however militant, would change the poverty that threatens the animals with extinction.

Just outside of the Serengeti is Olduvai Gorge. There our human ancestors lived more than 2,000,000 years ago in a landscape that looked much the way it does today. This land around the Serengeti may be our basic home ground. In contrast to Europe and Asia where, during the past millions of years, humans were temporarily hindered in their advance or chased away by severe climatic changes, here in East Africa, there have always been some areas where the climate and water supply have made it possible for humans and animals to live and evolve uninterruptedly.

That's why the fauna is so unbelievably rich and complex—because it is old.

It began in the forest. Once all of Africa

may have been one dense forest. Giraffes walked in the forest, but they didn't have long necks then. We swung by our arms among the lianas and munched raw baby birds and grubs. A species of giraffe, the okapi, still lives in the forest, or rather, after a phase of living as a savanna animal it has once more become a forest creature. The okapi with its short neck is virtually the same after 40,000,000 years, since the forest has kept it in constant security all that time, while the giraffe has adjusted to new conditions outside the forest. That happened when the climate changed and the forest thinned out. The forest was replaced

The Masai have killed many of the remaining rhinos in Amboseli National Park. Other poachers there use different methods, but the Masai hunt with spears.

by the savanna, and the savanna, stretching out before me from the terrace by the pool, is where humans evolved their ability to walk on two legs. The giraffe got a long neck instead.

We and the giraffe both adapted to the savanna environment. We humans seldom consider how much we have in common with animals. The way we are connected

with the earth, by our evolution and our needs, is no different from the way they are connected with it. We have similar origins. We are part of the same creation. How can we imagine that we can live according to our own laws? We must look around with open eyes—for a few brief instants dare to see the world around us with the humility in a giraffe's eyes.

("What a blue-eyed romantic this author is! He imagines that knowledge about life and life's laws is more important than integral calculus. Does he really believe that there'll be justice in the world if we just go out and pat the giraffes?")

Well, at least give it a try! Other ways are impractical right now. For over 2,000,000 years, humans and animals and flowers have evolved together—on the Serengeti plains and since then over the entire globe. It was when we separated ourselves drastically from our environment that the destruction became decisive and fatal. So then, what is more natural than to try to discover the rules for survival written in nature? We were there when they were first established. We can't get advice for the future anywhere else.

Perhaps paradise still exists. A dizzying thought. But the experience of 2,000,000 years clearly tells us—memory is unfathomable—that the day when, because of our incompetence and forgetfulness, giraffes, zebras and antelope no longer exist on earth, time will have run out for humans too.

Is that why the giraffe looks down at us reproachfully? ∎

THE RHINOCEROS AND THE MINISTER FOR THE ENVIRONMENT

This time the photographer decided to retreat, although the rhino seems to run at a human more from curiosity than irritation. A rhino very seldom attacks. It is nearsighted and wants to check whether a human is near, which it learns best from scent. As soon as it picks up the scent, the rhino turns to one side and runs off into the bush. Notice how its ears stand up like funnels to catch every sound. Its nostrils also seem to be sniffing.

Cautiously the black rhinoceros, also called the hook-lipped rhino, pokes its incredible head into the bush. It eats mostly bushes. In several national parks, the rhino is frightened of people, because even when it is in the protection of the game reserve, humans are still the rhino's mortal enemies. (It has hardly any other enemies and is peaceable when left alone.)

However, if you manage to get very near a rhino and its bush, if you succeed in approaching upwind so that your unpleasant human scent drifts in another direction, and if the buffalo weaverbirds happen to be silent for a second, then you just might hear how a rhino bites and chews. Just listen to how well it chews its food! See how elegantly it eats! It sticks its sharp snout into the bush and clips off, let's say, one little twig. It chews calmly and quietly and swallows (obviously) before stylishly trimming the next good cigar. And so forth.

An enlightened human notices that the rhino never nibbles more of its bushes than it needs to live the good life. But few humans have tried to understand where the limit is for the good life for ourselves and our community. Our over-consumption of food stuffs and material objects has become a threat to our very existence.

People who have assumed the responsibility for our part of the environment in the critical seventies cannot or will not understand this. "We have to increase our productivity to create still better reforms and still

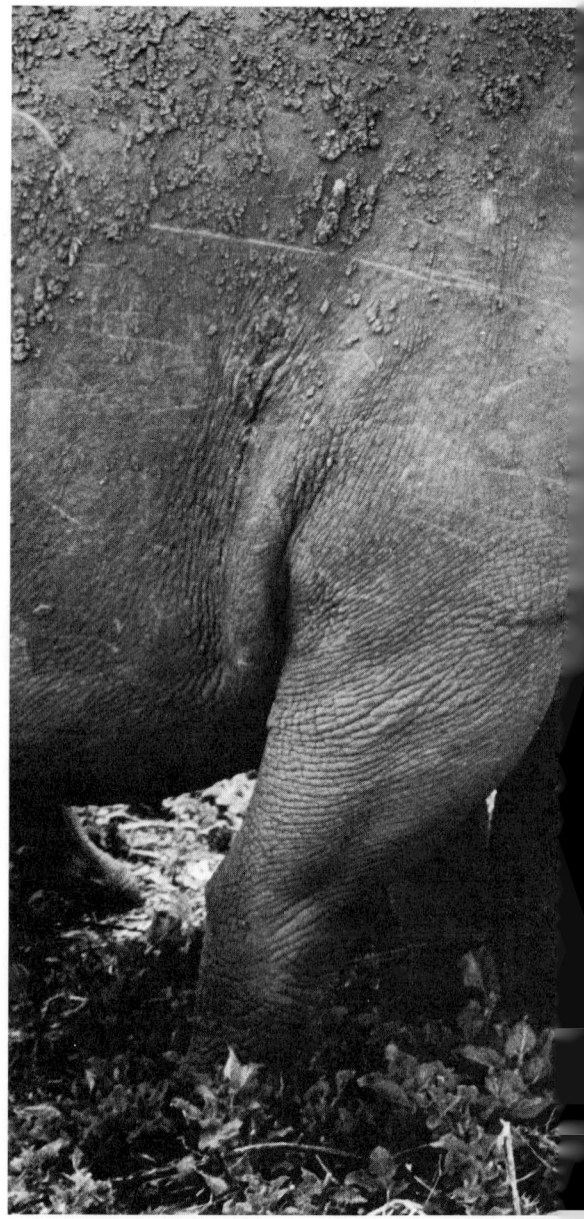

The rhino is a solitary creature. The only lasting bond exists between mothers and their young. Here two walk together grazing at the bottom of Ngorongoro Crater. The white rhino is a grass-eater, while the black rhino eats bushes. If you look closely at the picture you will see that the vegetation is dominated by small shoots of bushlike plants which the black rhino likes.

FOLLOWING PAGE:
Here's dinner served up for a giraffe or a rhino. The acacia thorns are needle-sharp and longer than the leaves that they protect. Both rhinos and giraffes eat these twigs with great relish, though they first select new twigs on which the thorns are not yet completely hardened.

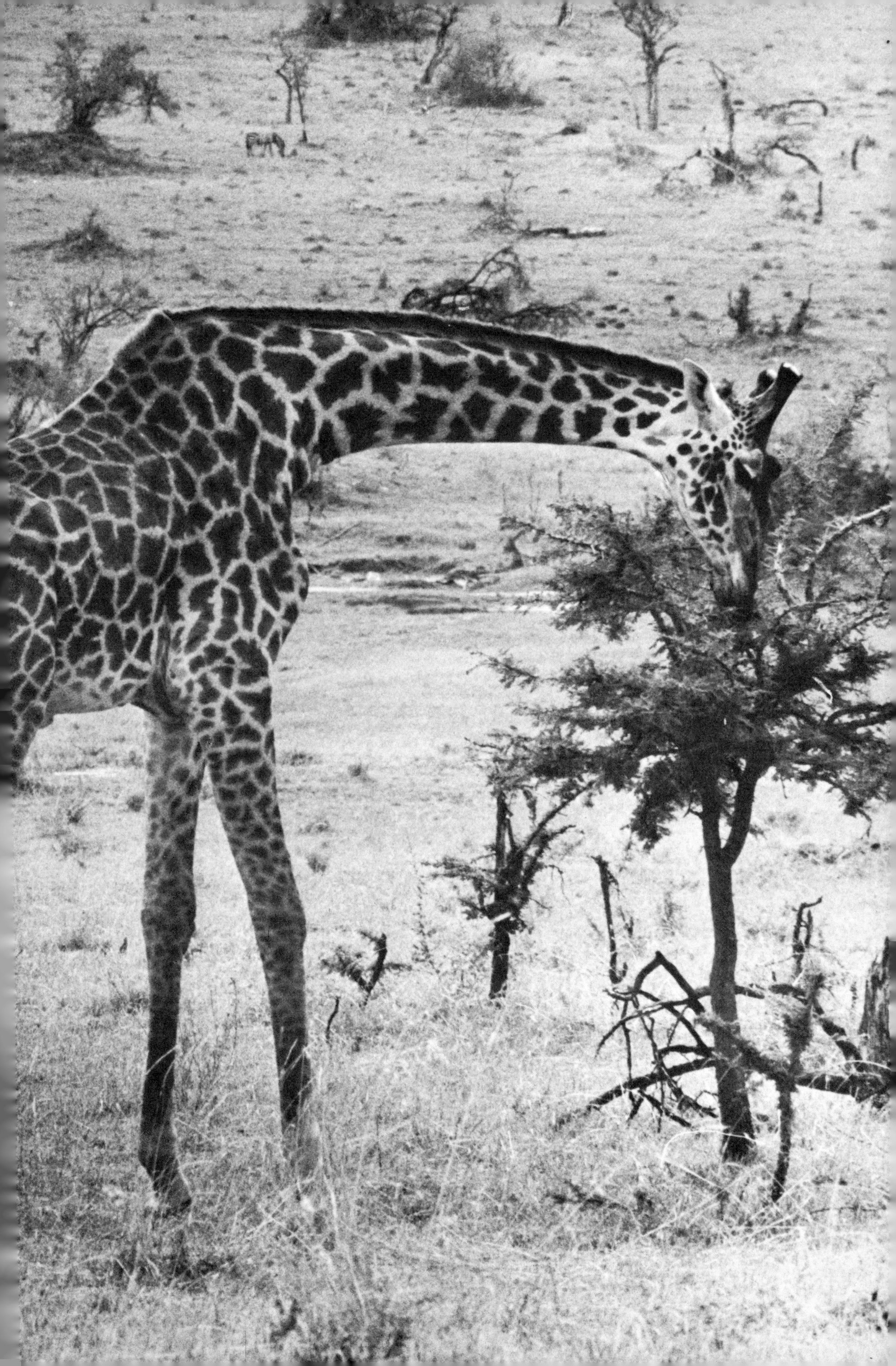

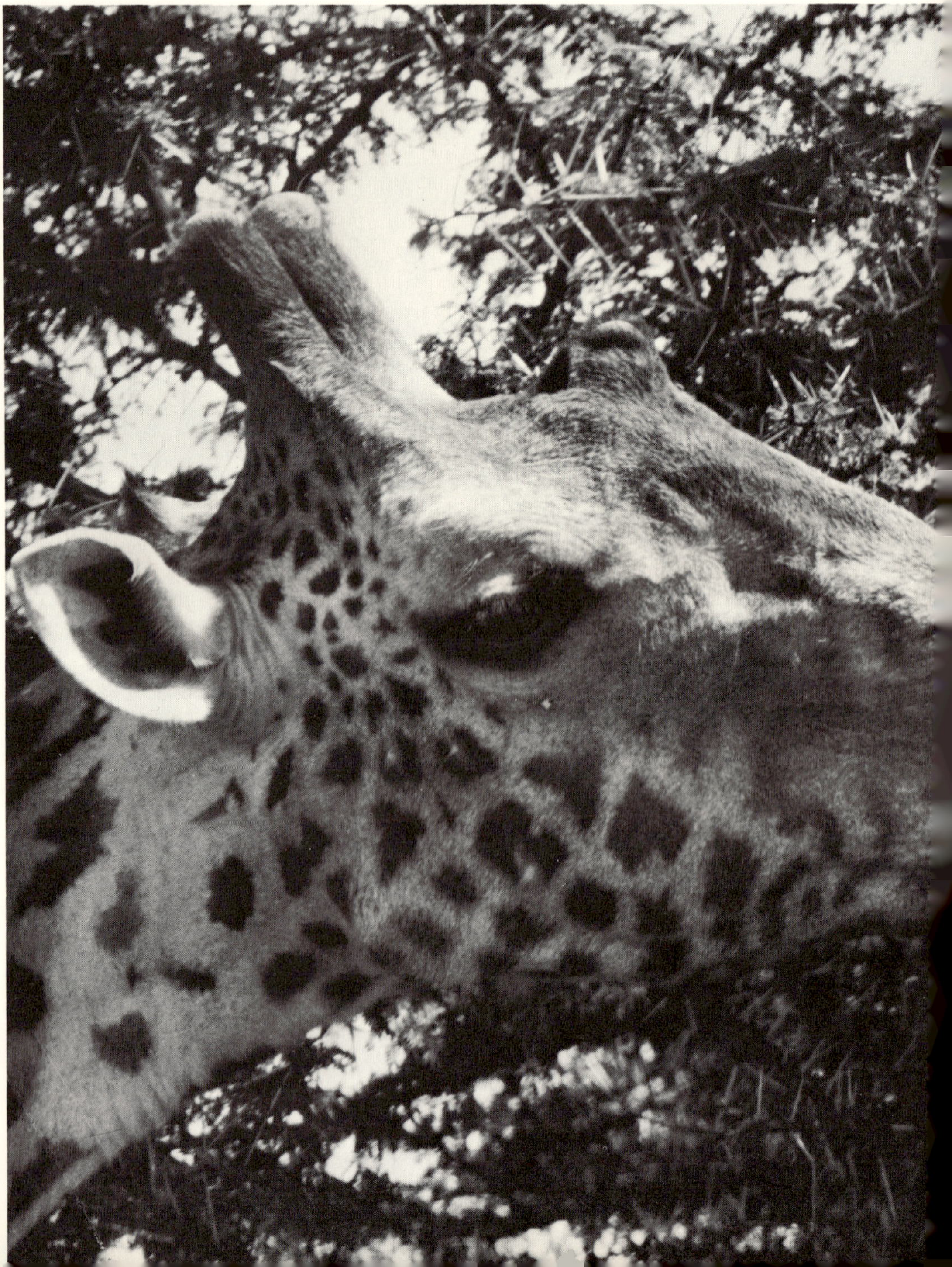

Thorns are one way the acacia protects itself against being eaten up by giraffes. Trees and tree-eating animals have evolved together. It is in both their interests to avoid exploitation.

Sticking out its tongue, which can measure four decimeters, the giraffe grabs a twig. Its tongue and lips have evolved a hard rubbery protective surface against thorns.

In addition to thorns, the low-growing whistling thorn, easily reached from all sides by browsing herbivores, has evolved a kind of gall that serves as a dwelling for stinging ants. These ants bite and irritate the animals that browse too long on any one tree.

better resources in order to improve the environment we live in," said a Swedish environmental minister on February 4, 1973, and the environmental ministers in all the other affluent countries say the same.

If he felt a twinge of hesitation, it was well concealed in that beautiful speech he gave.

I'll spell this out more clearly.

This is how one rhino in Tsavo National Park spent a day, observed from dawn to dusk by the Swiss research couple, Rudolf Schenkel and Lotte Schenkel-Hulliger:

6:30–8:10	Eats and moves slowly northward.
8:10–8:30	Follows an animal track without eating.
8:30–10:05	Leaves the trail and eats persistently without moving in any definite direction.
10:05–10:15	Walks over to a tree and remains standing there in the shade.
10:15–10:30	Leaves the tree for a short walk. Returns.
10:30–3:55	Lies down and rests.
3:55–4:00	Gets up, stands still, takes a few steps almost in place, then lies down again.
4:00–5:50	Lies under the tree.
5:50–6:30	Gets up, starts eating and goes on eating until nightfall.

The research team stresses that the rhino's daily rhythm is not at all stereotyped. This rhino's day may not be typical but one thing is obvious: when the rhino was not eating the bushes, they were spared. The rhino did nothing in particular, except walk slowly north and rest under a tree, for a total of eight hours and five minutes out of the twelve daylight hours. Its productivity lasted three hours and fifty-five minutes.

A famous ecologist, Charles Elton—a pioneer and very perceptive man—pointed out in one of his publications that many wild animals "spend an unexpectedly large proportion of their time doing nothing at all, or at any rate, nothing in particular."

This is important and worth remembering about the rhino as well as other animals. Fighting over territory, struggling for existence, competing over resources, are exceptional states in many (most?) animal communities. Humans are quick to see these kinds of behavior as typical in nature. People want to see their own unrest, their own inequitable striving, their embittered ethics of competition played out in their environment, so that their own asocial behavior might be justified throughout creation (thus confirming the notion that humans are masters of their situation and legitimate lords of everything else besides).

But in the jungle, no "laws of the jungle" prevail. The struggle for existence more closely resembles training before a championship sports event. No small elite is formed, but rather teams of individuals train together, knowing and respecting each other's abilities and skillfully avoiding confrontations.

Inactivity is a rule in such situations. This has a great survival value. Those who rest conserve their energy, don't squander their resources more than they have to or put themselves in unnecessarily risky situations. Ecology teaches us that the environment is as important as the people and all the animals who live in that environment. The blades of grass in a field and the soil under the grass must be treated with the same care as the butterflies, rabbits, sheep and people who live off the field. Similarly, people now feel that starvation and poverty are conditions that violate human rights. Starvation and poverty are caused by lack of resources. But many people live in excessive luxury. The resources exist. Those who have the resources overconsume them "to create still better reforms and still better resources" (for themselves).

The lesson of ecology that started the universal environmental debate has been only partially understood by environmental ministers and a handful of other people in important positions in the world. They have understood that natural resources (environment) make people rich, just as the rhino is rich in an environment with a wealth of bushes. But they don't seem to want to understand that lack of resources makes people poor and life miserable, and that when natural resources are used up, the environment will no longer be able to make people wealthy.

The environmental minister's speech was irresponsible because he didn't try to talk about how great the scope is for reform or about problems of future productivity in Sweden and throughout the global human community. His speech was carefully nuanced but all he offered his fellow citizens was blind faith.

And no one else, aside from the clergy, is trying to stake out a path to save humans in their environment. Hopeful and confident, we kneel humbly before the sacred sphinx in an expanding desert called progress.

The idol of progress does not permit a second thought. Whatever can be exploited will be exploited now, instantly, by whoever manages to get the resources to exploit.

Why haven't we learned the rules of exploitation? Why isn't part of our education devoted to the ethics of exploitation? It involves a sensitive way of living together with our essential resources. It involves morality just as much as getting on with other people.

Our Western civilization (which for a long time has been extensively imitated by the rest of the world) has over the last few centuries been driven, developed and elaborated by the conviction that man's role on earth is to exploit it to his advantage. Prosperity has arisen in a lawless situation.

So then what should we do? We could, for example, go rest under a tree and work out plans for the least possible production. There, under the tree with sunlight sifting through the foliage, we could reevaluate and politically focus our scientific knowledge and our technical capabilities. We could learn inactivity and devote a good deal of effective time to a redistribution of resources.

That's all! Learn to live according to the terms laid down by life, by the environment that is life.

During the eight hours and five minutes that the rhino rests from his grazing activity, the bush vegetation increases and improves. We need a comparable trial rest period, in order to figure out methods to order and protect our essential resources, because in our society there are no built-in protections against exploitation.

The whistling thorn (*Acacia drepanolobium*), one of the swollen thorn acacias, is an admirable tree. In East Africa, these acacias are keenly sought after by rhinos. A rhino can consume 250 of its shoots in a day. This doesn't sound like much, but the shoots are very nutritious. They can sustain huge creatures like rhinos and are also eagerly coveted by giraffes.

In fact, the acacia diet produces such a particularly high-quality milk that the nursing phase of a giraffe's baby is shortened appreciably. The baby grows quickly into such a strong, sturdy fellow that it can stop nursing after only six weeks and then wander off alone into the savanna.

But then take a look at these whistling thorns! We put barbed wire around a pasture and it's an effective barrier. Compared with the whistling thorn, barbed wire is as soft as mohair. This tree and a number of other acacias have long white thorns all around their twigs. The thorns of the swollen thorn acacias are like little spears, up to two or three decimeters long, those on the whistling thorn slightly shorter. The thorns are longer than the leaves which grow protected between them.

Obviously, the rhino doesn't bolt his food; he nibbles off one twig at a time, very carefully.

Thorns protect trees and bushes from being eaten. There are even more acacias in Australia than in Africa, but on that continent the acacias have no thorns. There are no large tree-browsing Australian animals, so thorns are not needed.

Two scientists, J. B. Foster and Paul Martin, have taken a closer look at the tall, thorny umbrella acacias which the giraffes also work over eagerly. Numerous large thorns appear up to a height of five meters, but above that both the number and size of the thorns rapidly diminish. Five meters is as high as an average giraffe can reach. Above that the leaves do not need thorn protection.

A comparable observation was made by the Swedish professor Ingemar Ahlén in a study of the common Scotch pine. The pine needles are particularly sharp and pointed when the pine is young and within reach of elks. Needles are less sharp on taller, older pines with higher branches which cannot normally be reached by an elk. Here we also

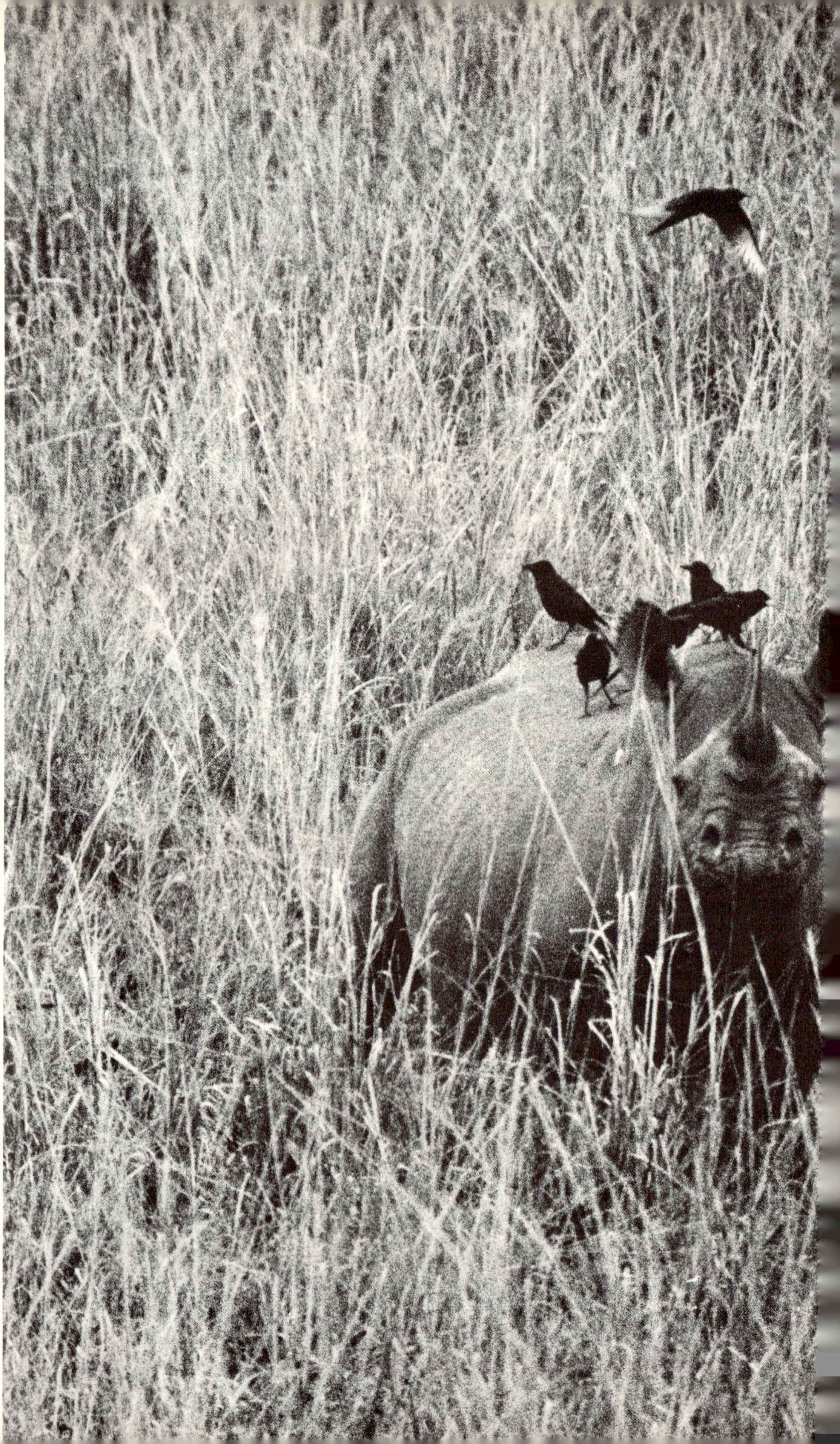

have the explanation for why elks are often seen foraging out in bogs. Such areas are very poor in nourishment, so the pines grow slowly. Instead of fine, lofty trees, low, stunted ones take shape. These old trees lack a young pine's sharp needles and yet can be reached by the elk.

Thus, three factors in the rhino's and the giraffe's lives could properly be called protection against exploitation. The rhino takes it easy under a tree for just over eight hours out of a total of twelve. This is the very best way to economize resources. The trees have evolved sharp thorns, a protective adaptation against exploitation. The third factor is that the tree's leaves and shoots are ex-

In Uganda, rhinos are often accompanied by birds like magpies, called piapiacs, which have learned that hundreds of insects are stirred up when a large animal passes by.

FOLLOWING PAGE:
Oxpeckers scramble over a rhino's back. This species of bird is completely dependent on the parasites of the large savanna animals. You see the birds riding the rhinos, clambering up the giraffes like woodpeckers, clinging onto impalas and gazelles. The animals provide food for the birds which simultaneously rid the beasts of flies and ticks, and the warning cries of the birds alert their host animals to approaching enemies. Oxpeckers never seem to stay on elephants, who manage without them. On the other hand, elephants are often accompanied by herons and yellow wagtails that eat the insects stirred up in the elephants' path.

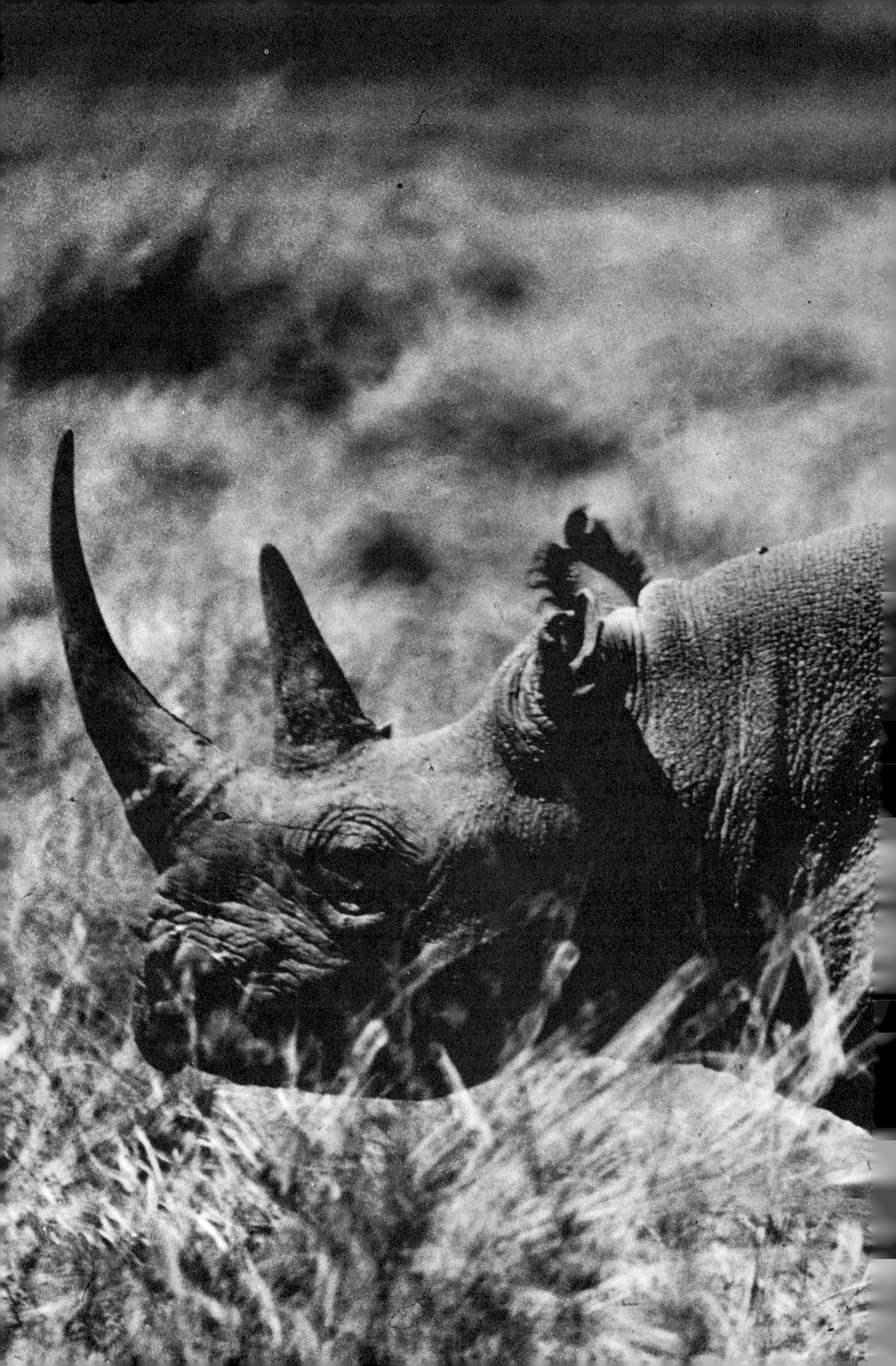

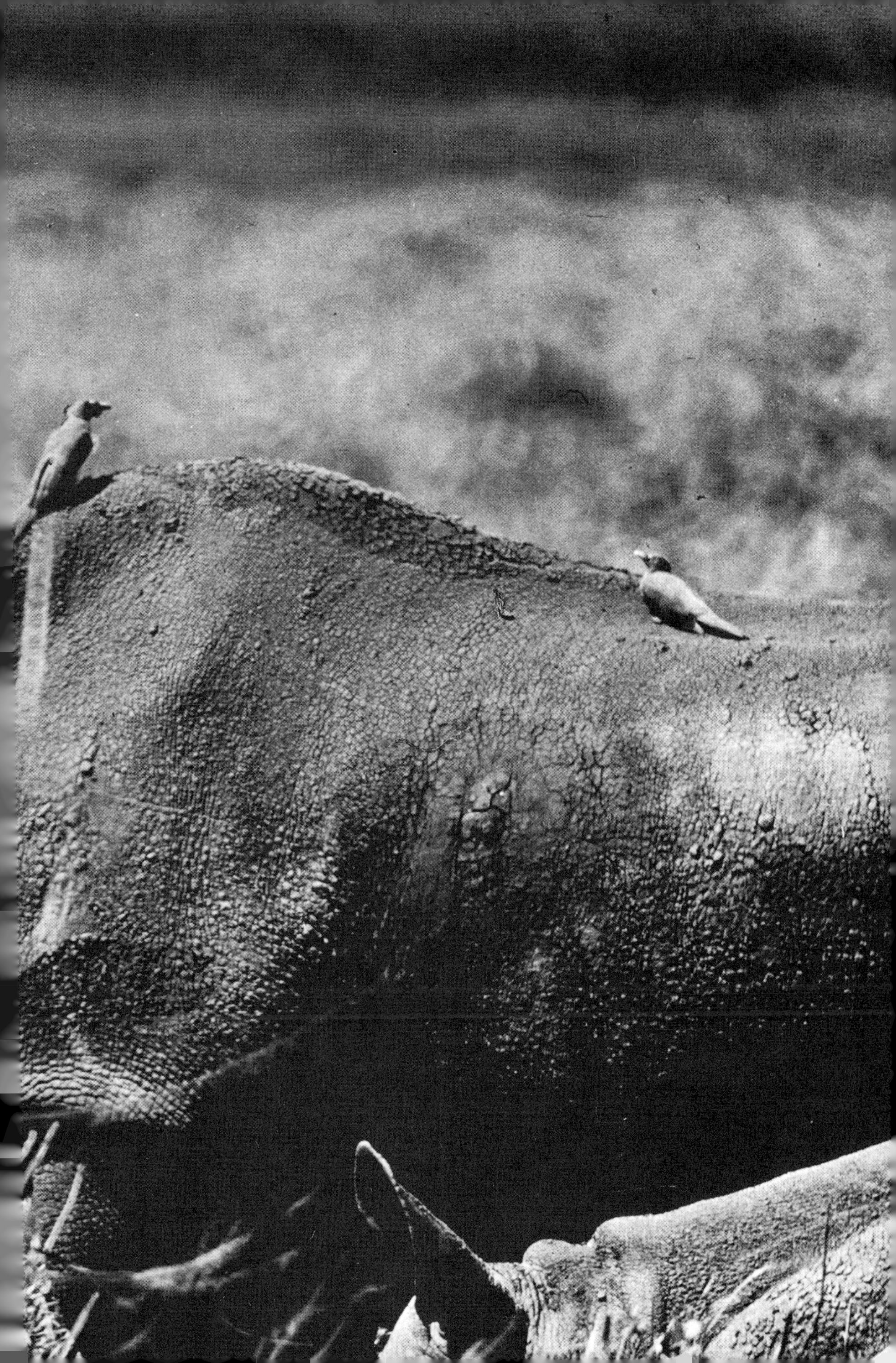

Of course, the rhino's face is beautiful! Its distinctive features and harmonious forms are like an old, gnarled tree stump. Why in the world does it look like this? The answer is hidden several million years back in time.

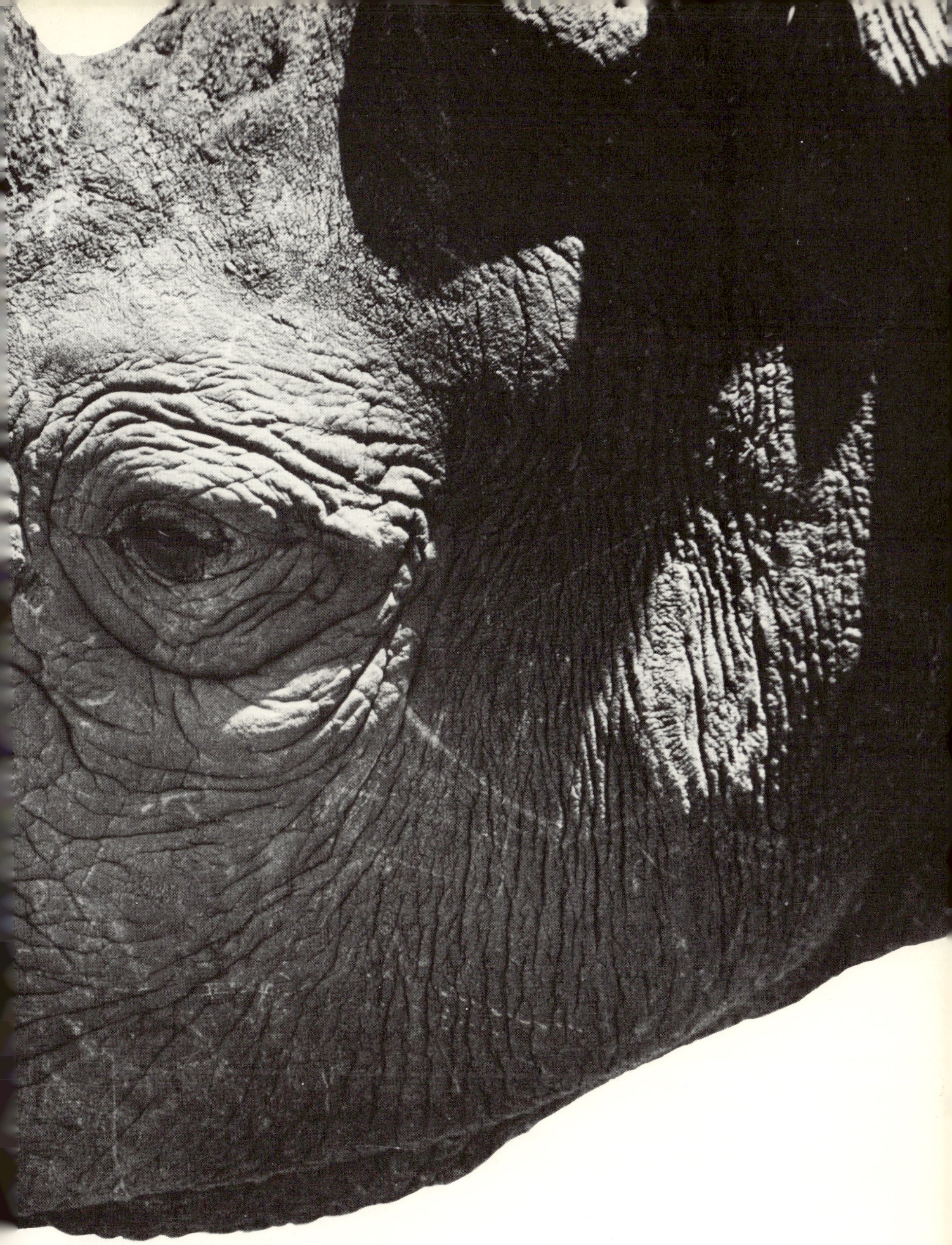

tremely rich in nourishment. Generosity in quality is a protection against undue encroachment in the environment.

However, it is important to notice that the protection against exploitation is not particularly effective. It is not a matter of preventing but rather of controlling. Both the giraffe and the rhino eat the whistling thorn with pleasure despite the formidable thorns. In an area where the whistling thorn is the principal food source for the large browsing animals, the trees are all worked over and thinned out by them. An unnaturally large animal population—one which for some reason cannot move away—results in an acute exploitation of trees and shrubs. This happened in East Tsavo during two severe dry periods in 1960–61 and 1970–71. During each catastrophic drought, about 300 rhinos were lost out of a total population estimated in 1960 to be about 1000. During the hard times, the effect on their eating was drastic. Their need was worsened considerably by the elephants which, in their distress, gradually caused a total destruction of the tree and bush vegetation.

While waiting for scientists to evaluate the ecological stress factors in Tsavo at that time, we can state only that at least in more normal conditions, the protection of the environment is well and truly built into this system of giving and taking organisms.

Time studies of giraffes eating whistling thorns have shown that, as a rule, an undisturbed giraffe contents itself with browsing for no more than one hour and forty minutes per tree.

Why? Why doesn't it eat up one whole tree at a time before moving on to the next —probably also an acacia? These are low trees, seldom as high as five meters. The giraffes can reach every part of them.

At the base of many of its thorns, the whistling thorn's stipules are swollen into round, plum-sized galls. These are excellent dwellings for stinging ants, which build their nests in them. When the wind blows over the savanna, the dry, brown galls act like whistle pipes. The wind puts its lips to the round ant entrances in tens of thousands of acacia galls and fine flute music streams out over the district.

This explains the acacia's name. I would really like to hear that music sometime.

It is plainly an advantage for the acacia to have the ants move in. At the base of the leaf shafts, the acacia secretes nectar. This has nothing to do with the tree's pollination. It is obviously there for the ants. The acacia offers the ants both food and a place to live. What service do the ants offer in return?

Through his binoculars, the time-study man could see that the giraffe's presence and drastic treatment of the tree stirred up the ants more and more, causing them to scramble out of their dwellings in increasing numbers. The angry stinging ants crawled all over the giraffe's muzzle until finally they covered the animal's whole head. The giraffe couldn't take it any longer. It was forced to interrupt its meal and move to another tree.

About an hour and forty minutes had passed.

The thorns' protection is complemented by the ants', both insuring that many trees share in assuaging the animals' hunger. This kind of protection is a vital part of nature's dynamics, commonly known as the ecological balance. We are probably idealizing when we assert that such protection, guaranteeing harmonious, peaceful evolution, always exists. And it is absolutely absurd to demand a similarly considerate, one-sided restraint of human activity in the environment. Surveying the global eco-system we may sometimes justify drastic and irreparable exploitation.

But this cannot continue if we don't know what we are doing, if we don't maintain a clear idea of the consequences of our interference. Maybe we do. Maybe we intend to destroy our world. If we don't, we might learn survival behavior from nature. In human civilization, there are no built-in guarantees that everything will gradually find a balance.

The environmental minister thought that continuous productivity creates better reforms and still better resources to, as he said, "improve the environment we live in." This is supposed to mean that if we fight on with our exploitation and consumption of resources, we will promote and improve our living environment. By consuming our living environment, the living environment will be improved. This is the ethic of suicide pilots.

Our increased prosperity occurs by consuming an increasing amount of raw materials and energy, wearing out soil and forests and depleting the oceans of fishes.

Compared with munching acacias, our increased prosperity often involves consuming resources that don't renew themselves.

We have to develop environmental protections such as those the acacia and the rhino have worked out for themselves. Until we have developed and accepted such rules, our forward march into the future will be devastating—and without gasoline. ∎

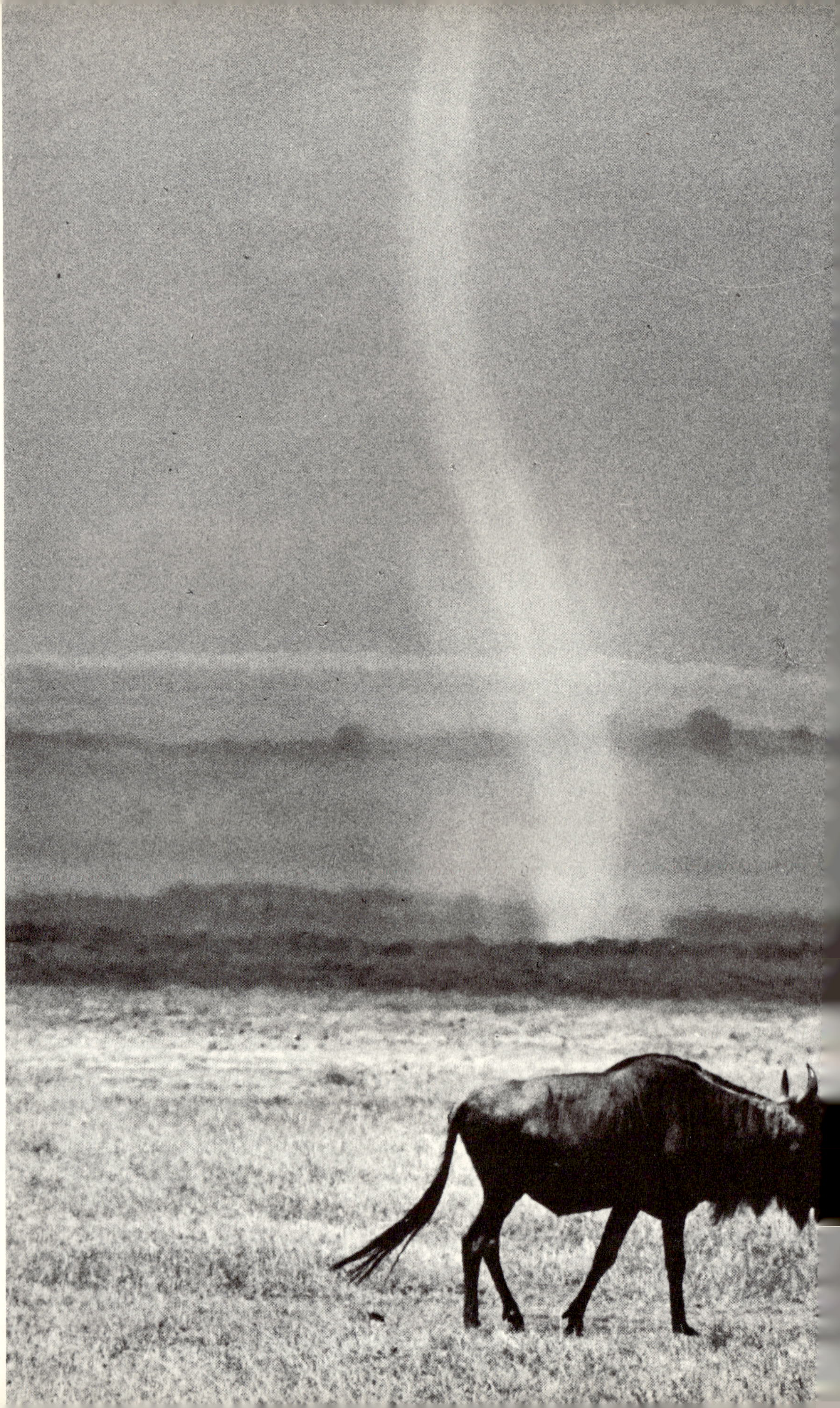

A SINGLE BLADE OF GRASS

A swirl of earth blowing away—a dust devil—scatters small portions of the savanna's soil where the grass cover has been worn down by overgrazing. When the sun is intensely hot, these dust devils wander constantly over the savanna. Wherever the grass is sparse, the spiral draws up the dust.

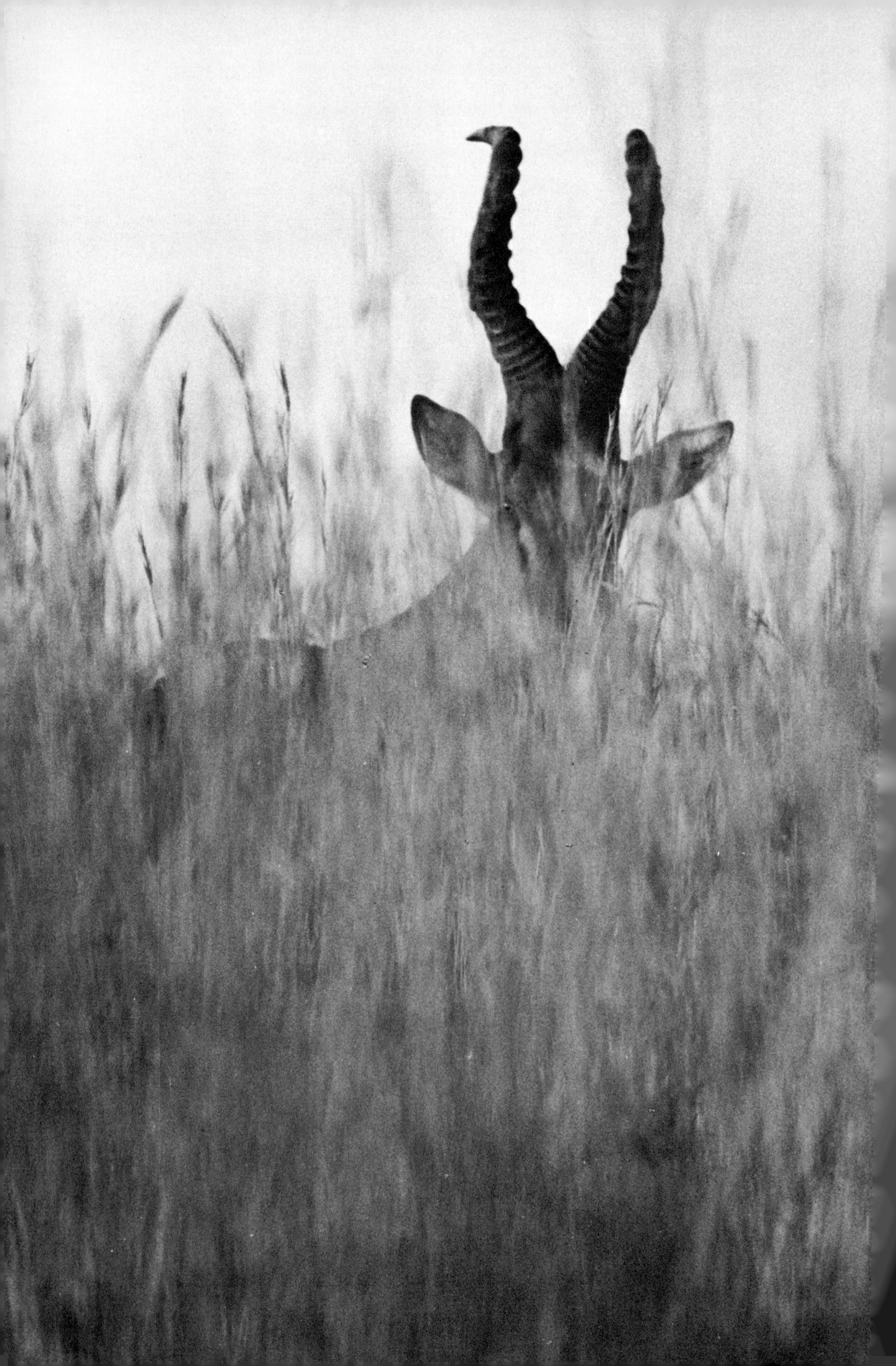

A dust spiral rises from the plain in front of Mt. Suswa in Kenya's Masailand. The very earth is being drawn up from the sunbaked plain in the form of a question mark. It is estimated that every year for every square kilometer Africa loses 715 tons of earth through wind and water erosion.

This is an apocalyptic mean value for destruction of earth on the African continent, but it tells us nothing at all. Catastrophes happen all the time: inhuman wars, famine, death from disease, traffic accidents, environmental poisons. We can dismiss them from our minds—all the more easily because they are absurd and unacceptable. Tragedy must be personalized for us. (The ordinary enlisted man as a murderer. The eyes of one starving person. Kill the malaria mosquito with your bare hand. Detroit's human victims. A little Japanese miracle with twisted limbs.)

As with single accidents, large-scale disasters often arise from the combination of what appear individually and over a long period of time to be harmless false conclusions, negligence, shortsighted necessity, local decisions, etc.

The dust whirls away down Kedong Valley and disappears in the sun's haze like an evil spirit released from its bottle. Dust devils, as these spiraling winds are called, wander over

Each rainy season the water cuts deeper. It carves furrows and washes the soil away, down brooks into rivers. Land once lush with grass is now in liquid motion. The rainy season colors the watercourses golden or red, fills the power station dams, causes flooding, and culminates in massive mud clouds in the ocean, colored like fire—or blood.

Here is a Jackson's hartebeest in the tall grass that still measures time for man and animal.

the golden plains in the dry season. Scattered before the wind, elephants, antelope, lions and warthogs, familiar dairy cows and nomads, farmers and agricultural experts all seem to disappear into the cloudless sky. Up in dust goes the whole crew from Noah's ark.

The plains look so hopeless. Wind rustles faintly in the acacia groves. Is the bare ground cracking before my very eyes? I throw a stone. I rub the golden grass between my fingers. I reflect (an instinct for self-preservation?) that there are indeed possibilities in this exhausted, destroyed grazing land. Something is still being squandered. A person still squandering resources is not totally impoverished, even though he's bound to be so eventually.

After the rainy season, the Indian Ocean where the rivers emerge is rusty red. The surf over the coral reefs glows like fire with eroded earth. Perhaps no global environmental destruction is more radical and thorough than soil abuse.

This is a developing land. I pick up a fistful and hold it in my cupped hands. It sifts away between my fingers and the wind carries it off. When the earth is destroyed, time has run out. On this bare, devastated land, there were once great herds of wild animals. Then people came with their cattle. The herds can still be seen where there's enough grass, but thorn bushes have grown up where they walked.

Climate dictates the limits of the possible use of these arid regions. Humans and their cattle exceed that limit so that neither wild herbivores nor tame cattle can exist there—nor people. It is difficult to distinguish between desert and fertile land—and land that hides its potential under a shabby garb of thicket.

After the rains, these plains turn green with lovely grass and the shrubs blossom. Then for a short while, everything looks very lush. Such is the rhythm. This alternates with lengthy periods of extreme drought, when the environment shrinks to bone-dry desert conditions. Then, abruptly, the dry season ends with heavy, welcome rain, and once more the greenery bursts out. Animals and people are integral parts of this continuum; each time of need in the savanna puts an arduous strain on them. This causes the environment to be overtaxed so that each time some minor damage occurs, it is difficult if not impossible to repair. A lengthy phase of alternating good times and hardship can eventually result in extensive areas of earth becoming totally destroyed. This has happened in all the drought areas in the world. They were once minor ugly flaws that became magnified. After 10 or 100 or 1000 years, they have developed into great catastrophes. How did it start?

I walk along, sucking on a grass stalk since I don't know what to do with my thoughts. I chew on it too; the stalk is dried out. How does a blade of grass wither on the African steppes?

After the rainy season, there's plenty of water in the earth for the grass roots to drink. The blades of grass, thirsting in the heat, need water to grow and to have enough strength to bear flowers and seeds. A blade of grass sweats in the sun; quite soon the grass returns the water that the earth lent it. The water drifts away as steam in the breeze.

Then the grass withers to straw.

But the grass itself doesn't die. It merely sleeps. Down in the earth, the grass roots sleep; embedded in dry leaf sheaths, new shoots are resting. When the rains return, the savanna grass turns green again after very few days because its root system is vast and effective. One single wheat plant can have 80,000 meters of densely concentrated and richly branching roots to suck water in rapidly. There's no time to lose. Water doesn't stay still and soon the sun's heat is very strong.

Where today can we find a landscape that human beings have not affected? A bushland district in Tanzania is being cleared. It was covered with such a dense thicket that only rhinos could have got through it—if there were any still around. Within that area, where both cows and people would be torn and scratched bloody if they tried to penetrate, artificially-made water holes were found, indicating that long ago cattle-herding people had driven their animals to graze there.

We know a little about how such a change takes place. Usually the reason is that the grassland has been damaged and destroyed by overgrazing and by burning the grass excessively. This has probably occurred for as long as these areas have been inhabited. In 1956, for instance, the cattle-herding Masai on the arid plains of this part of Kenya had 330,000 cows (actually cow-equivalents: for the sake of simplicity, five sheep or goats are counted as one cow). In 1958, they had 378,000 and in 1960, the number of animals had risen to 450,000.

Grass is one of the most important renewable resources on earth. It is because of grass that people live. But the Masai owned twice as many animals as these grasslands could support. The overgrazing was too drastic and so in 1960–61, three-fifths of their livestock died and the people went hungry. Many died of starvation. A severe drought added to the overgrazing, creating an acute catastrophe in Kenya.

Since then, people and animals have recovered their strength, hunger has been appeased, and the number of grazing animals has again increased excessively. A new catastrophe is anticipated here and on many other grasslands where people struggle so desperately to improve human conditions but where the resources are too limited to support an increasing number of people and animals.

Overgrazing can have the same effect on the area's water table as an appreciably higher annual rainfall. That is, the water balance can change to favor bushes over grass. As a result, the bushes take over more territory and the grass retreats. Under the thorny bushes, soil is often bare and washes away in rills when the heavy rains set in or it blows away when dust devils darken the sky.

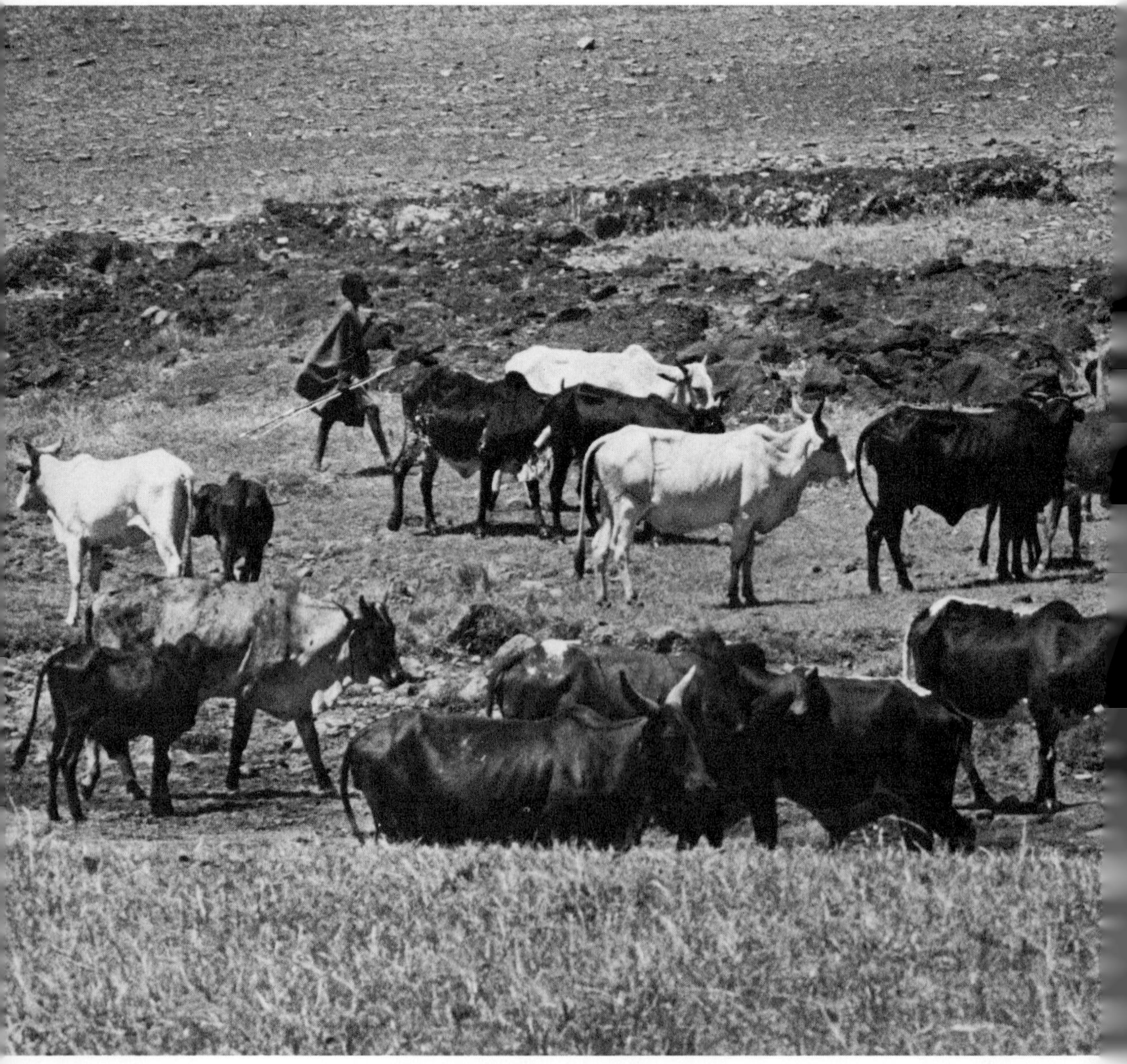

A savanna can produce—from sunlight, water, air and minerals—23 tons of grass per hectare. Nine tons of this can be grazed without causing damage. This yields 2.7 tons of beef. There are definite limits for the nomadic culture's expansion, but their population still increases. They need more animals, although the land cannot support more.

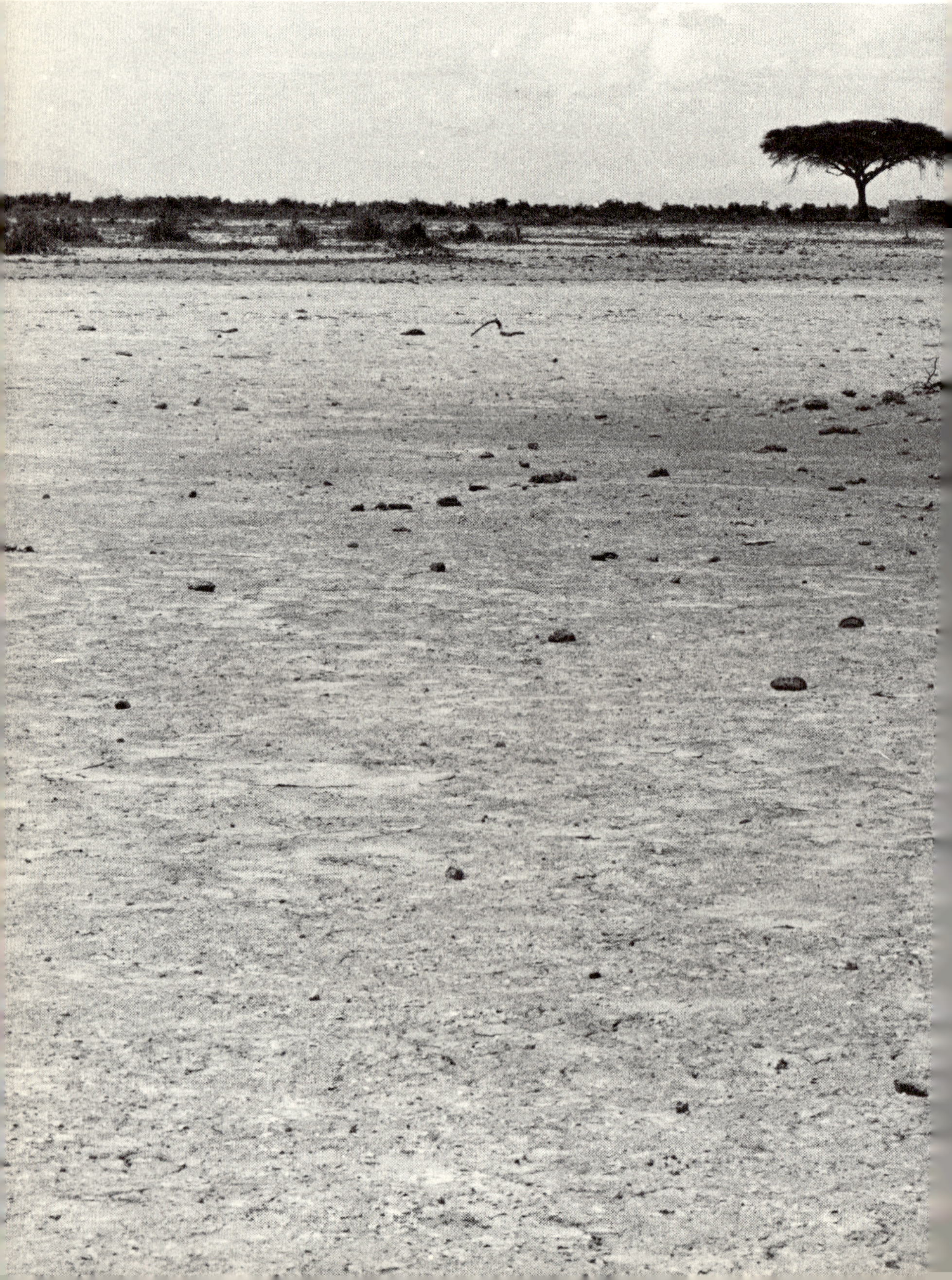

Grass doesn't grow here anymore. The savanna is barren. Once fruitful, it has become desert. In East Africa, you occasionally see large, uninterrupted savanna areas totally lacking vegetation as in this picture. Usually the damaged earth presents a mosaic pattern under more or less dense bush.

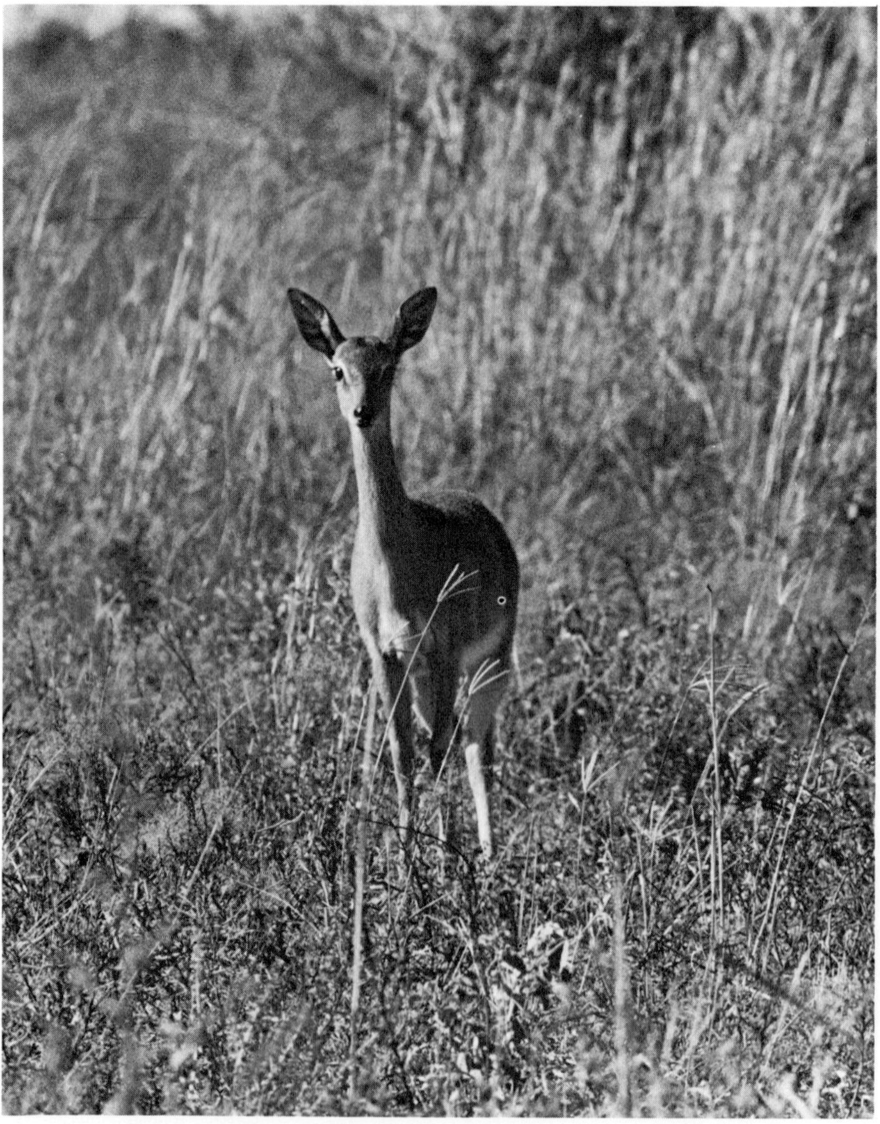

This is an oribi, one of 37 antelope species in Tanzania. It also lives in Uganda and Kenya. The abundance of Africa's beautiful animal kingdom can be measured in many ways. There are 289 species of land mammals in Tanzania. An equally large land area in Europe has less than 50. Perhaps no country in the world has as many species of animals as Tanzania. There are 10 different kinds of squirrels. There are 800 species of birds breeding in Kenya, 260 in Sweden. Why does East Africa have so many more species of animals than Sweden? The African environment has remained stable for a very long time. While Sweden's animal world was decimated by glaciers, Africa's plants and animals were able to continue evolving in a fertile ecosystem. Europe and Sweden are struck by winter, the annual return of an ice age, while Africa's animals can go on all year long accommodating themselves to every possible ecological niche that unconstrained, evolving nature has to offer. There is another crucial difference: the European fauna is drastically reduced because humans have altered that environment much more dramatically.

When there are many species of animals, specialization is also greater. As a rule, different species don't compete; each lives, mutually dependent, in its own niche. This limits their ability to adapt to an altered environment. They cannot change their niche, partly because each niche is occupied and partly because their species has arisen and maintains itself on the terms dictated by its specialization.

That is why Africa's animal kingdom is so sensitive to environmental change. The threat of extinction hangs heavier over these animals than over the fauna of a more impoverished environment.

When there are many species, there is a need for great variation in form, color and behavior. It is important to keep closely related species excluded from the threat of hybridization—which threatens each species—and so genetic barriers are built up with the help of characteristically magnificent colors and beautiful forms. That is why the African birds are so much more varied than the Swedish birds . . .

. . . and why the oribi is so beautiful.

FOLLOWING PAGES:
An experience can be fleeting in its beauty but last forever in one's memory. Here you see a group of kob antelope, two black-headed herons and a sand martin hovering over the road. It saddens me to realize that we frightened these creatures as we bumped noisily along the road in Uganda's Kabalega Park.

Here are the same three female kobs as in the preceding picture. The kob is Uganda's characteristic animal, called the Uganda kob. There are 10,000 in Kabalega Park and another 10,000 in Ruwenzori. The impalas, the most common antelope in Kenya, are replacing the kobs where they have been almost totally killed off or have disappeared for other reasons. The kobs' behavior is radically different from that of other tropical mammals. The males defend small individual territories within a larger group territory. The females are allowed in freely but other males are excluded. The kobs' practice of defining small plots of land occurs only when the population density is high, when many of the same species must share the same space.

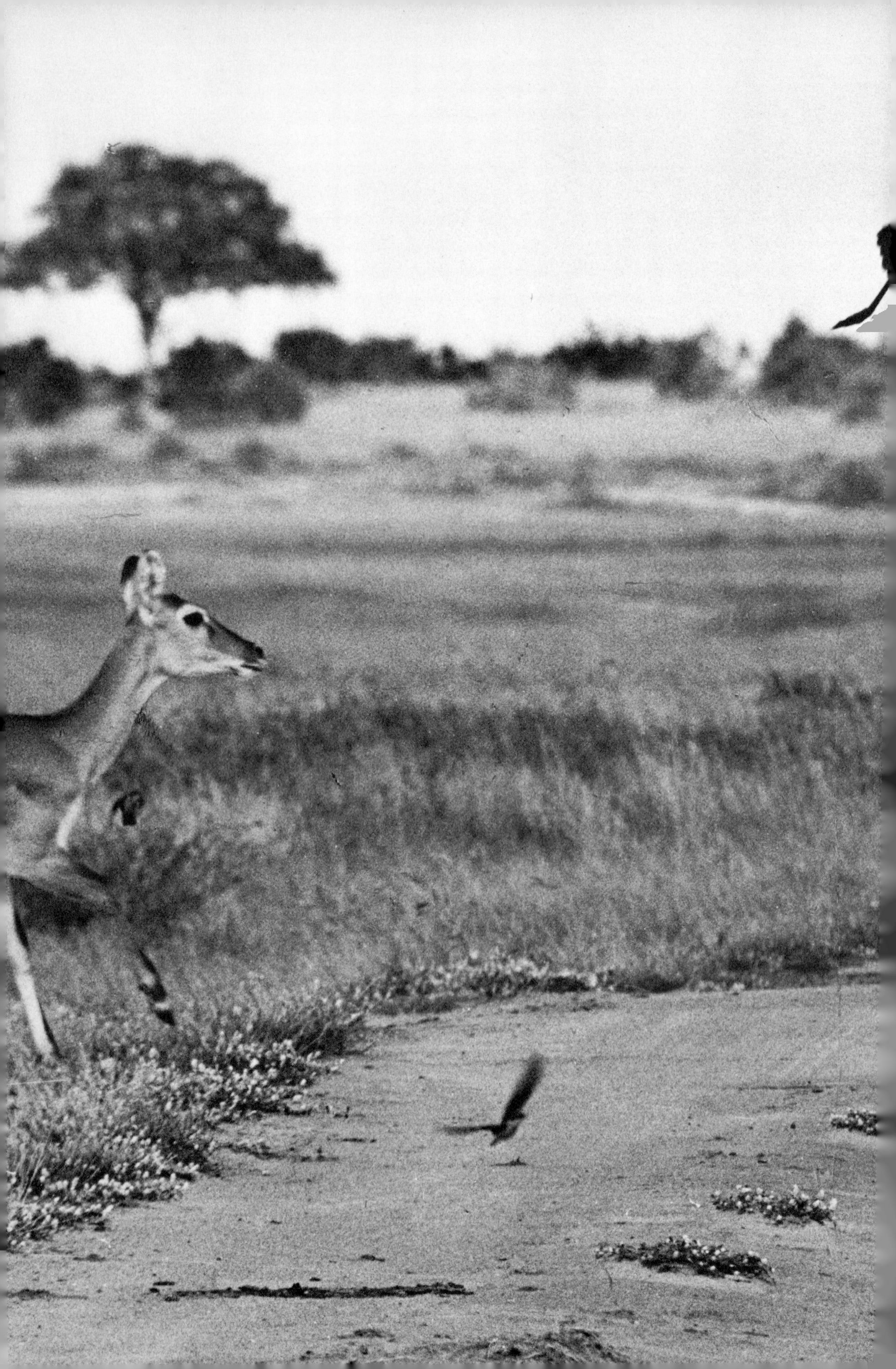

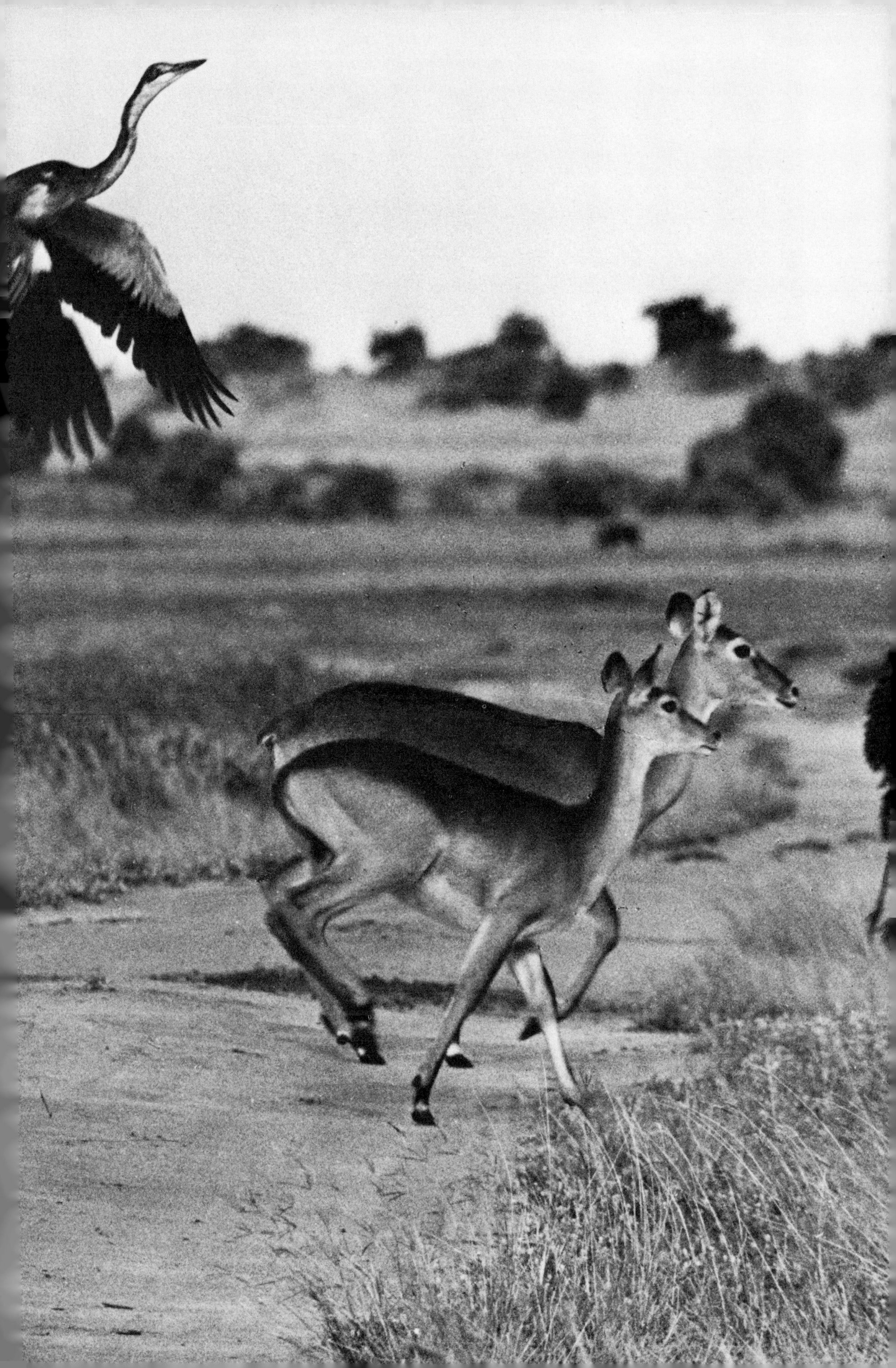

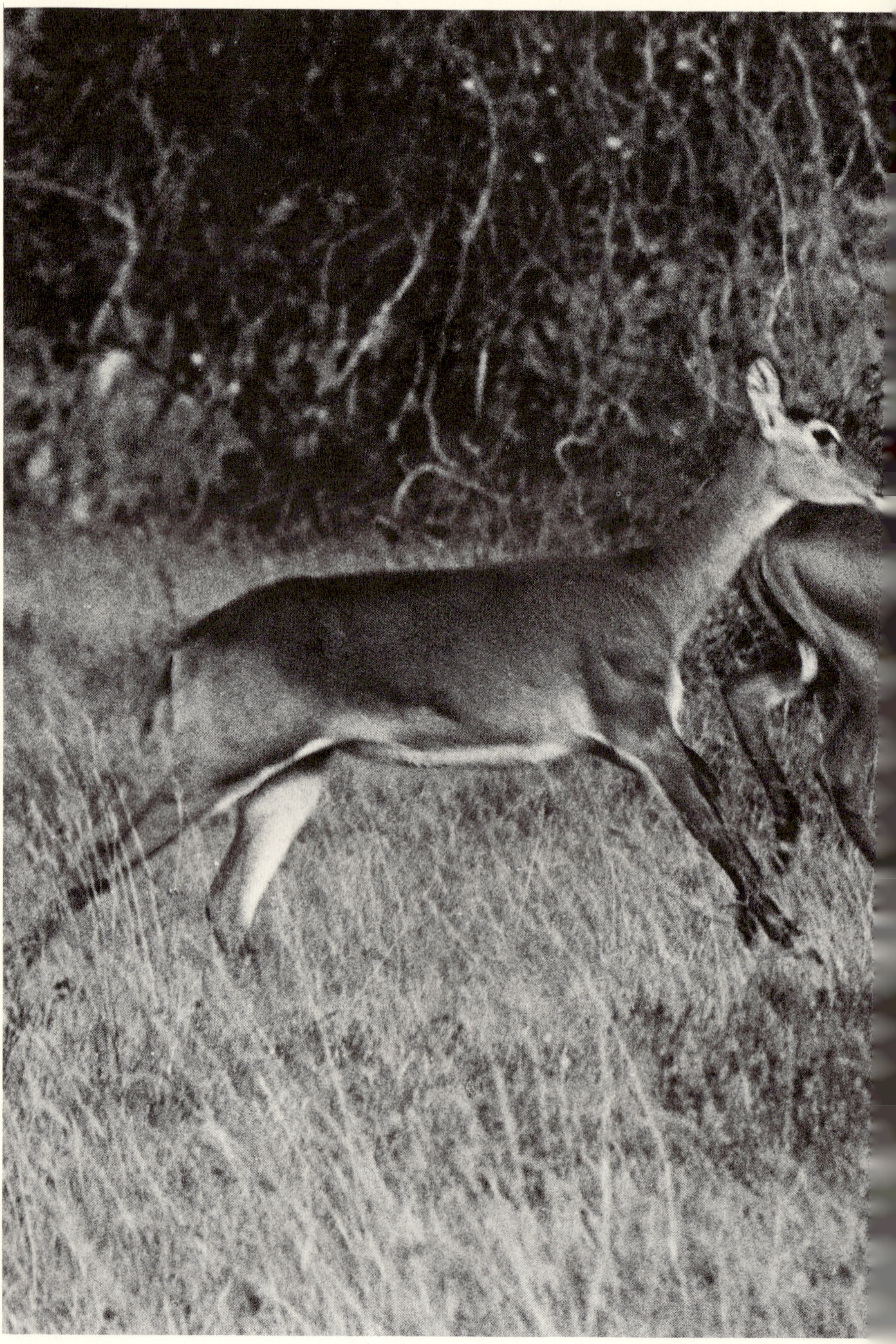

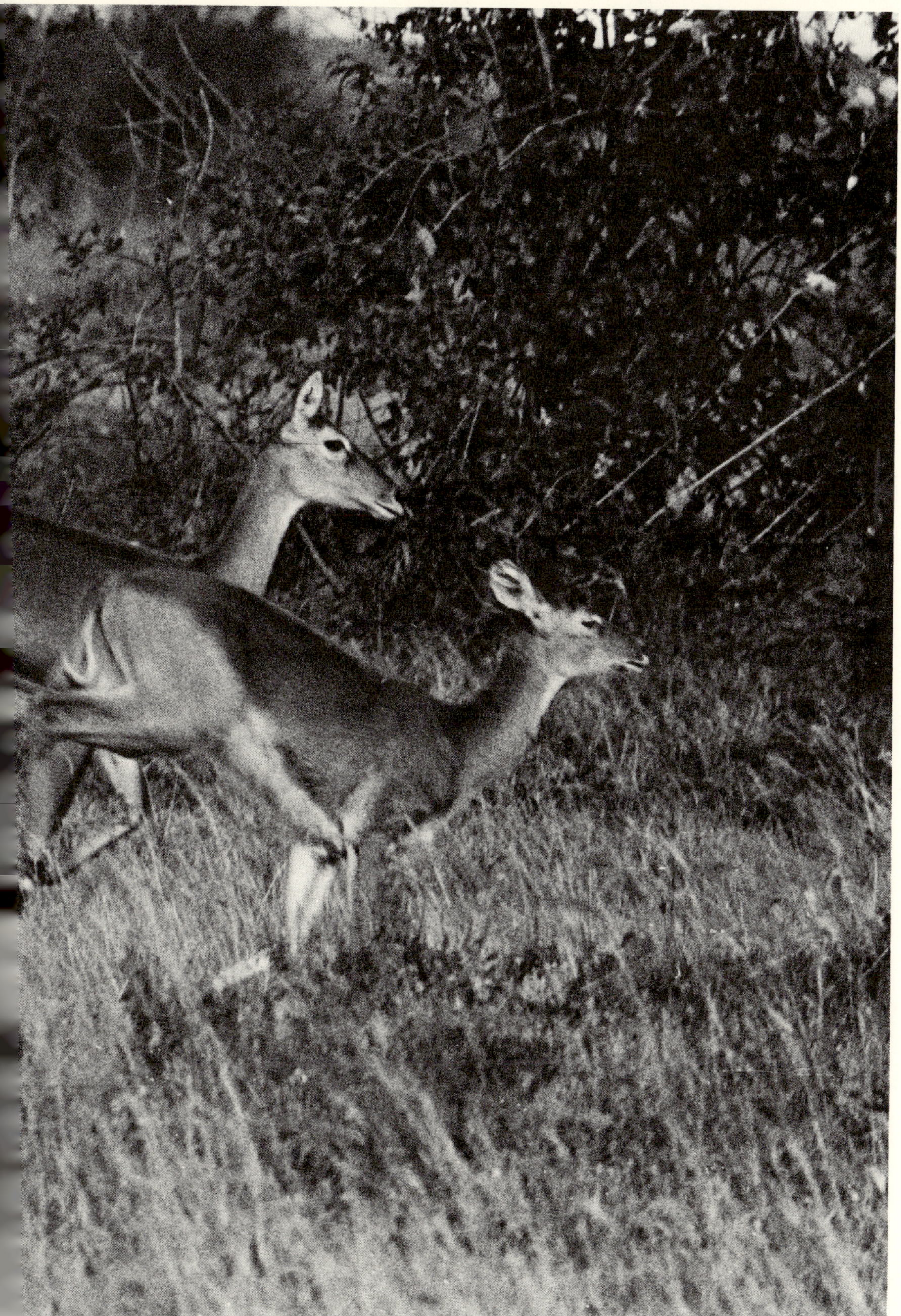

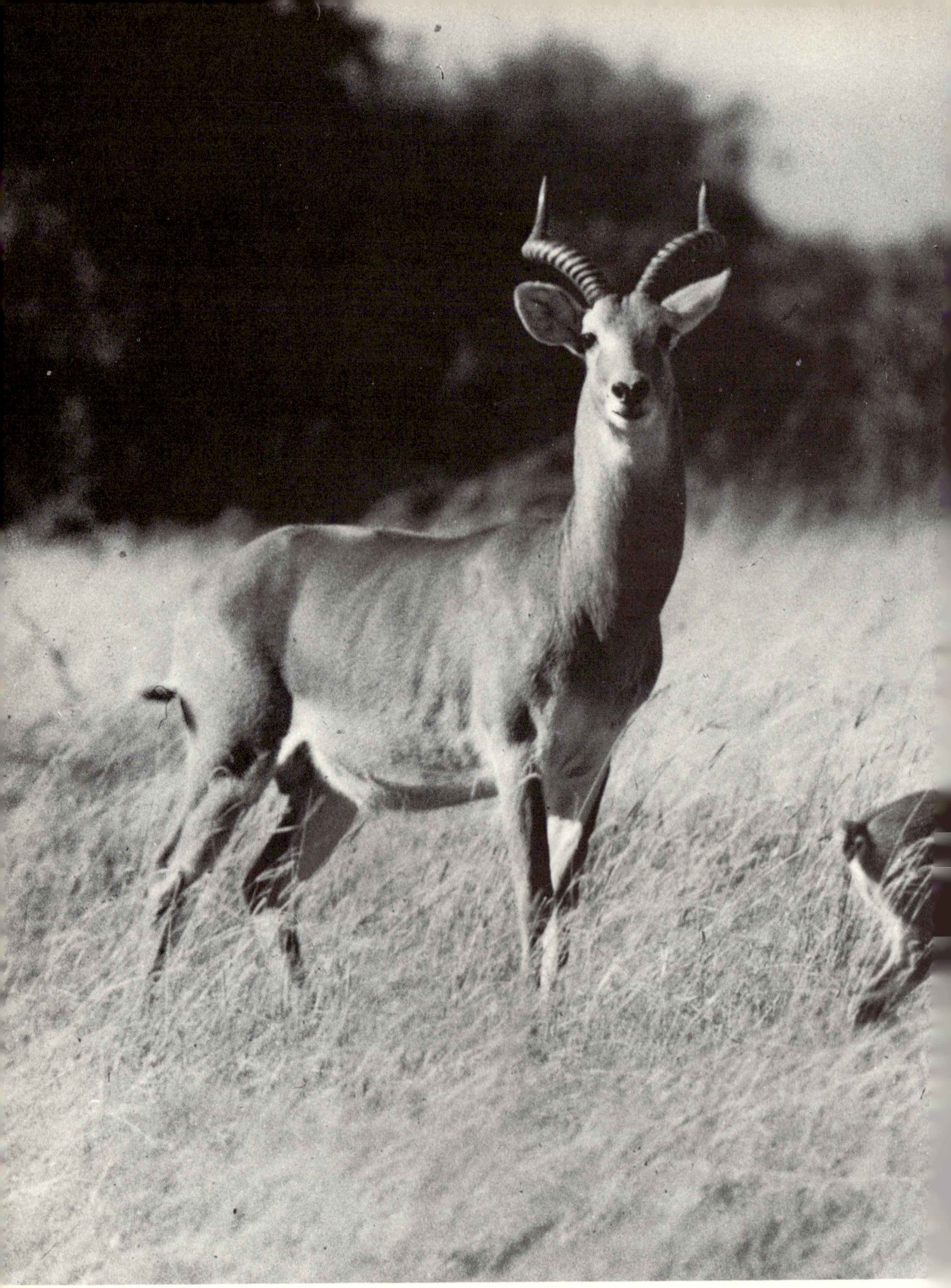

Right now, as I jot this down in my notebook, a morning shower has fallen on Mombasa and a scent seems to rise right from the cement steps of the Catholic church where I'm sitting, waiting for the sunshine to return. Fleeting as the scent after rain are the thought and the feeling, the questions and the answers—the basis for action and passivity. For a brief instant, a human being becomes a cluster of accidental impressions. So weak are the forces that most profoundly alter the world.

A cattle farmer has 100 cows. He should have only 50. He and his animals are hardly noticeable to the outside world. But together with all the other cattle farmers in the arid regions of the tropics, he exploits 5,000 hectares of grassland, and altogether their scattered herds of cattle constitute half of the entire world's tame livestock, producing a third of all the meat and a fifth of the world's milk production. These grazing lands are the largest land reserves left for the meat production for an increasing world population. *If* the grass could be improved, *if* the yield could be increased . . .

But, instead, gradual destruction. The gap becomes rapidly ever greater between the resources nature has provided and the possibilities for improvement that science and technology can offer.

A male kob surveys his territory. Other male kobs are chased away but an oribi is allowed in.

"It is not unlikely," writes McIlroy in *An Introduction to Tropical Grassland Husbandry*, "that the natural grasslands of the tropics, when improved and adequately exploited will form major centers of livestock production in the world."

But while these plans are being made, the grass thins out to its bare roots and desert comes. Barrenness spreads, as it has since the time of Abraham in the extensive Arabian, Indian, Chinese, North African and American grasslands that were once green. With insufficient rainfall, desert also comes to the remaining grasslands. The possibility of these grasslands supporting mankind diminishes as our need increases.

Environmental destruction seldom comes quickly or dramatically. It never happens in a uniform way. The future is killed in small bits, piece by piece. In the zebras' and antelope's recent homeland, through which we tourists pass on our way to and from the national parks, a hopeless future is written on the earth and grass by each hoof and muzzle of every individual cow and sheep and goat.

In fact, hooves even more than muzzles tear up the grass cover of the land. In the dry season, the animals' mouths bite the grass so hard that new shoots are injured. Tussocks die, leaving bare patches of earth. Hooves beat down on these patches and sod until the earth is hard-packed. The welcome raindrops only bounce off the bare, hard-trampled surface, making the earth even more impenetrable. Instead of sinking in and contributing to the grass (cattle, wild animals and men), the water runs off the land. In Karamoja in northern Uganda, it has been estimated that overgrazing and trampling of the earth diminish the absorption capacity of the earth by 40 percent. A half-desert climate can be created by land abuse despite a relatively adequate rainfall.

A favorable savanna climate also promotes bush vegetation, which can take over when the grasslands are abused. In the dry season, dust devils sweep up whatever topsoil has not been washed away already by the rains. The remaining naked earth is too compacted to let grass seeds take root among the trees and bushes. Without competition from the grass, shrubs and trees can overrun the savanna with their thorny thickets.

We don't know how extensive natural transitional zones between desert and woodlands have been, because humans have altered the landscape everywhere. Along the desert frontiers, the desert increases. The steppe is the driest grassland, shifting into desert. A savanna, with somewhat more rainfall, includes bushes. Vast bush regions of this sort, resulting from overgrazing, extend over much of Africa.

What solutions to this spread of bushland are there? The bush burns poorly, since the grass is sparse. The bushes could be uprooted by bulldozers, which would be very expensive, or could be killed by defoliants. These methods are being tested. There are also cheaper attempts which combine people using clearing implements, controlled fires and goats—which feed on the bush. It is a desperate fight. This sort of attempt was made in Kenya. It went on for five years, and the input and effect have been evaluated.

After two years of burning, mechanical clearing and extensive goat grazing, a great deal of grassland has been reclaimed—any other result would have been strange—but, viewed as a whole, the trees and bushes also gained during the experimental period. Two types of trees that dominated the bush were not at all affected by two successive burnings. Finally, after a third burning, which included additional fuel from dried, cut bush, individual trees of both problem species began to die. The attempt was discontinued prematurely with the bitter conclusion that this combined effort might be significant if complemented by tree-killing chemicals.

A raindrop is not large. A dust devil on the dry steppe makes a cloud no worse than smoke from a campfire. A cow's hoof causes no landslide. An uprooted blade of grass doesn't ruin a pasture. A three-year-old

Bush and thorny thickets cover half of Kenya today. This is, to a large extent, the result of humans overworking the environment for a long time. Now humans must clear new grazing land or reclaim pasturage that disappeared under bush. This is a tremendous undertaking. The bush must be chopped down and dried. Trees and larger bushes must be burned to produce charcoal or used as firewood. Then the landscape must be burned.

starving in a devastated area of Africa doesn't lessen the romping fun at a children's party in Sweden. It is nevertheless on this level that great tragedies are played out and the possibilities of life decided.

Where shall we look? Wherever shall we start to put the crazy world back on the right track again? We can start by looking around us. We can steady ourselves by picking something to focus on. Then we find a blade of grass, a raindrop and a dust devil. Grass —a single blade of grass—measures time. The future of all mankind is being decided in the treatment of each blade of grass, over mile upon mile of land that is being destroyed. ∎

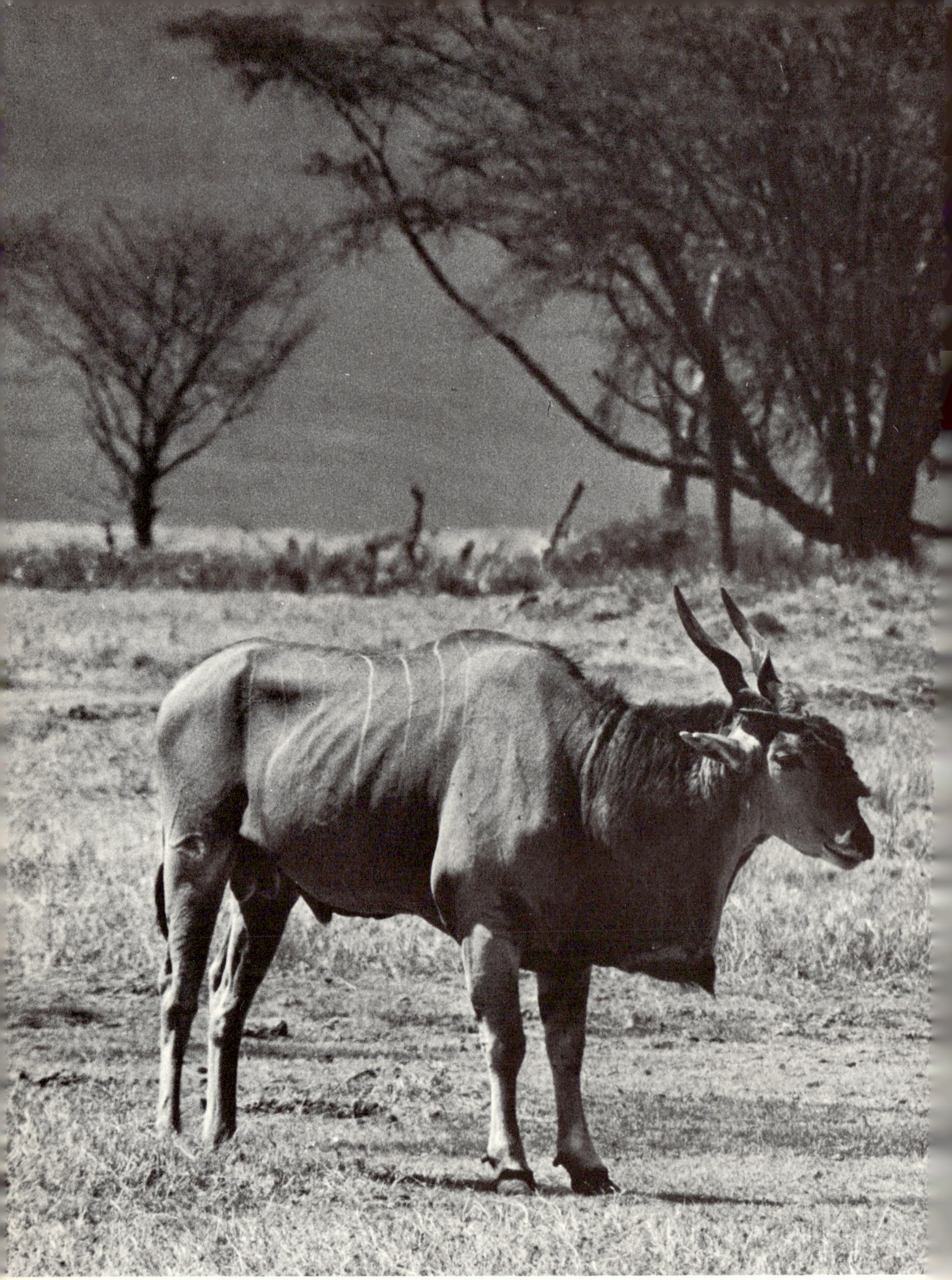

SHADE IS THE TREE'S THANKS FOR HELP

You, human, are the acacia fruit sown in the dry season when the land lies blackened by fires and the eland drinks the shade under a tree.

At noon, the eland searches for shade. It follows tracks where the land has been worn bare. It doesn't need to drink as long as it can find shade.

Acacia tortilis, the umbrella acacia, drops its fruit when the rainy season is still far off. This fruit will stay there; it is not supposed to be distributed by the flood waters. It will stay on the savanna, which is at once forest and meadow.

When this acacia drops its spiral-shaped pods, the surrounding grassland is often burnt, covered with ashes from the grassfires lit by people. They singe the land and the trees drop their fruit into the ashes.

The fruit is covered with soft flesh rich in nourishment. Impalas, giraffes, the beautiful, stocky elands and domesticated cattle come to eat this fruit. They don't have much else to eat: the new fresh grass shoots won't sprout from the burnt land before the rains. The acacia fruit is also picked up by the slender antelope; they eat the rich flesh, but the hard pits travel unharmed through their bodies.

It's the dry season: the sun beats down. At noon, the eland and other animals seek out the shadiest trees. Following almost invisible tracks worn by hooves, they rest under trees where the ground has been so trampled that no grass grows.

The antelope distribute the acacia's seeds both along the tracks and at their resting places. There the tree seedlings have a chance of surviving the otherwise overwhelming competition of the grass. Umbrella acacias are found in broad belts around the open plains that are or have been the territory of antelope and other herbivores. In the undamaged parklike savanna, many of the trees are these large, shade-giving umbrella acacias.

These trees and the animals live in mutual dependence. The trees produce ripe fruit when the animals need food most. The trees add a scent that attracts the animals to the fruit's tasty and nourishing flesh. The Animals spread the seeds to places where the acacias have a good chance of surviving. Many don't make it. These trees are always sparsely scattered. Their widely extending branches dispense shade liberally. The fruits that have passed through the antelope's stomachs have a better chance of germinating than those which have not been eaten. They are concealed from seed-eating insects within the animals' droppings.

This is one of the innumerable interconnections between forms of life on earth. No one is alone, no one can manage independently; no one is master, not even of himself. That is the rule. The eland can survive the dry season without drinking as long as it can find shade under a tree. It plants its own tree and shade is the tree's thanks for help.

Cut down that tree and the animals can't survive. Kill off the animals and then the trees can't survive.

Humans are part of this system. They can't extricate themselves. They are also a piece of the puzzle of the environment. Humans burned the grass and then the animals could find the fruits more easily.

We venture out into the savanna, this

mosaic of relationships and equalities. There's no way to be totally informed about the whole mesh of interrelationships in the savanna. Like forest and meadow, lake and ocean, this ecosystem functions as its own particular cosmos. It took shape in primeval times; its history is as old as the constantly changing life cycles within it.

In the distance, a herd of gnu looms like a mirage in the air, raised by the shimmering sunlight. Far off, a grassfire smokes up the sky. We don't know how much of the savanna was formed with the help and intervention of humans. But we do know that for thousands of years people have been important participants in the savanna's community. The East African national parks—beneath the high mountains—are all in the savanna, if our definition of savanna includes plateaus, prairies and the bush.

Usually, savanna means an extensive grassland scattered with tall trees. According to this capacious definition, the savanna comprises the transition between desert and forest. It is hard to define the edge of a desert, but the edge of a forest is often very distinct.

The savanna evolved from the forests that in prehistoric times extended throughout Africa. Climatic changes were unfavorable to the forests. Hundreds of volcanoes lit forest fires which spread across East Africa, clearing the way for the savanna. Humans followed, lighting more fires, gradually clearing the forests for cultivation. People still use fire to keep the savanna open. We encountered these fires everywhere on the horizon during the dry season. Vast tracts of East Africa are burned each year, as long as there is grass to fuel the fires. If the grassfires were to cease, the area would gradually revert to forest. In the national parks, where grass is not burned for cattle grazing, there is a policy of controlled burning in plantation areas because often the savanna could not exist without fire. Hence people have been and continue to be one of the savanna's most important participants.

Following in the tracks of man came the great wild herds of gazelle and antelope, buffalo and zebra. People have hunted them but also contributed to their welfare. Humans are largely responsible for the origin of the enormous herds of wild herbivores and thus indirectly for the lion and other beasts of prey on the savanna. People and animals evolve all the time interdependently, serving each other as do the acacias and the elands.

It is really so simple but we still don't understand and that's why we ruin the earth. When will humans, who can go to the moon, realize that we finally exist only because of the resources written in the grass on the earth? No civilized humans, however perfectly developed their synthetic industry, can survive if they lose the ability to listen to the grass and the trees and animals, and return in kind to them what they give us.

Part of the savanna in Tanzania is grazed

Trees in the savanna offer their foliage to animals seeking shade at noon. Animals need shade. Many of them might not be able to live if they weren't in the shade occasionally. On the savanna, an acacia's crown is unusually broad. There are many reasons for this. Wind has a drying effect, and trees cope best if they can offer the minimum resistance or obstacle to the wind. A broad, shady crown also protects the tree's roots by keeping the earth damp beneath it. Furthermore, giraffes that eat the leaves won't reach more than the edges and undersides of a tree with an extensive crown of leaves.

But surely the tree has also evolved its shape because of the presence and influence of the animals. They fertilize the earth under the shady tree with their droppings. They eat the tree's fruits that have fallen to the ground. The fruit is easy to find there because the shade has thinned out the grass.

FOLLOWING PAGES:
The savanna is burning, but the animals don't flee in panic. The topis in this picture remain calm despite the flames and smoke in the grass and bush around them. They are used to fire constantly breaking out in the dry season. Their grassland environment has to a large extent been created by fires, often lit by people. In a way, people are responsible for the enormous herds of antelope and other animals that live on the savanna. If people were to stop burning the grass, the forest would return. Topis could not survive in the forest.

Hundreds of thousands of gnu graze on the Serengeti plains.

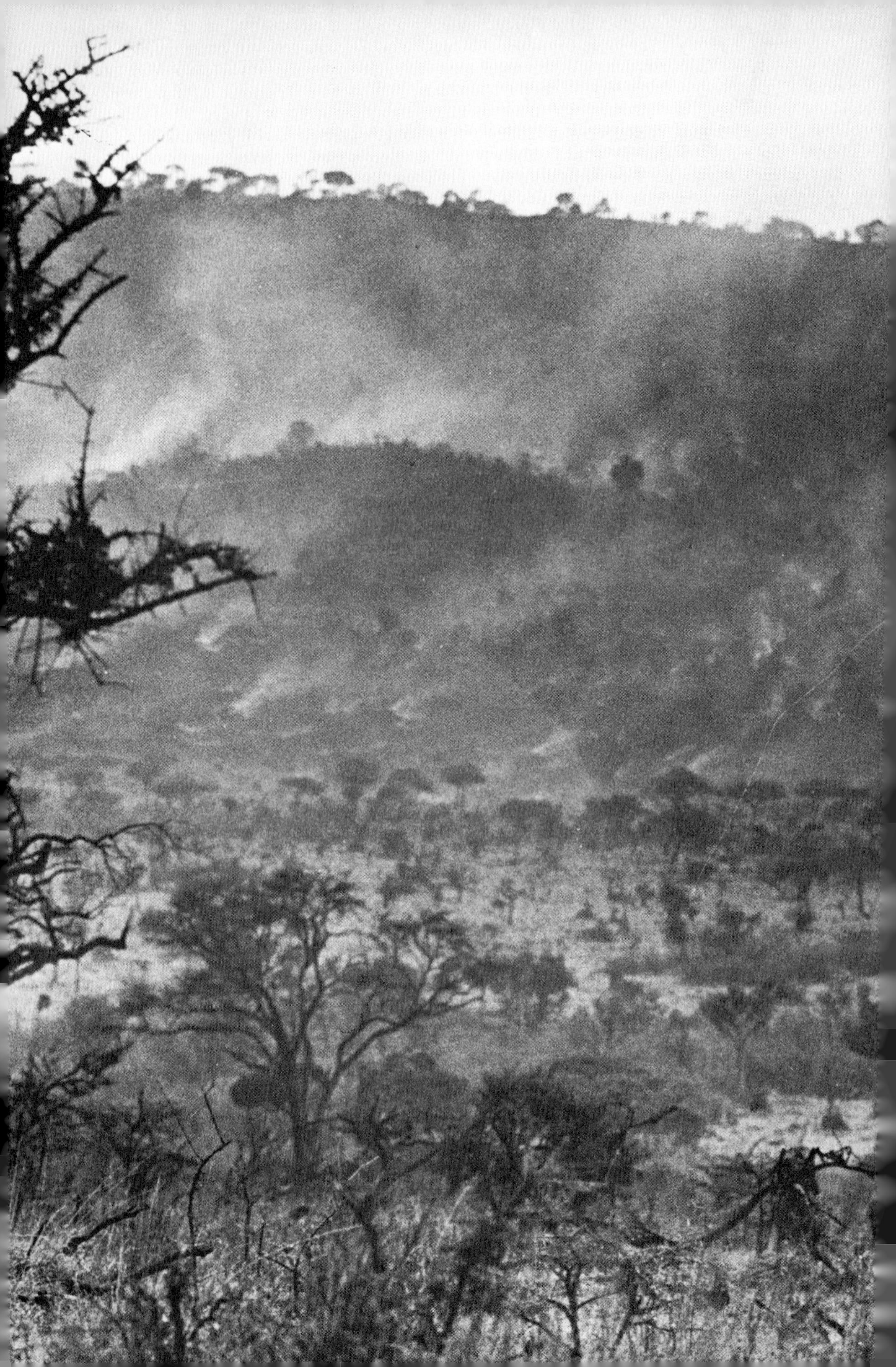

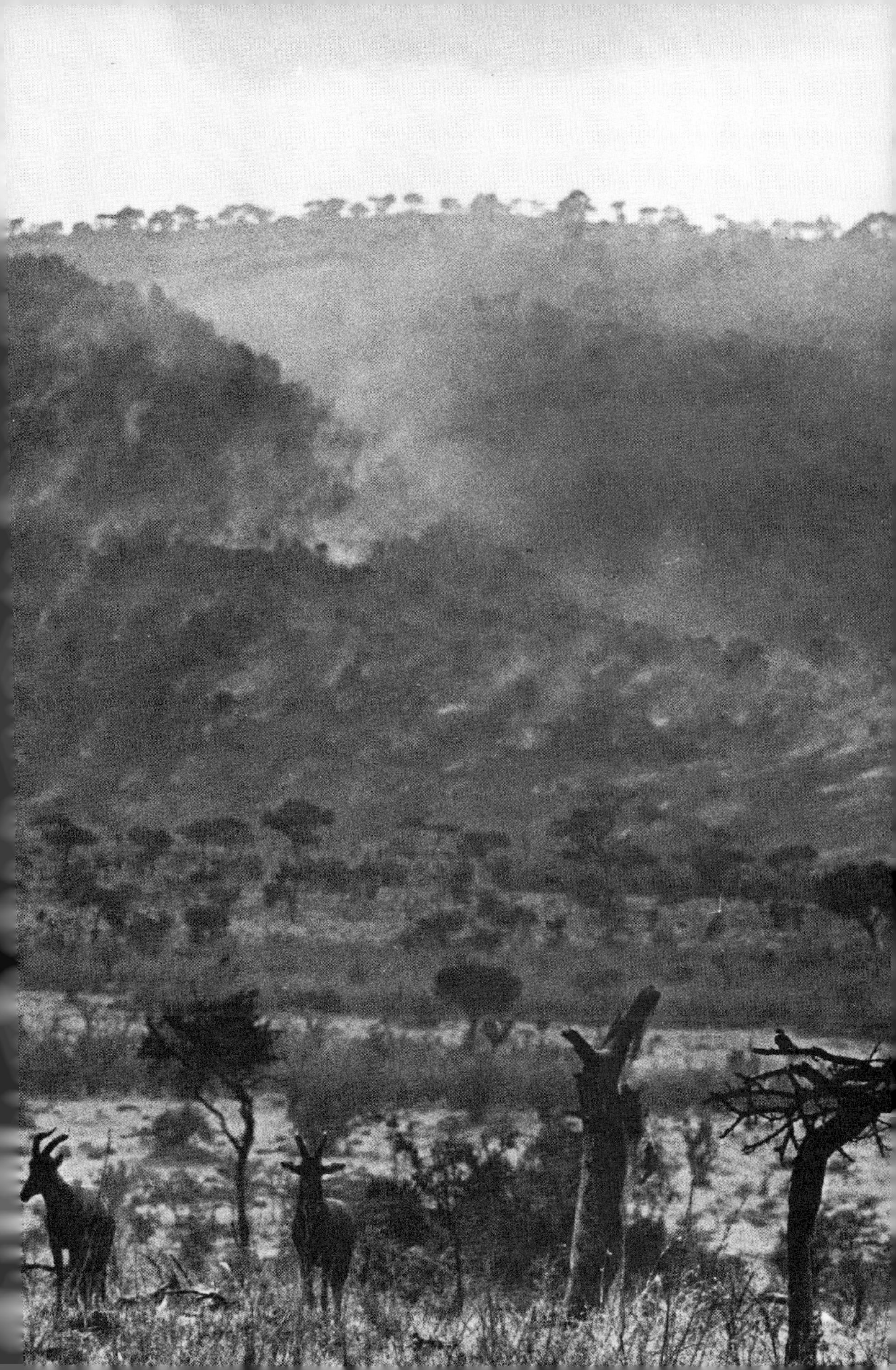

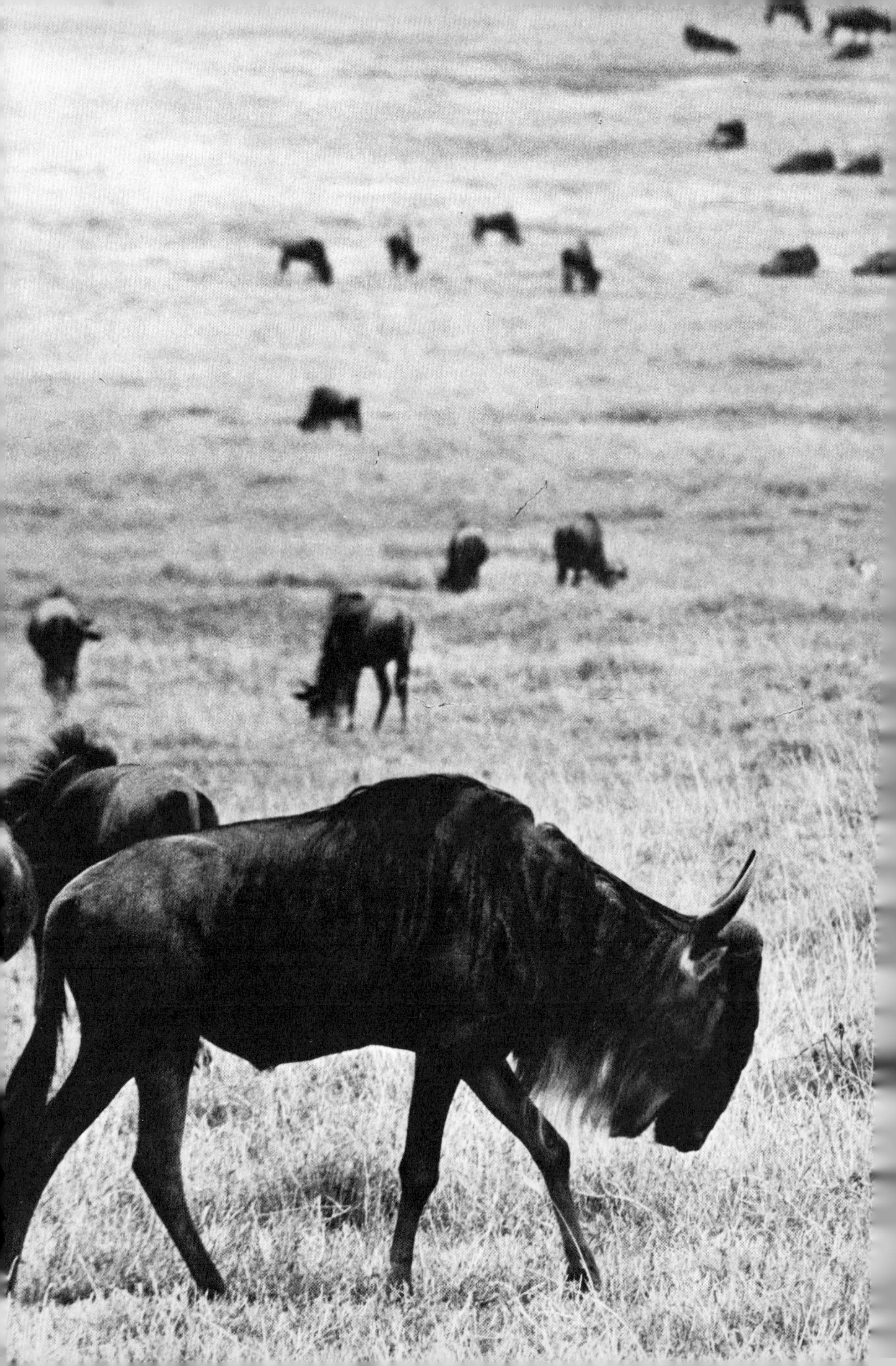

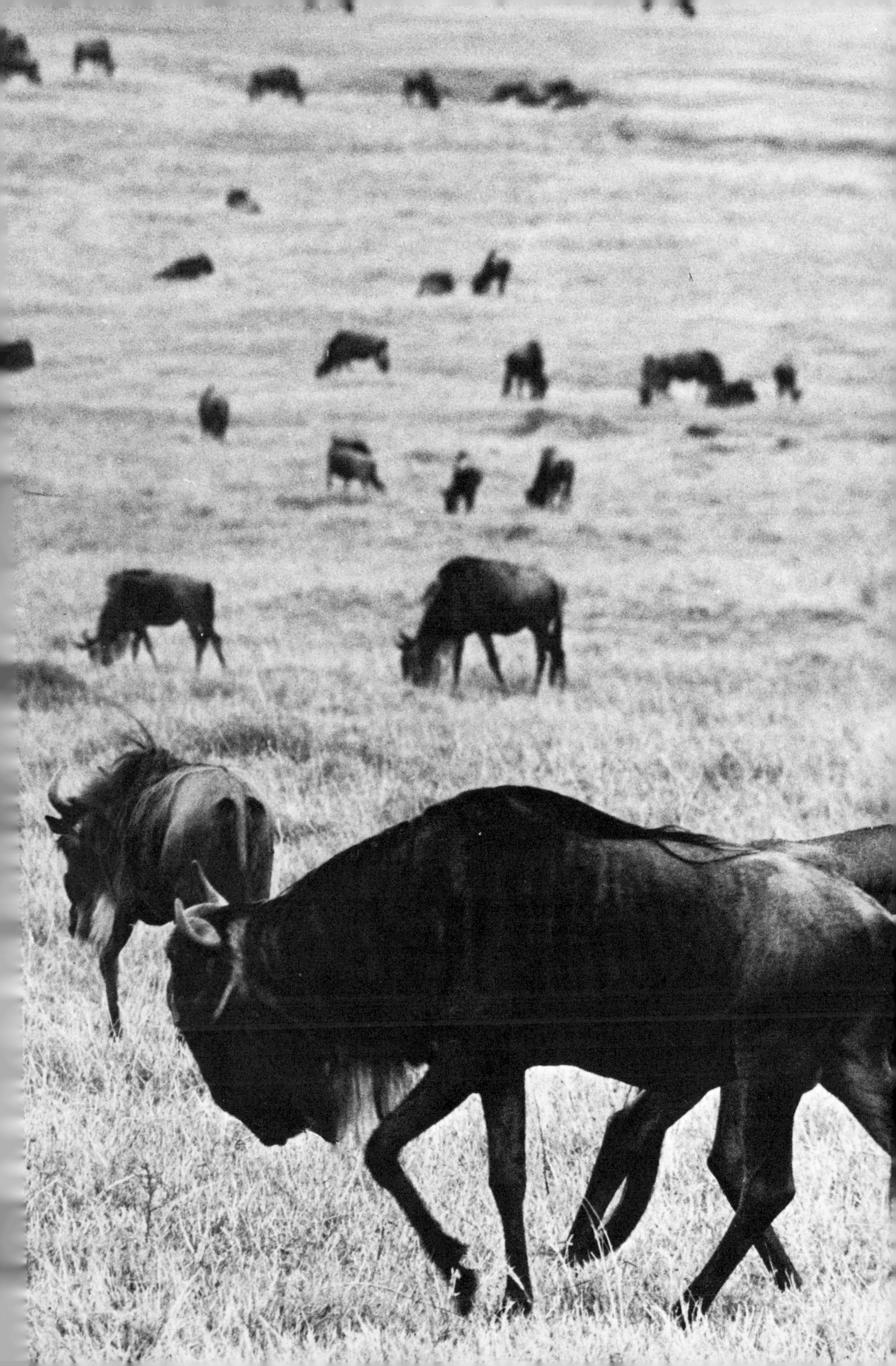

by ten times more cows and goats than the grass can support. Hundred-mile-wide forests in Africa are chopped down without making sure that they will grow again. New land is cleared for cultivation every day, but at the same time just as much arable land is destroyed when the earth is used until it is so impoverished that it can no longer yield a crop because it is not given any time to rest.

An ecosystem, for example the savanna, is a social community, a rather closed society. Community members produce goods and distribute them among themselves. The sun rules the society but does not have full control. Its power as the constant recreator of life is unconditionally balanced by water. A range of other essential resources are as important as water for life. The most important besides water (hydrogen) are carbon, oxygen, nitrogen, sulphur and phosphorus.

The ecosystem flourishes only when all these are present together under the sun. Then green plants are produced. The quantity of life that the sun can create in the ecosystem is determined by the supply and distribution of the six basic substances essential for life. In fact, we can measure the resulting primary production of grass, trees and plants exactly. Animals live off these and the number of animals—the secondary production of the ecosystem—as well as the variety of species, are completely dependent upon the amount, composition and variation of this primary produce. That is the way it is on the savanna and in all human societies as well.

Suppose, for example, that the Serengeti National Park were a balanced ecosystem. Then there would be no more animals in the Serengeti than the grassland and the sparse groves could adequately provide for. What do these meadows, trees and bushes, so thin and bare, in the dry season, really offer? They support, for example, 2,000 elephants. Elephants in the Serengeti amount to 3.6 million kilos of meat as a balanced annual produce, assuming that the average weight of an elephant is 1,800 kilos.

But all the other large herbivores in the Serengeti—gazelles, antelope, zebras, giraffes, rhinos—weighed a total of 116 million kilos when this count was made at the end of the sixties, and since then the number of animals in the Serengeti has drastically increased.

It is useful to measure nature's creative force in living weight, because then it is easier to understand that there are great possibilities but also absolute, definite limits for the production of life. We realize that the savanna is a community that produces great riches, not only in beauty. However awesomely weightless a Thomson's gazelle appears, it does weigh 16 kilos and is a product of tender grass.

Cattle-tending people are traditionally part of a natural ecosystem. For every square kilometer, the savanna's primary production is considered to be capable of supporting and nourishing 25 people together with other animals, including everything from butterflies to elephants.

But in Europe, because of modernized, industrialized land cultivation, the crops yielded by one square kilometer can support more than 2,000 people. Could the difference between these two figures be a measure of Africa's underdevelopment?

Ninety percent of tropical Africa's savanna is marginal land unsuited to cultivation, producing a very low yield as pasturage for livestock. This would be true of a naturally-balanced ecosystem. But if larger amounts of the six essential life substances that are lacking (carbon, hydrogen, oxygen, nitrogen, sulphur, phosphorus) could be added, then perhaps the savanna could be changed into an artificial ecosystem with a corresponding increase in productivity. This is what has been done in European agricultural districts.

It is not correct to say that the African savanna—most of Tanzania and Kenya—is worthless marginal land, until the following possibility has been tried. We must test the plausibility of conquering the enormous difficulties involved: sweltering sun for months on end, violent rains, water that evaporates rapidly and leaves salts, soil that erodes easily, a yield that is difficult to control and a multitude of diseases and noxious insects. All these demand great resources of knowledge, technical skills and money: in short, industrialization.

Even the desert can flourish and yield rich harvests. Artificial ecosystems can be created in what appear to be impossible contexts. It is often "only" a question of money, raw materials, energy and great knowledge of agricultural sciences and ecology. However, it cannot take place by disregarding the laws governing an ecosystem. Just as natural ecosystems are balanced, so artificial systems must be balanced according to soil, climate and crop conditions. With great resources and truly relevant ecological knowledge, the savanna could conceivably be changed into permanent agricultural land.

It is quite another problem whether the rich wild fauna, this priceless natural heritage, could exist in an agricultural landscape. But on the other hand, wild animals cannot proliferate abundantly if people are denied a corresponding prosperity. That too would be an imbalance—for the whole world is one large ecosystem. Studies of small neutral ecosystems like the savanna provide the basic knowledge for us to adjust the global imbalance, which could also be called inequality or injustice.

At one time, grassland rich in wildlife also extended over North Africa, Egypt and the Tigris and Euphrates valleys in western Asia. Today these are deserts and semi-deserts. From grassland, they became grazing land and then artificially-irrigated farmland. Even if major climatic changes contributed, it is likely that human mistakes in agricultural measures have been the main cause for this total desolation. It came about gradually, in the form of minor injuries done to the land over thousands of years, and larger, disastrous damage done during wars and difficult times.

Humans did not live successfully within the terms of the environment. They sold their future to the desert and that future is our present. The impoverished Yemen, once fertile, was known as "Arabia Felix." Somewhere along the line, the wild herbivores and the lions disappeared.

Tropical Africa has not been destroyed so far. Severe problems of development have struck relatively recently. We know very little about its earlier history, but we can read some of the results of history in the landscape. We can venture to say that the East African savanna is by and large a cultivated landscape and that vast areas of it have degenerated to barely fertile bush and semi-desert as a consequence of humans forcing the land to yield in the past.

Most of the overstraining of the savanna occurred during colonial times, when the British, Germans and other Europeans stole the best land and forced the Africans out to marginal land which became rapidly de-

When an ecosystem has been firmly established, it is practically indestructible. Natural catastrophes—or human interference—are needed to break down a society evolved by time, material resources and life expressed here in the beautiful zoning of buffalo and zebra in the Serengeti grass.

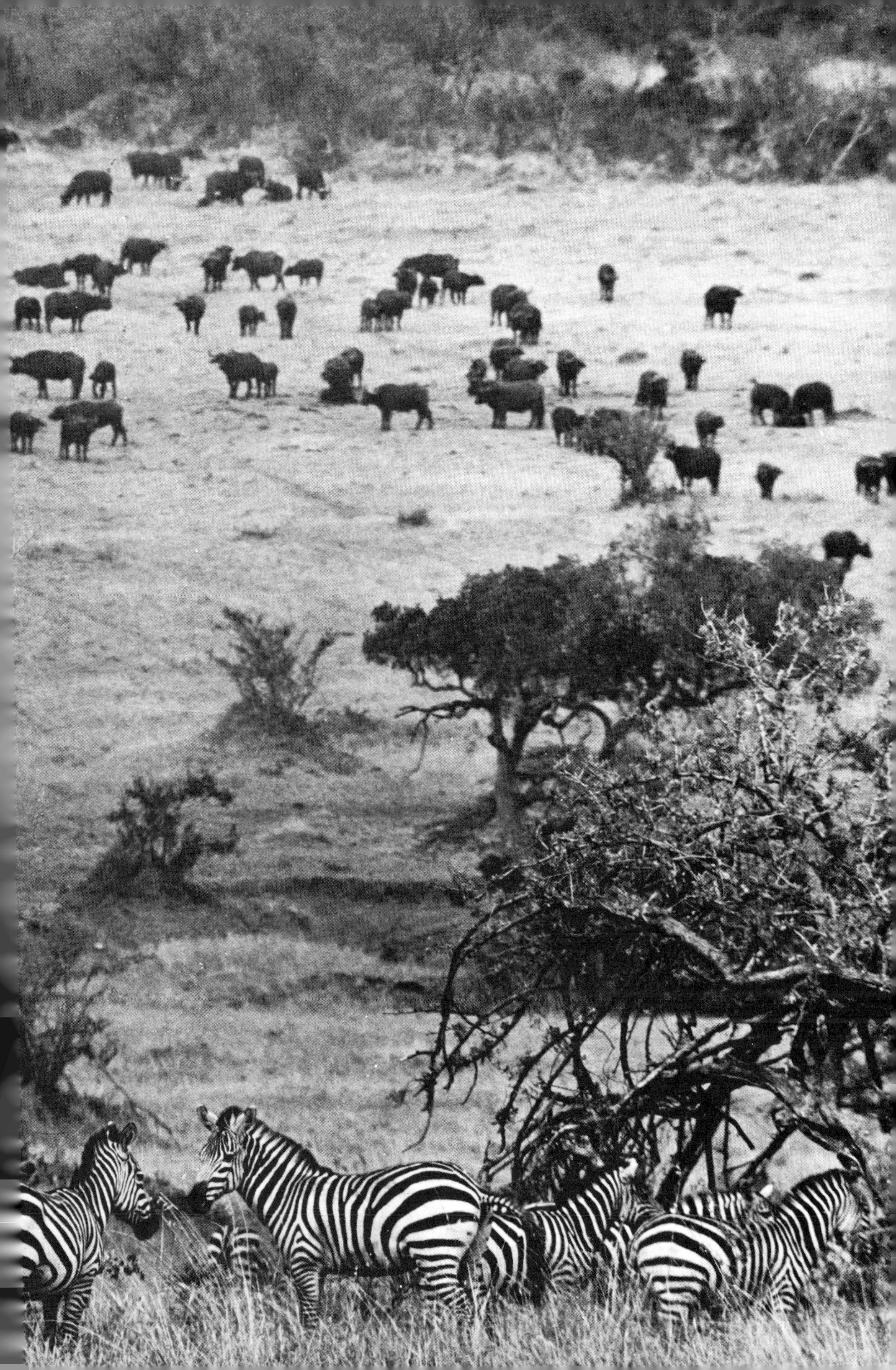

pleted. The cattle-tending Masai and other nomadic tribes who base their cultures on exploitation of extensive grazing lands had their freedom of movement restricted. It was further restricted by cattle plagues and tsetse flies.

These people were locked into the plateaus and dry valleys. Gradually they got help: wells were dug to provide water for their livestock; their thin animals came to benefit from the fruits of modern veterinary medicine. The people themselves received some medical attention, but the grazing lands didn't become any larger just because there were more people and their cows produced more calves. Today they live with far too many animals on land that is rapidly being broken up and gradually destroyed.

Why do thousands of people die regularly in severe floods in India and Bangladesh? The floods are caused by rains rushing over the earth without being soaked up, because the vegetation has been ruined. When the earth lies bare and hard-packed like a cement floor, it cannot absorb the water. Once this catastrophically-destroyed earth supported grass and trees and animals, but humans had no way of supporting their chil-

---

The sun's heat makes the air shimmer on the hot savanna and results in highly contrasted color patterns like the giraffe's and the zebra's that can blend in and fade out the animals' contours. The patterns on these animals definitely have a protective function.

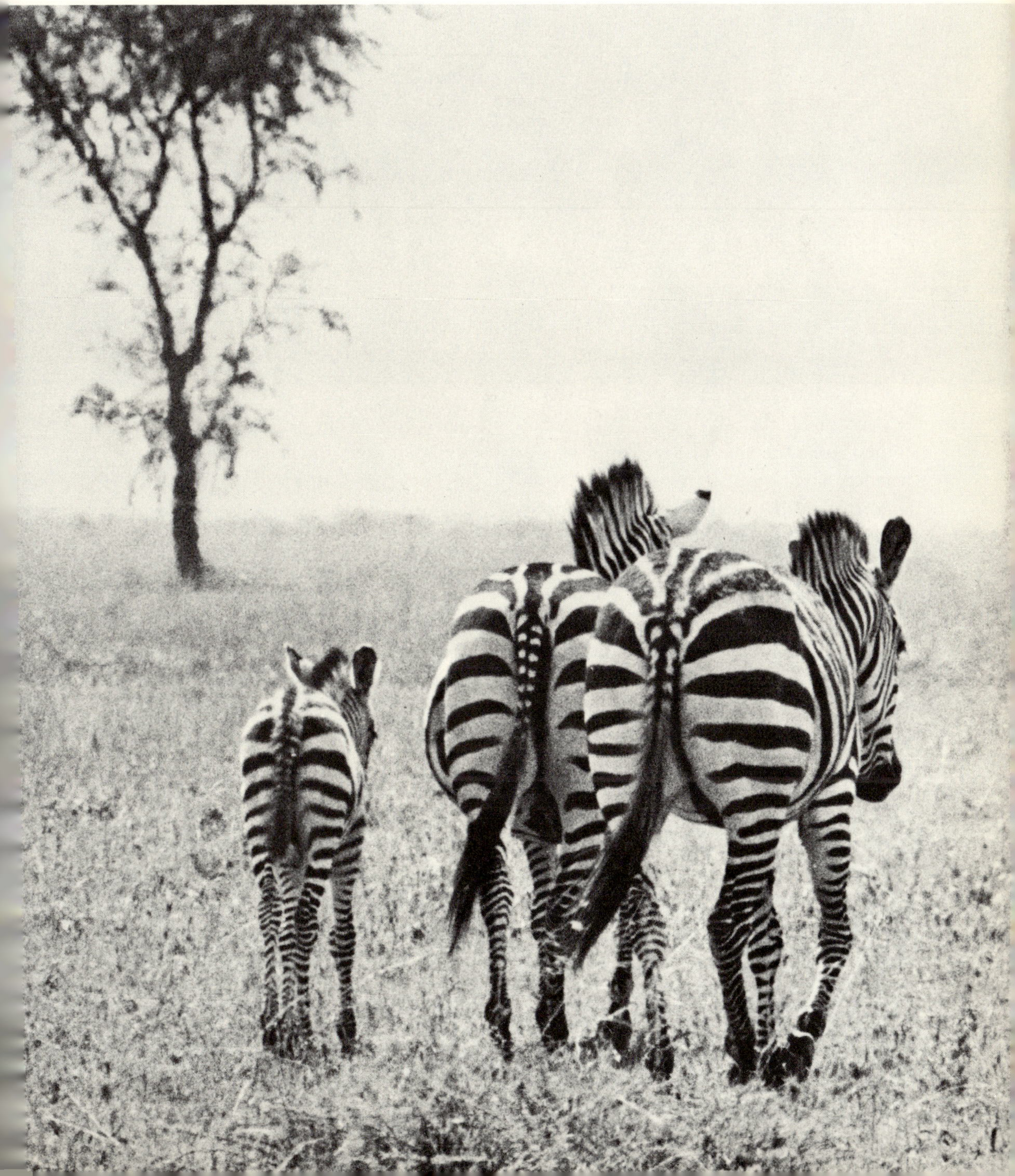

dren and no choice but to exploit the earth. So they broke the laws of the ecosystem. As secondary consumers, they took more from the earth than the earth's primary producers could give and tolerate. Then the givers of life—the sun and water—became the enemies of life.

The humans had no choice. They couldn't get food any other way, because those with plenty lived in another world and did not share. These flood and famine catastrophes will continue and worsen as long as an imbalance continues, because helping out after a catastrophe is only charity; the earth is already dead. Are we really aware, we who talk about environmental protection, that global environmental destruction probably reaps millions of human lives?

We know where the surplus and the resources are, so it should be possible to repair many of the damaged environments. It is also possible for us to use our knowledge of how the earth should be farmed and developed so that people can support themselves on it without making future harvests impossible. Every possibility is still wide-open—the solutions cry out from the eroded corners of the earth—but the rich world cuts down its aid for development and at the same time increases its extortion of resources and men from underprivileged lands.

I sit down in the shade of an acacia in the Serengeti. I feel at home there. A herd of zebras passes a short distance from me.

Zebras move and graze in family parties. There are often five to eight animals in a group. The stallion is the chief, but the leader of the family is an old mare. She walks first, choosing the way between water holes and grazing lands. After her come the foals, arranged by age with the youngest first. Recently added family members come last. The stallion walks by himself, slightly apart from the rest. This ranking order may be maintained for an entire year.

Why do I feel such security in the wilderness? Because I feel in my whole being that prolific nature is indestructible in its harmony, in the unity of all living things. I feel part of this community, and I'm not afraid of the lion. But my intelligence tells me that just as people destroy each other, so do they also destroy nature. The Serengeti will certainly die unless better directions for development are given to Tanzania. This is true all over the world. For instance, unless strict limits and regulations are established for industrialization in eastern North and South Carolina, the offshore islands and their wildlife will be destroyed.

Imbalances are impossible to adjust from either end of the spectrum. Too much development is just as bad as too little. The environmental debate should have taught us that, for underdevelopment and overdevelopment are the two ground rules of environmental destruction. Economists find that the rich nations of the world can continue to become richer only as long as the poor nations become increasingly poorer, because the size of the earth and the yield of its resources is fixed. It is high time to channel surplus in the direction of equality among people and nations all over the globe. Studies of nature teach us that this is necessary.

There's a scent of heat and animal droppings under the tree where I'm sitting. From somewhere comes the shriek of an unfamiliar bird. The zebras walk across the still living earth. ∎

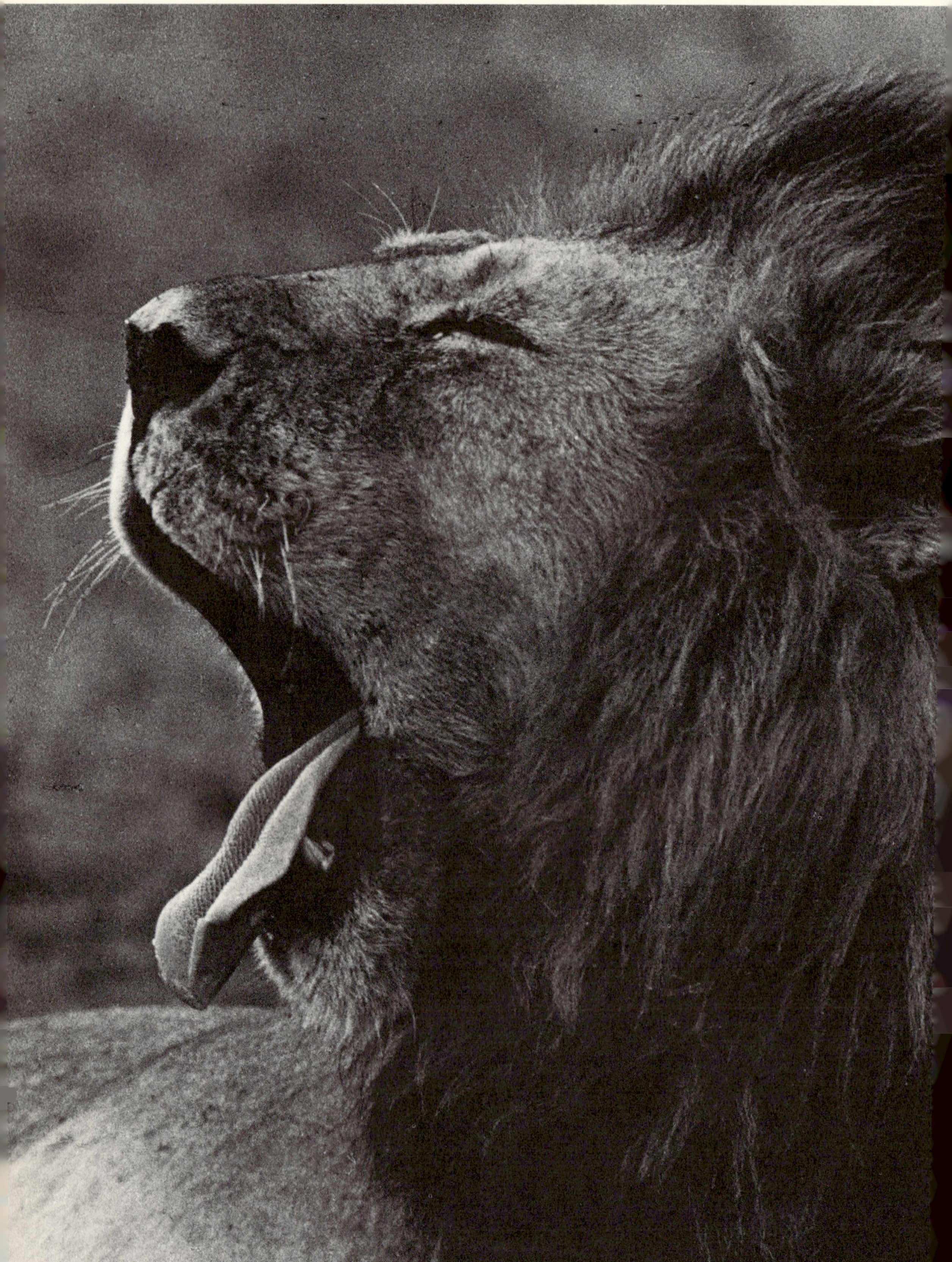

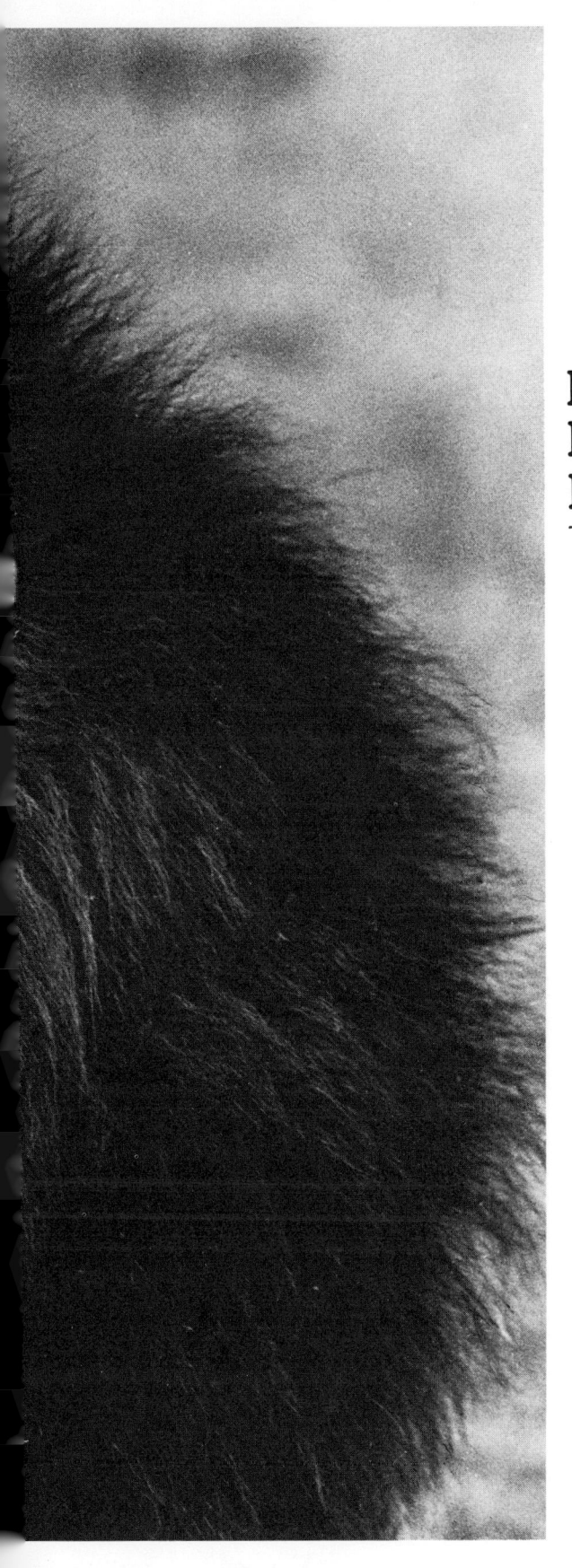

LIONS HAVE A HARD TIME

The lion, king of the beasts, kills innocent babies of its own species. The lioness is a bad mother. She takes all the food she wants herself first; her babies take second place. Infant mortality is high—50 to 90 percent —in lion families. The hyena is at least as good a hunter as the lion. Lions often chase hyenas away from the hyena's kill. There are about 1,000 lions in the Serengeti and more than 2,000,000 game animals. And yet the lions are often in need and their cubs starving. Why?

If you pitch a tent in one of East Africa's national parks, you'll turn in really early. You sit awhile by the camp fire, drinking tea. But you won't head off for an evening stroll. It's not a good idea; it's not allowed —and it's not tempting. The darkness is dense, and you know that out there in the night lions, buffaloes, hippos and other obviously dangerous animals are prowling about.

Instead, you get up early. Morning in Amboseli: we were up at five, with the first signs of dawn. We had gathered wood the evening before. We stirred the embers and blew a breakfast fire to life. We fried eggs, boiled tea water and stretched out on the dewy grass to follow the sun's ascent of Kilimanjaro's snowy peak.

Four lions were sitting in a palm grove nearby, staring at us. Young lions. We were the only campers there. The lions came over through the high green grass between us and the palm grove, bounding, playful, looking quite nice. Two of the lions were males. We saw the first signs of their maleness growing around their faces. They mooched off into the trees.

We joked all day about our lion visitation. You feel rather exposed when you camp in Africa. Around the hotels in Amboseli, there are huge warning signs forbidding guests to leave the hotel grounds after nightfall under penalty of a fine. There are no such restrictions for campers. They have to follow their own judgment out in the bush with the wild animals.

In the game wardens' reports from East African national parks, which as a rule are published in the African newspapers, you read all the time about people torn to death by lions. Someone going down to the lake to fish meets a lion on the way. Someone having a glass of wine on his verandah dozes off during the crickets' evening concert only to wake up to find himself in a lion's jaws being dragged out of his easy chair.

Jonathan Kingdon in the first part of his magnificent book *East African Mammals* refers to an attempt to analyze the circumstances in which a lion becomes a man-eater. It is, as a rule, young lions, still unskilled hunters, that attack men. People are easy to catch and offer very little resistance.

Lions often have a hard time; it is especially difficult for them to get food after the rains when the grass is so high that warthogs, bush pigs and other smaller game—a young lion's main diet—can hide.

We were thinking about this in Amboseli when we returned to our camping site. We

Why does the lion roam around our tent?
What causes the lion sometimes to become
a man-eater? We had occasion to think that
over at our camping site in Amboseli.

intended to go out into the bush to gather wood for our fire. The grass was really high. The lions that had visited us in the morning had been young. Why were they prowling around our campsite? How hungry were they?

But, we told ourselves, they just happened to be walking by. Surely they had moved off somewhere else by now.

We hadn't walked more than three steps from our tent toward a grove of trees where there were dry branches, when we saw a lion, scarcely visible in the grass, glaring at us, ready to spring—or so we thought. A young lion, probably famished, since the grass was so unusually high. Here were the best conditions for turning a lion into a man-eater.

And where were the three pals from his pride? We looked around the grass and thickets as darkness fell. We couldn't go get wood after all. We quickly struck our tent and set it up a good distance away, near a road where the grass was shorter so that we could see further. We went to sleep without dinner.

Another time, in the Serengeti, the grass was shorter. There we lived protected by lamps, guarded by a night watchman. That was in Seronera, a community inside the national park.

"This is the wild animals' kingdom," said the night watchman. "We people stay here on charity. There's a good chance a lion is lying behind the nearest bush or even among the houses. Because you're not used to this,

A warthog and its baby wander along, grazing.

I'll make sure that you don't amble off on a dubious walk in the dark. It could turn out bad."

We laughed at him. It did sound funny. But early in the morning we drove through the sparsely-settled community. People were walking along the streets and there suddenly lay a lioness by the roadside. On a rock, with a home in the background, her mate was stretched out comfortably. We stopped, looked, photographed, quite amazed. Passersby on the road hastened along. We couldn't stop thinking of the zoo at home.

Suddenly the lioness stiffened, got up, stood still as a statue, her tail twitching eagerly. Her eyes stared off into the distance. We followed the direction of her gaze. A warthog family of two sows and five little piglets was wandering along, eating grass a ways off.

The lioness started slowly in that direction. The nearer she got, the slower she went and the lower she crept. She sank down gradually into the grass so that she finally seemed to be walking on her knees. Suddenly she was off, and the piglets didn't stand a chance.

With a quivering, dead, bloody piglet in her jaws, she went off and lay down in the shade. We sat in our car to watch her eat the piglet. First she lapped up the blood. Then she tore the baby to pieces, lowering her eyelids as she chewed. Her mouth was covered with blood.

It was 8:30 in the morning: the lioness' breakfast. In the afternoon, we came across a pride of lions, numbering no fewer than 25. They were all lying around, taking it easy in the particularly intense afternoon sun. A carful of tourists was already there when we arrived. Then more tourists drove up around the pride, stopped awhile to marvel before they drove on.

We stayed there for several hours. Nothing much happened. It takes patience to study lions. It isn't at all unusual for a lion family to laze and sleep day and night on their sides or on their backs in the same place. Lions seem able to take any amount of heat from the sun. Lions that have eaten don't hunt. They save their energy until it is needed.

There are about 1,000 lions in the Serengeti. Two hundred are solitary, following the big wild herds. These are outcast lions that haven't a place in the home or hunting territories claimed by the 800 group-living lions. Those of us visiting the national park saw perhaps 30 lions that were used to tourists. It's a good feeling to know there are still 970 lions roving around in paradise, undiscovered by tourists.

We know quite a bit about how the Serengeti's wild lions live. A lion field researcher is almost always stationed at the fine research station in the park.

The Serengeti's lions ought to be able to lead a good life. They are surrounded by about 2,000,000 game animals. Their primary food is the gnu, although they sometimes choose to kill a zebra. There are at least 160,000 zebras. Or a gazelle. There are undoubtedly 1,000,000 of the various gazelle species.

A number of years ago, an estimate was made of the annual consumption of the 700 lions then in the Serengeti. It was calculated at that time that there were 330,000 gnu in the Serengeti. The lions killed 3,800 gnu a year. They ate 2,000 zebras, 600 buffaloes, 400 Thomson's gazelles, 400 impalas and 400 ostriches. Plus a number of giraffes and lots of small animals.

All in all, these 700 lions ate approximately 1.2 million kilos of meat a year. A lion can down 30 kilos of meat in a day. The annual consumption per lion was 1.8 tons.

These are fantastic statistics—and yet the lions sometimes suffer from not having enough to eat. Are lions such poor hunters? One of the answers is that the Serengeti is large (13,000 square kilometers) and the herbivores are clever. Gnu, zebras and gazelles move to different parts of the park depending on their grazing.

Lions, on the other hand, generally keep to the same area. The lions' living standard is determined by access to game in their own hunting territory. The lions' inertia forces them to experience periods of real need when their meat supply is grazing out of reach, a number of miles away. Some researchers think that lions are stationary because their young can't keep up with them in lengthy wanderings. It could also be said that this arrangement maintains a good balance between lions and game.

Studies in various East African national parks show that the ratio of lions to large herbivores is, as a rule, at least one to three hundred. The lions' hard life in the Serengeti, where the density of game is great, shows that lions are by no means more powerful than their game. As a rule, lions are forced to make many unsuccessful hunting attempts before they assuage their hunger. There's a continuing evolutionary race between beasts of prey and their game. The antelope have the lion to thank for their own alertness and swiftness. At the same pace as the herbivores develop cleverness in avoiding the beast of prey, the beast of prey must improve its ability to hunt. Obviously, an inferior prey would quickly disappear. The hunter always directs his efforts against the weakest.

Now a balance prevails between equally strong parties. The equality is a consequence of each being able to look after themselves. They exist with built-in protections against exploitation, just like the whistling thorn and the giraffe. There is never a risk that a beast of prey will destroy the basis for his own existence.

When people talk about the threat of beasts of prey, they are discussing situations in which human intervention has destroyed the natural balance. This can pose a great problem, but the beast of prey does not cause the problem by its bloodthirstiness or greed; people are to blame for having destroyed the natural order.

The lion family has to defend a hunting

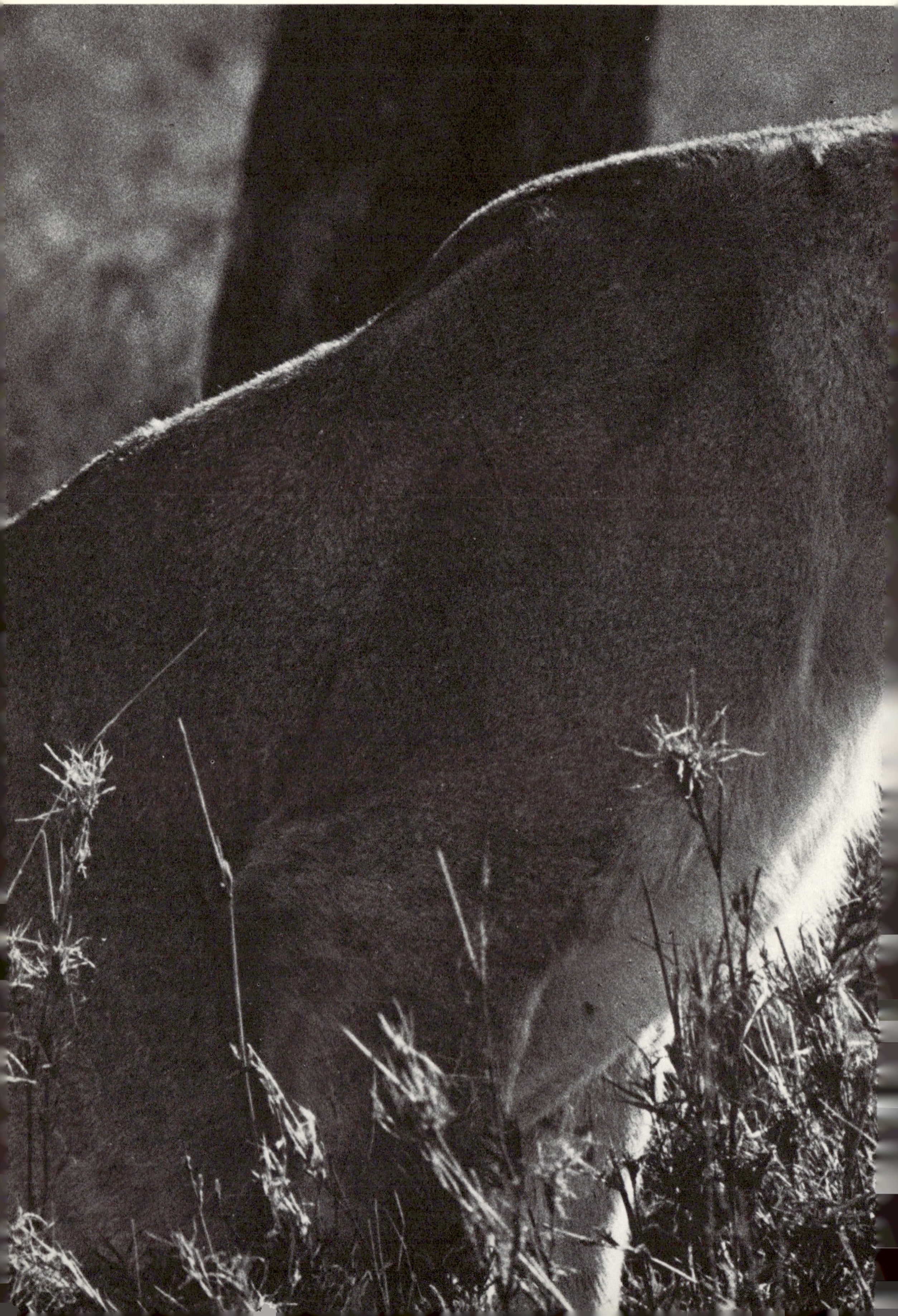

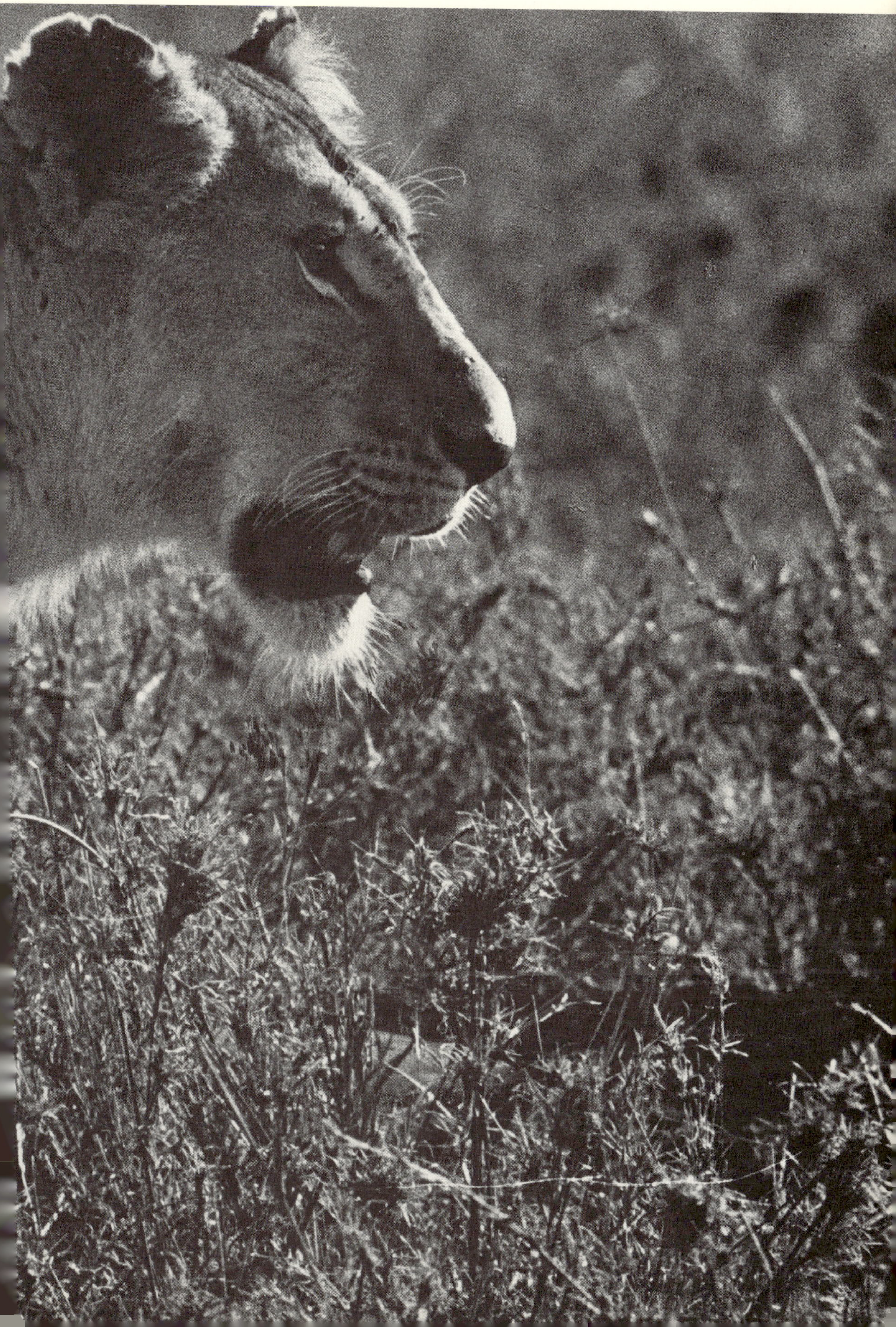

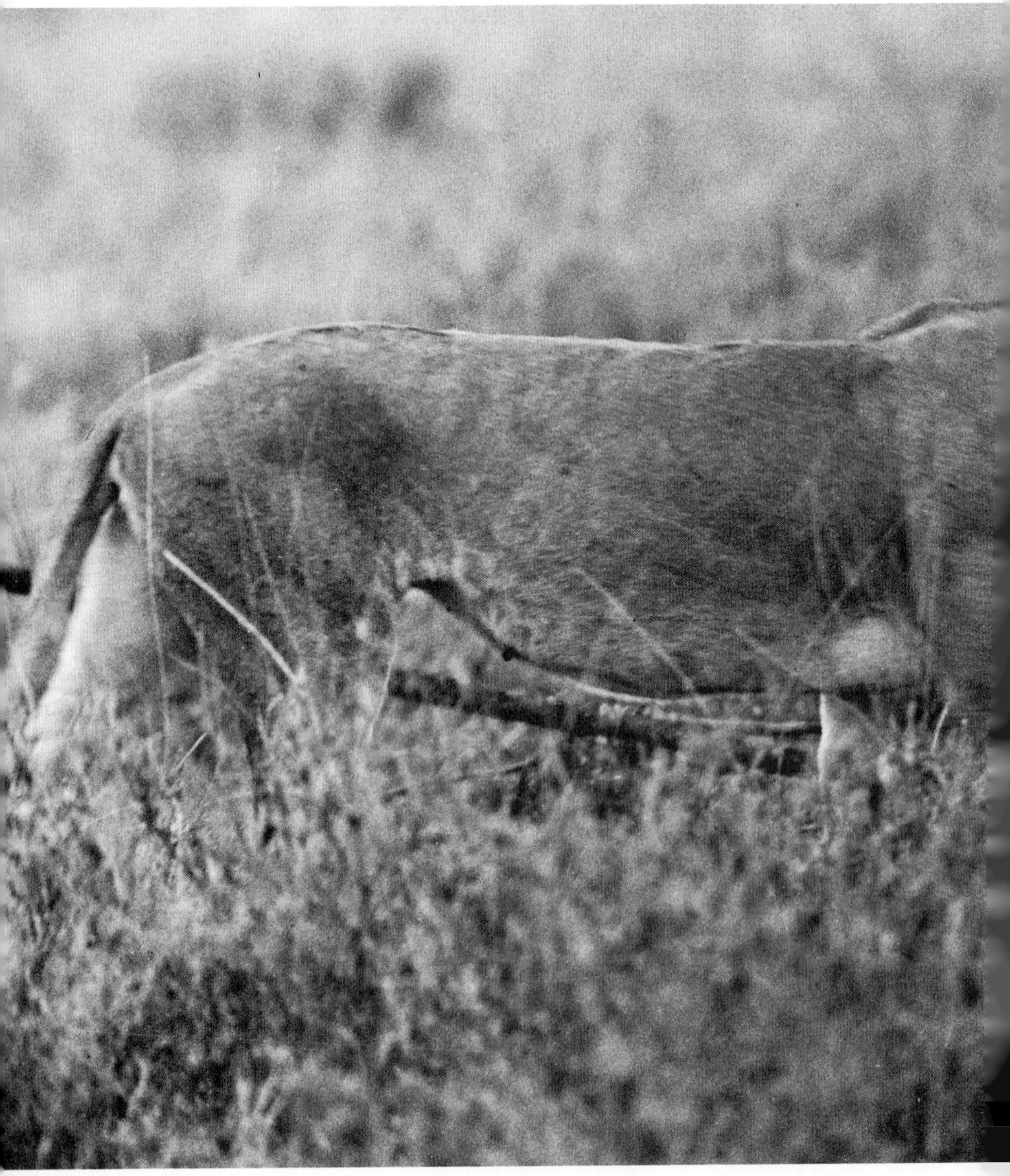

A lioness sees the warthog's piglets out playing and makes a decision. She creeps off through the grass, first slowly, then faster and faster.

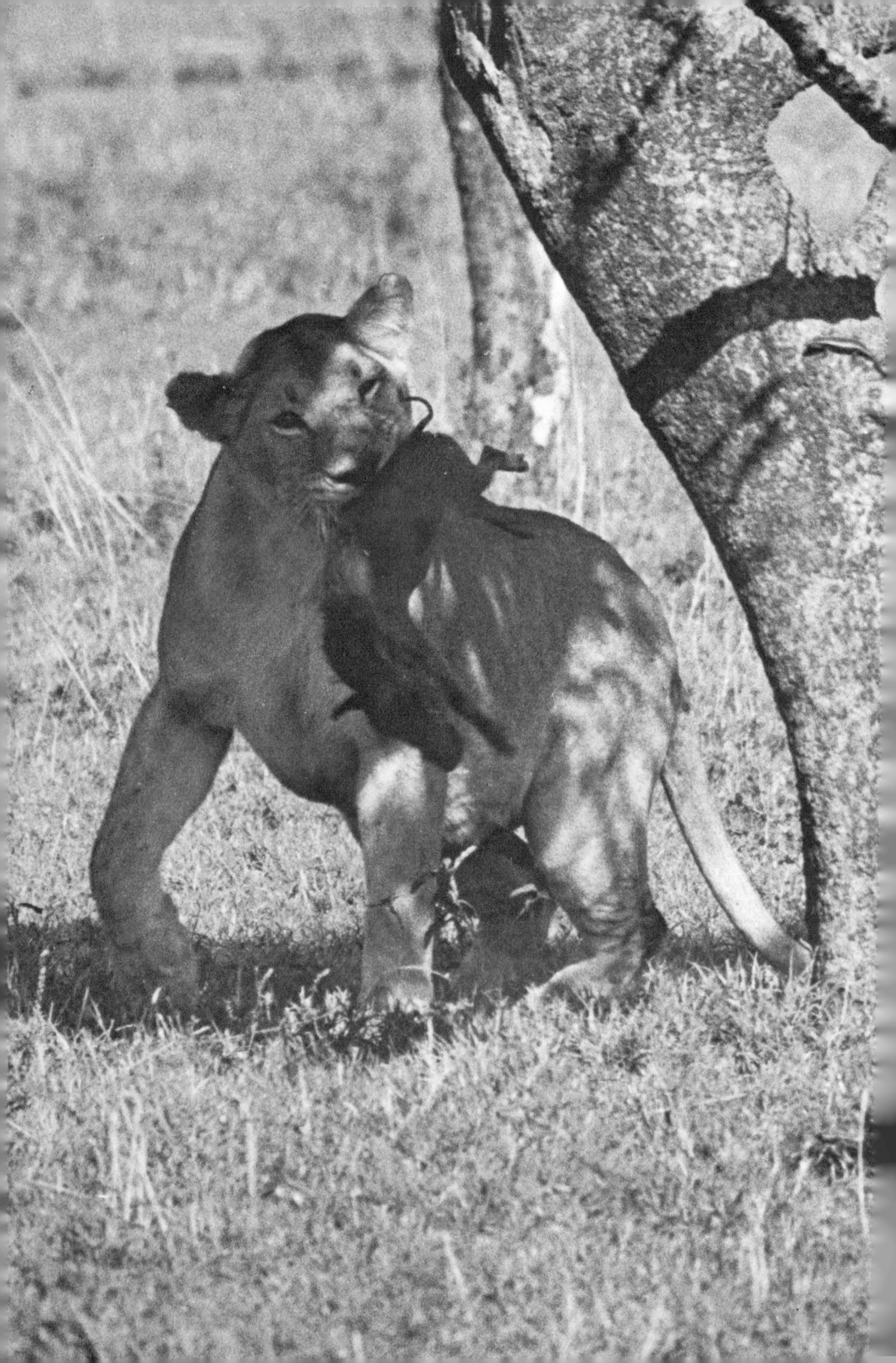

With a still twitching piglet in her jaws, she goes to lie down in the shade of a tree.

First she laps up the piglet's blood. Then she eats it with great relish. This was a lioness' breakfast one morning in the Serengeti.

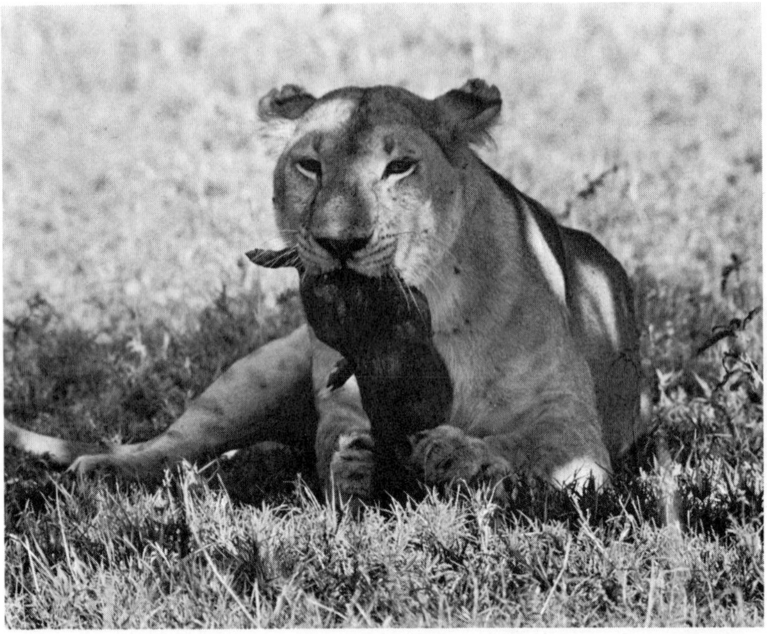

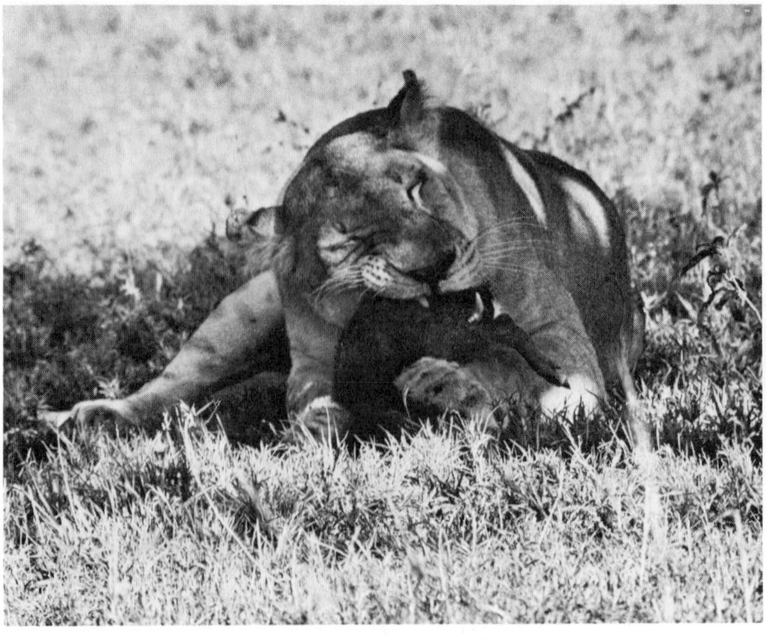

The day will come when a young male lion must leave the family circle and set off on his own. Eventually, he will join another pride in a new territory. To become a member of the pride, he may have to depose the male leader. This takes strength, courage and acts of aggression.

This may not be a mother and her cub. Lions live in extended families including several females; the young attach themselves with equal trust to both their mothers and their aunts. Each female looks after her own young first, but she also accepts other cubs, playing with them and nursing them if she can fit them in.

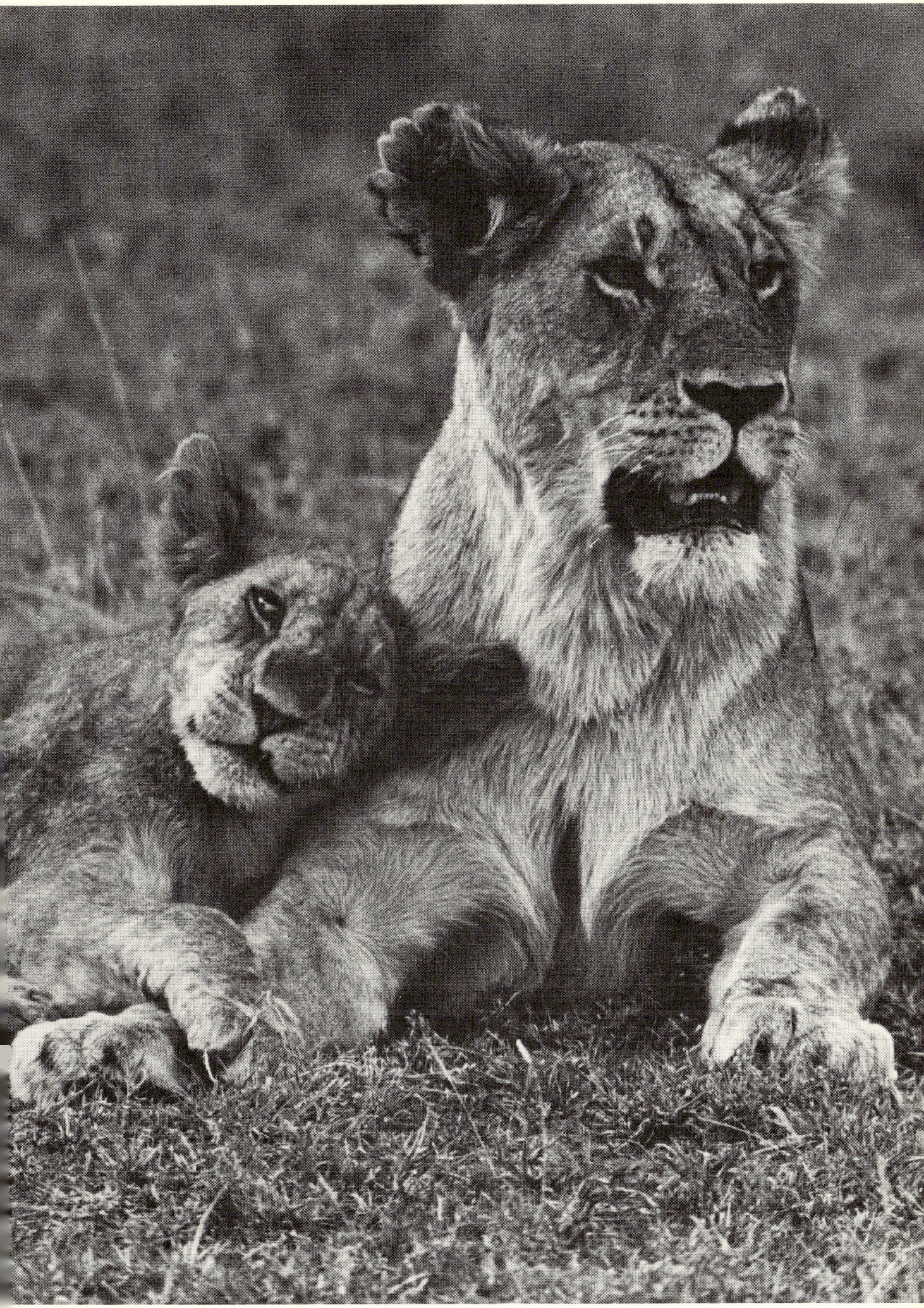

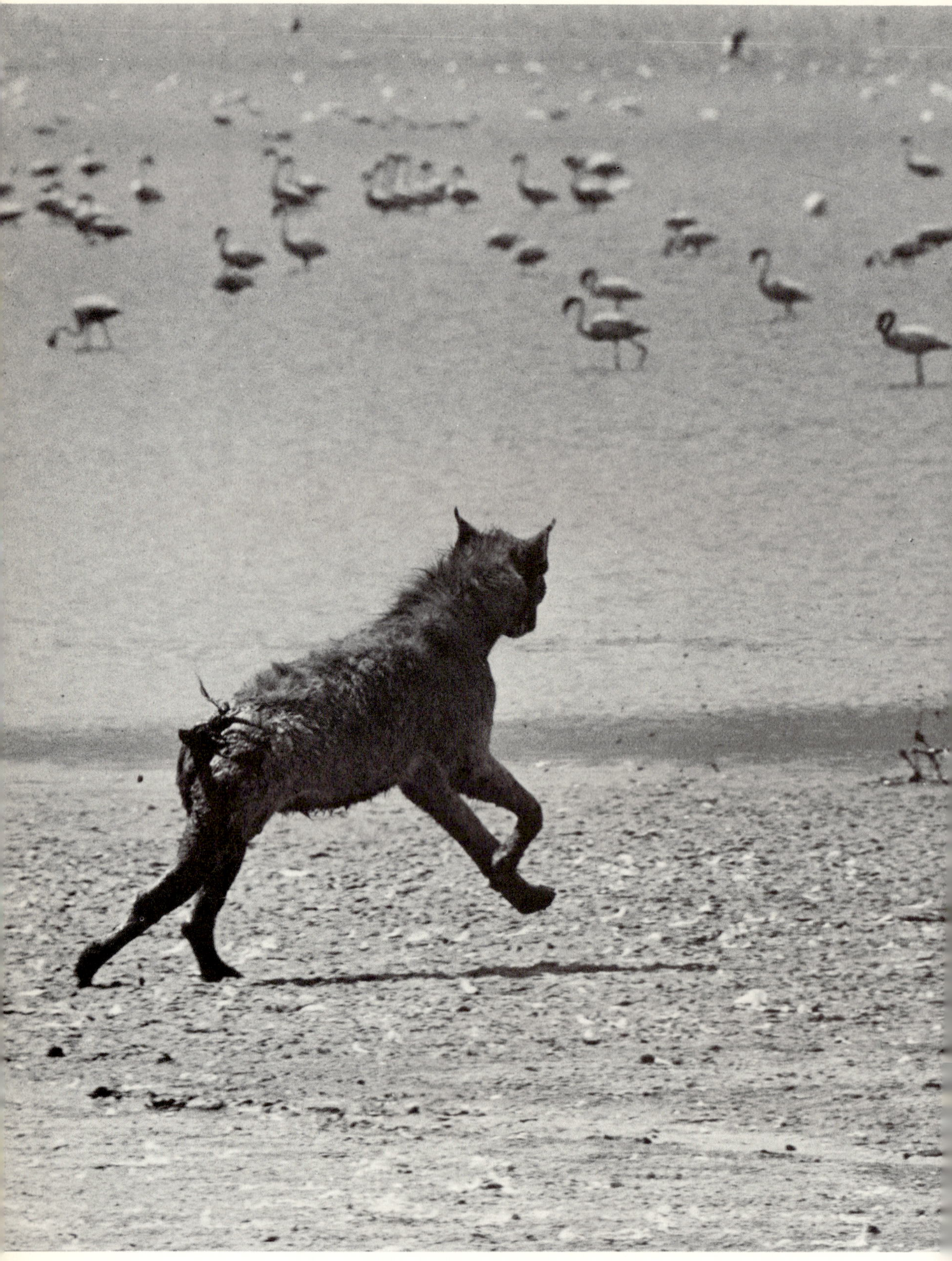

Spotted hyenas have a great time in the mud of the salt lake at the bottom of Ngorongoro crater in Tanzania. Good hunters, with stronger jaws than some other beasts of prey, they are often more successful than lions. A field researcher managed to follow the same lion at a discreet distance for 21 days. During this period on the savanna, the lion ate seven times and every time his nouishment consisted of food stolen from the hyenas. An investigation in the Serengeti revealed that the hyenas, which are three times as numerous as the lions, killed 10,000 gnu a year, while the lions took 3,800. If we admire the lion for its cleverness as a hunter, we must also admire the hyena for the same reason, and when we say that the hyena is a carrion eater, we ought to point out that the lion is one as well.

territory sufficiently large to nourish its members, even when most of the game is elsewhere. The males have the task of defending the territory. Of course, the territory is defended primarily against other lions, since these are their main competitors—they hunt the same game and have the same hunting habits.

Constant territorial fights are avoided because the lion stays basically in one place. But there are still many conflicts. However tender and caressing lions are to each other within the family, they are equally merciless and unsparing to members of other families threatening their security. Without one or several males to defend the family's territory, the pride would not survive. One pride contained two males, and one was killed in a fight. Left with only one male, the family couldn't sustain itself. Within two years, 24 of the family's younger lions died.

But a neighboring pride defended by three males supported 12 out of 20 young ones, which seems to be an unusually good number for a lion group. The young often die of starvation, deprivation or neglect. Or they are murdered.

An American field researcher, George B. Schaller, who studied lions for several years in the Serengeti, watched two males chase another male out of a neighboring territory. Then they hunted up the male's three cubs that were hiding in the bush and tore all three of them to death. They ate one of the cubs, left another and took the third with them as a kind of trophy.

If the male lion is a murderer and a cannibal, the lioness is a bad mother. She stays away hunting both night and day while her young are left alone. It is not clear whether the food she brings home is for them. When food is scarce, the lioness eats first. She hisses and spits at her cubs, pushing them away with her paws. After she has had enough, the cubs can eat, if there's anything left.

Human morality doesn't apply to lions—only to people. The king of the beasts kills innocent babies of his own species and lets his cubs starve, perhaps to prevent overpopulation. Population control takes grim expressions. It is a war of resources. This also occurs with corresponding grimness among men.

The lion's "bad sides" serve an ecological function. They are of value to the lion community. Naturally, they cannot live like people, according to rules of solidarity, unselfishness and mutual respect of individual rights. Humans could never find it defensible to live like lions. When that happens, humans deny their humanity, but they still don't become lions. They become empty instruments of evil, making mistakes about where they belong in both nature and culture. There are people like that. ■

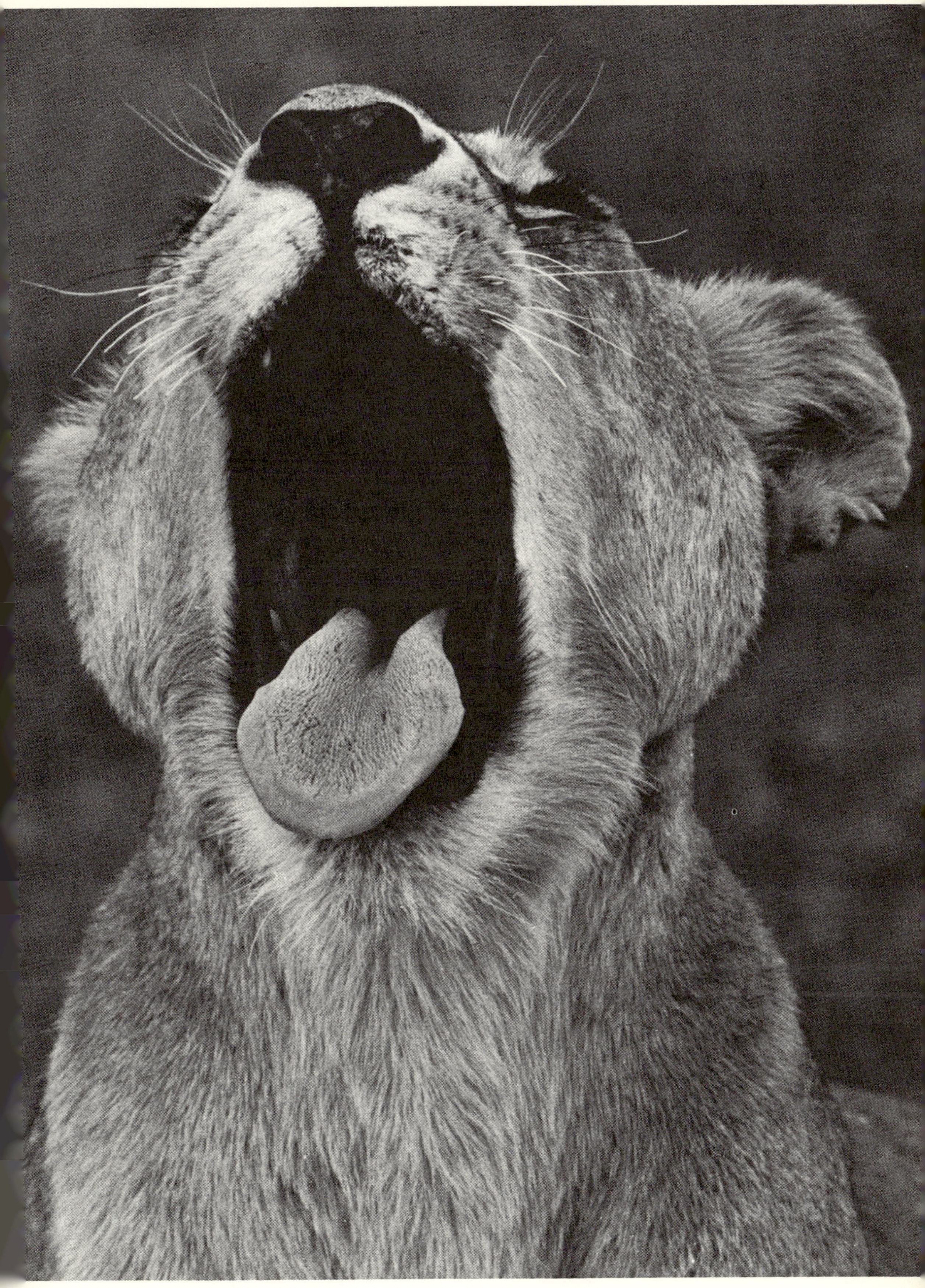

PERHAPS MY FAVORITE ANIMAL

The crocodile is a dangerous animal. He looks dull and apathetic lying around in the daytime on the beach, but when evening comes and he slides out into the water to hunt, the crocodile becomes dangerous. Notice how observant its eye looks! Crocodiles move astonishingly quickly. Floating in the water, they are said to be able to snap up a weaverbird flying past. Crocodiles have attacked and killed lions and rhinos. But lions have learned to kill crocodiles too. Also hippos seem to bite the tails off crocodiles that are too inquisitive in the home environment they share.

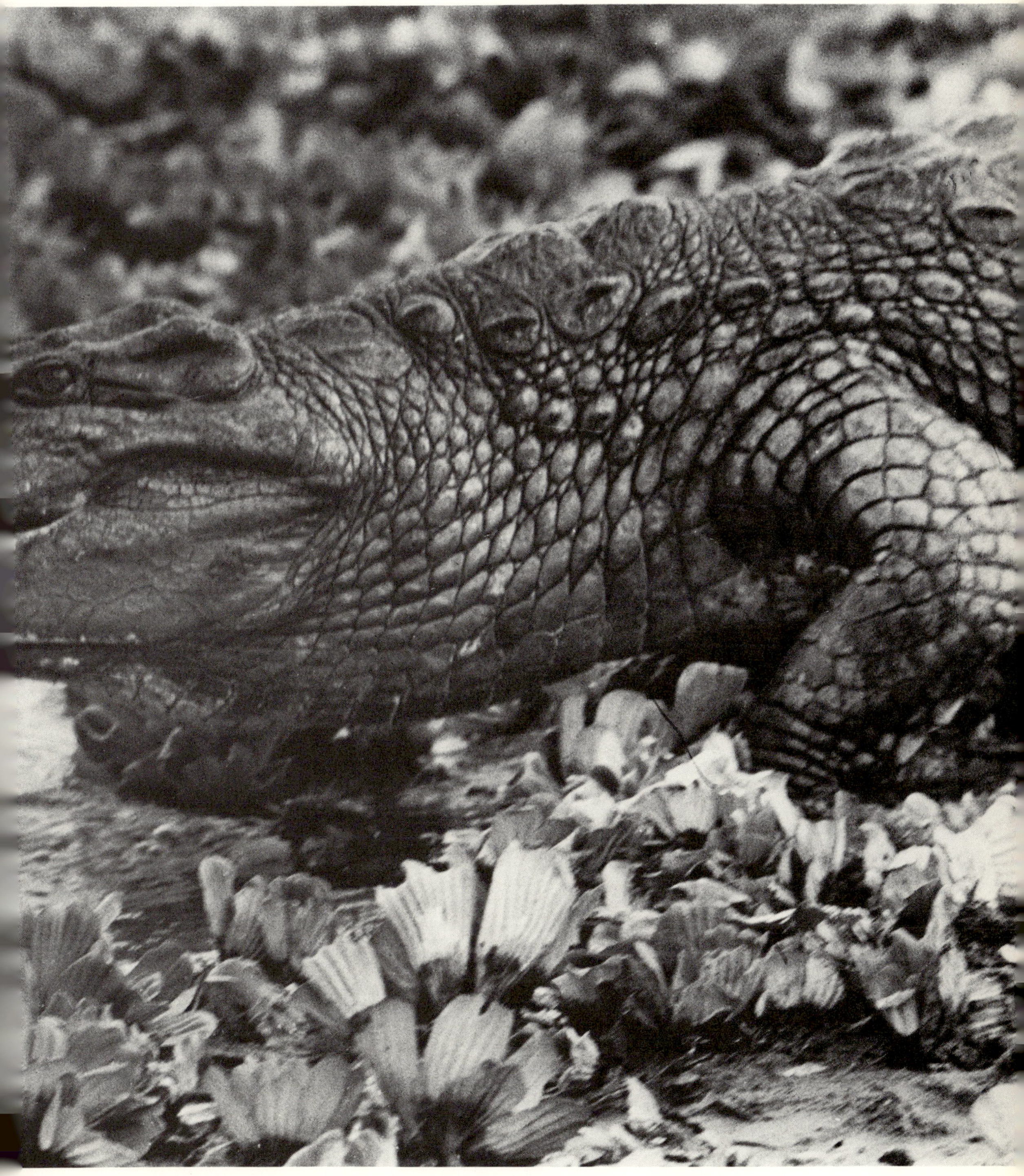

Sometimes I think that my favorite animal is the crocodile.

In everyday life, I am an environmental reporter. I disclose how we sabotage our air, water and grass. I look forward to knowing how people will behave walking down their little flowery path into the future. With factual information about possible detours—"sabotage" is only a shock word for headlines—I try to make the sinner repent. Directors and ministers of state sitting in their palaces talk about how environmental problems will soon be solved, while I jot down more and more notes. Sometimes I'm overwhelmed by despair.

I run out into the woods (as if that could help). There the last farmers are hiding out. They milk their cows for fun and from habit while they await death. The milk trucks stopped that route long ago; now they go only to animal factories and other big profitable industries in the plains. I walk far into the woods. Somewhere in there the monoculture thins out and I come across a meadow. In the middle of the meadow, protected by law, Noah's ark is still standing. In the grass amid the rubbish lies a discarded globe of the earth. I dream I'm sitting in the grass looking at the globe, that it bubbles and quakes, cracks and splits while the finance ministers veto increased subsidies for underdeveloped nations, and while the U.N.'s environmental Secretariat telegraphs gloomy position reports from Nairobi to Geneva.

A short distance behind me, in the last trickle from the Flood, lies a crocodile. It hasn't moved far from the ark. I'm delighted to get acquainted with the crocodile before it is too late for both of us. This creature found its appropriate place in life at a very early period and from then on never hesitated. A hundred million years ago (98 million years before man), there was a real future for crocodiles. They managed to establish a social model that has endured ever since.

Of course, an environmental reporter traveling through Africa naturally thinks that he will be able to find something resembling a model for successful evolution among the natural resources and human beings. In that context, meeting crocodiles is a disappointment, because it demonstrates the possibility of managing perfectly well for 100 million years without evolving at all.

We humans cannot learn anything from the crocodile, but it is an undisputed fact that this creature thrives in some places—as long as it's left in peace by impoverished Africans who know that rich old hags in the developed nations will pay a lot of money to put their powder puffs in crocodile handbags—once again a double evil, created in the chasm between rich and poor.

But the crocodile is the dream and the ideal, if you like. It lives in its highly specialized way in a static society, with no equivalent. Its life is the sort of utopia politicians prophesy in campaign speeches, where equality finally prevails and spiritual concerns occupy us most of the time, since material problems in some way—by themselves, automatically—have been removed from all of us poor beggars on earth.

This is the crocodile's world. The crocodile is the favorite animal of despairing optimists.

Its appearance is against it. It looks frightening, lying on a bed of beautifully-shaped Nile lettuce in the Victoria Nile. Jaws that strike terror in us gape wide-open. Its tongue is apricot-colored; tsetse flies buzz around its nostrils. Its teeth are well-worn. It keeps its tail bent. The tail is saw-toothed on top like that of a prehistoric monster.

The crocodile is a prehistoric monster still with us. In fact, according to fossil evidence, it looks exactly the way it did when dinosaurs were splashing around the sources of the Nile some 100 million years ago. The dinosaurs died out, but the crocodile managed to keep going.

It's a pity that such a frightening-looking creature should be a symbol of the success we are all striving for. Unfortunately, it is not an effective example, because we are so encumbered with prejudices about the crocodile that we think of it as a detestable beast. Actually, it is no better or worse than other animals. It deserves our admiration.

The Victoria Nile flows through Kabalega National Park in Uganda. Morning and afternoon excursion boats leave Paraa Lodge to visit the crocodile sandbanks in the river. Nowhere else in Africa or the rest of the world do so many crocodiles congregate.

This is a first-class tourist experience. The pilots steer as close as possible to the lazy creatures so that everyone can take good pictures.

Some of the crocodiles are a hundred years old and really should be left in peace on the sands for their last days. They refuse to go into the water even though the boats steer right at them. Sometimes the guide on an excursion boat throws a beer bottle at a crocodile's head, whereupon the creature slowly slides off into the water. I have seen this happen a couple of times. Disgust shone in my blue eyes as well as in the crocodile's red ones.

That is how miserably these creatures are degraded in the national park. So little respect is shown these creatures who have succeeded in living a good life on earth for hundreds of millions of years. I hope other tourists are also upset and feel that part of their experience of nature is ruined.

But perhaps not. It is hard to learn to love creatures that look like the crocodile. No one throws beer bottles at the more attractive deer and gazelles for the entertainment of the tourists. We see here an expression of the same blind contempt for beasts of prey that in Sweden has pressed the wolf, the wolverine, the owl and the eagle to the brink of extinction.

But why hasn't the crocodile changed, or why didn't it die out during its long history? It adjusted itself comfortably on the edge of the shore; from there it watched the world change and new species evolve and die.

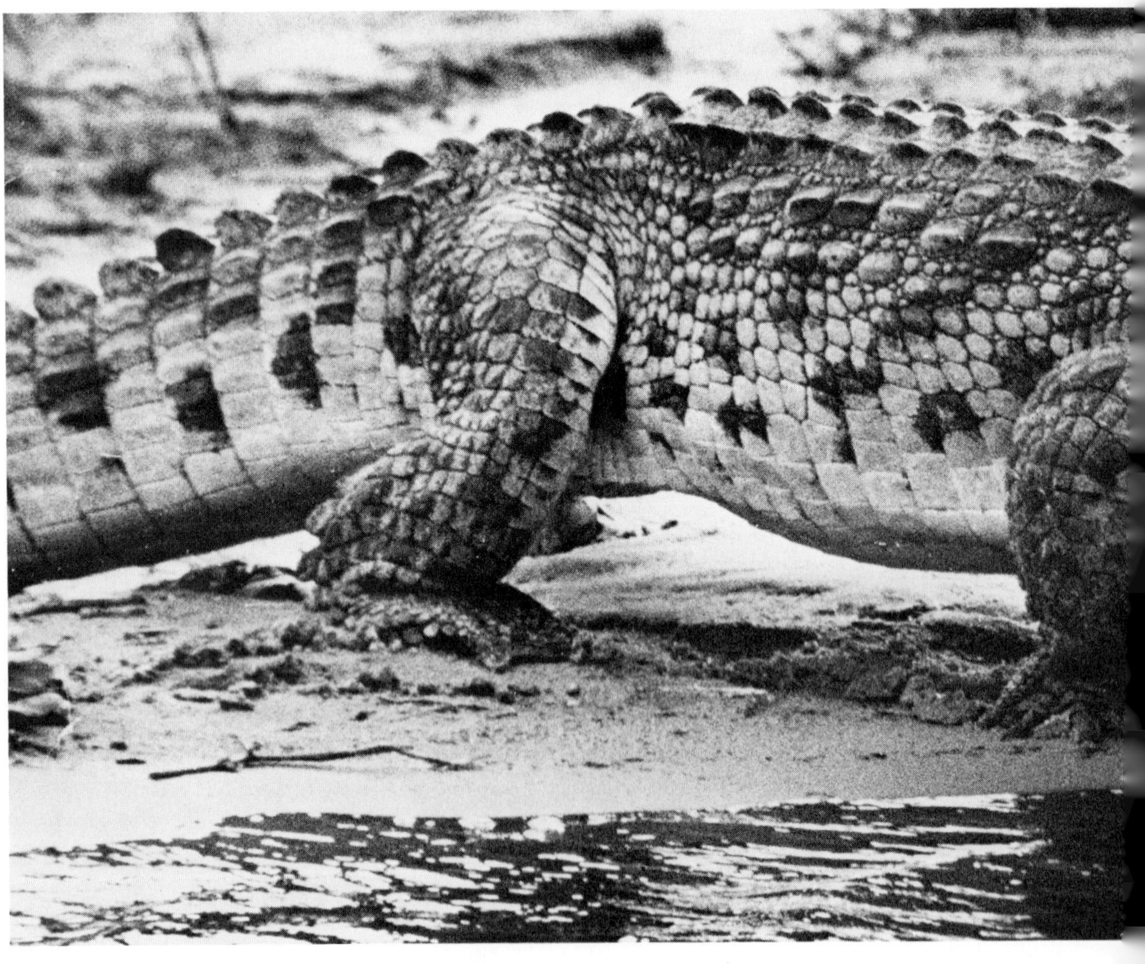

The crocodile specialist Hugh B. Cott pointed out that the crocodile doesn't walk with its legs turned out from its sides like a lizard, but rather like a leopard, with a light, springy tred, its back slightly arched, head low and tail trailing on the ground. However, otherwise it has little in common with the leopard.

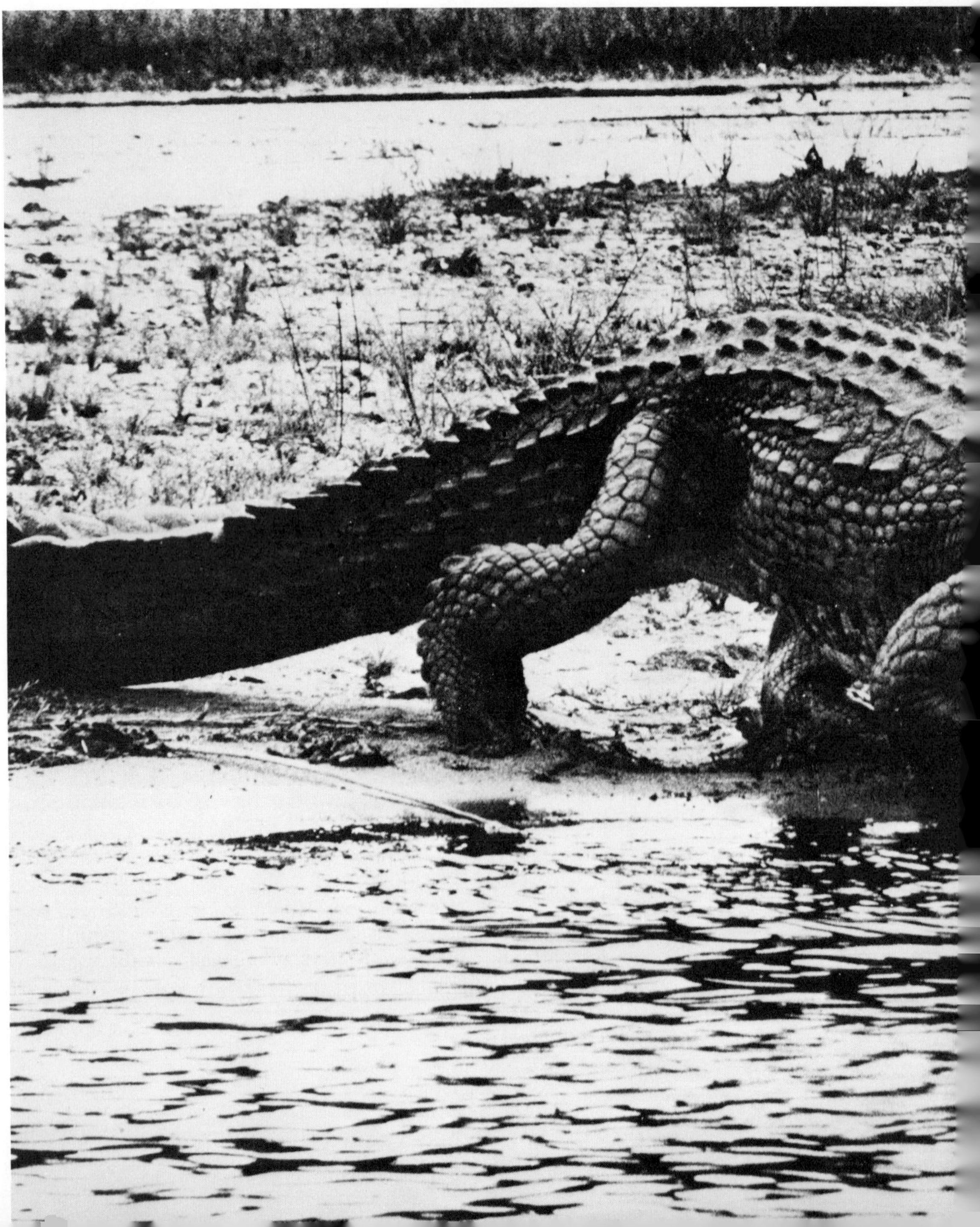

THIS AND FOLLOWING PAGE:
The crocodile doesn't lie around with its jaws wide-open just in case game might pass by. This is how crocodiles air their bodies. They have a problem with heat regulation. At night when the air is cooler, they go into the waters of the Nile, a constant 24° C all year round, day and night, in Kabalega Park. Just before dawn, they crawl back up on land. Then their bodies contain enough moisture. They lie out in the sun, until soon they become too hot. They can't get rid of the heat by sweating. Crocodiles sweat mostly through their open mouths, but that isn't enough. At midday, they hurry into the rivers to absorb fresh moisture. In the afternoon, they return to land again and, if it is sunny, they start gaping.

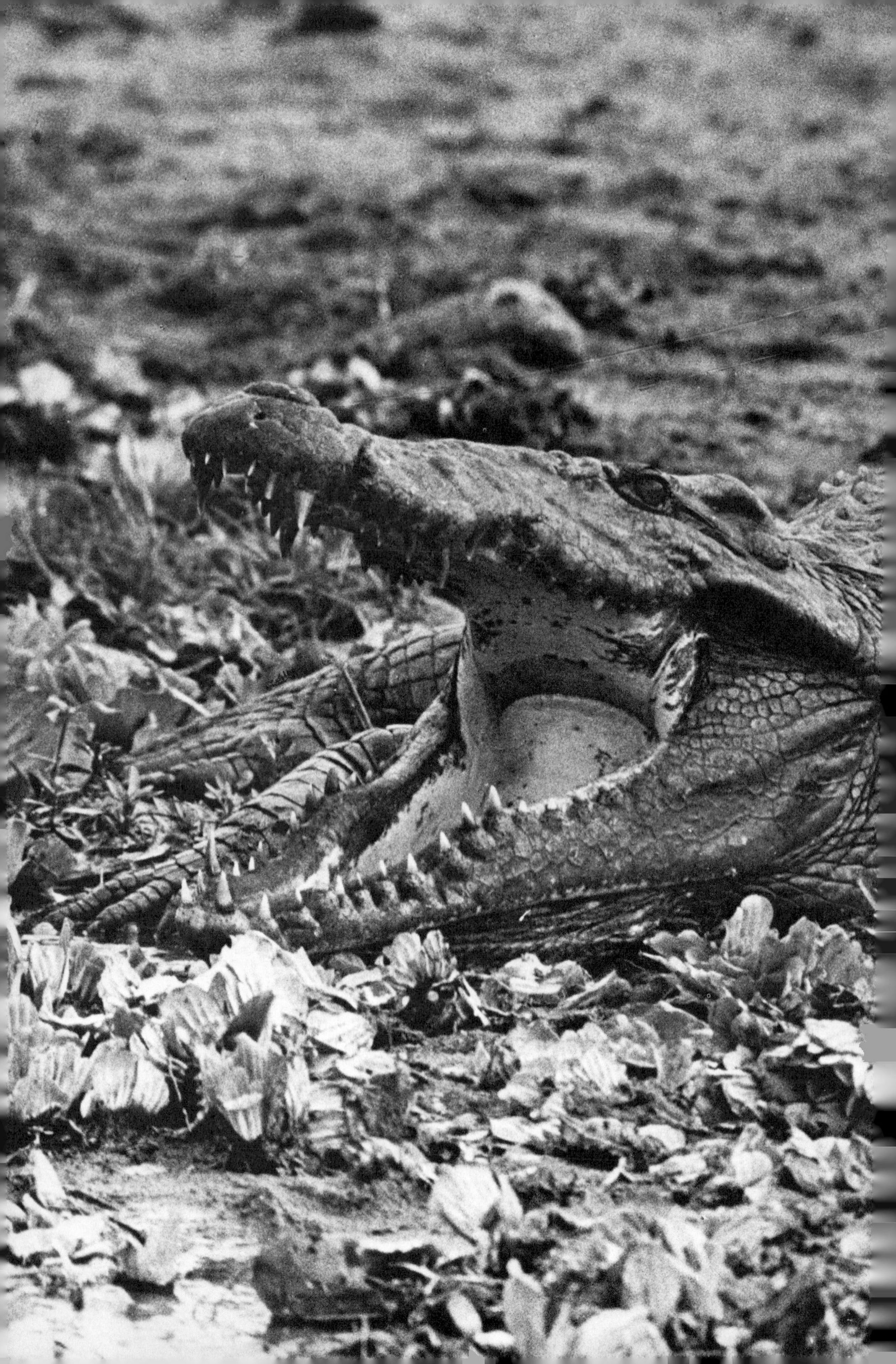

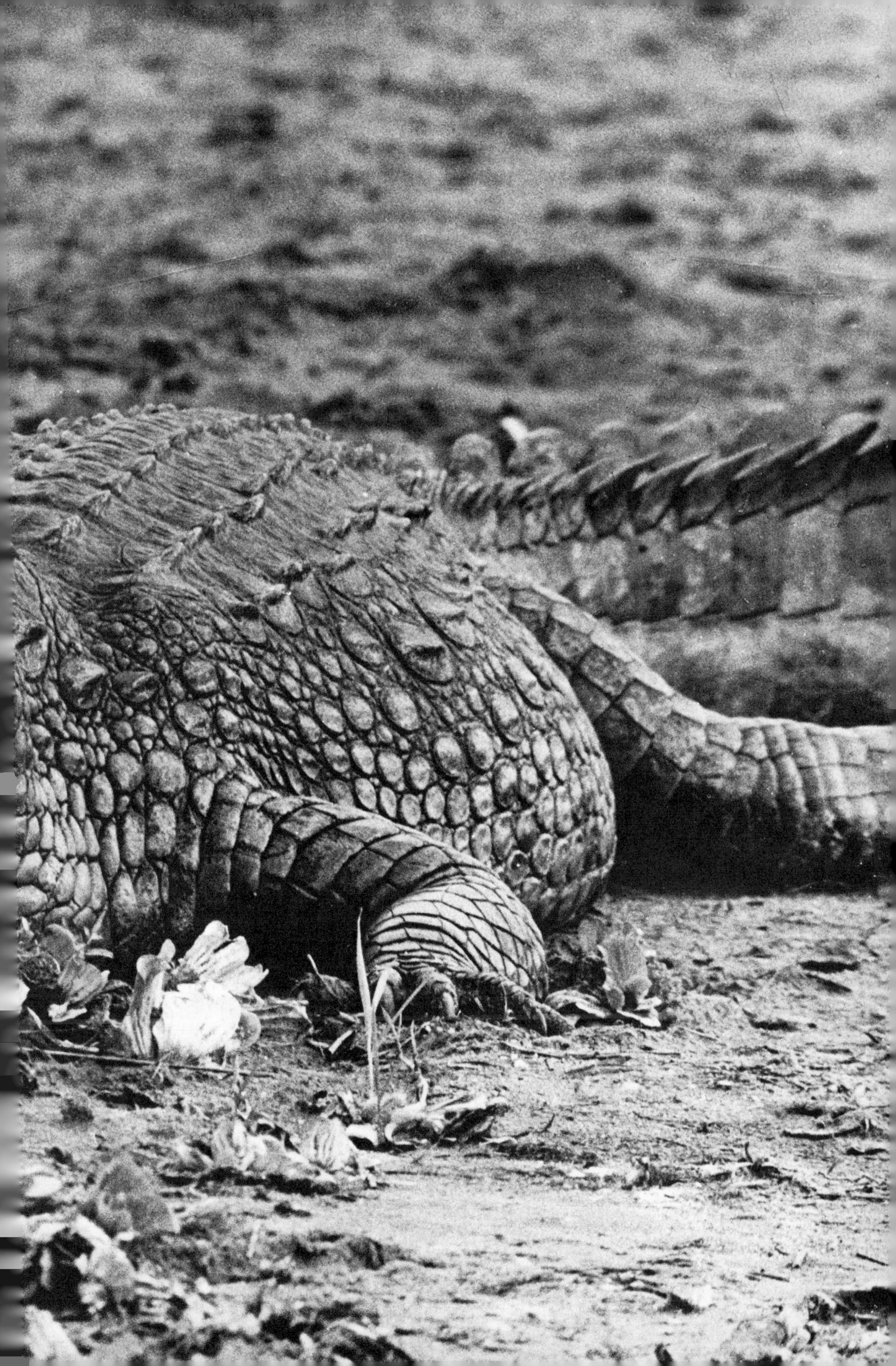

The environment was altered by more or less violent geological and climatic processes, and since the environment changed, the living organisms changed according to the process we call evolution. In order to survive the environment's shifting stresses and strains, plants and animals must constantly keep adapting to altered conditions.

Sullen and archconservative, the crocodile has avoided every change, perhaps because the environment it found for itself has remained unusually stable in crucial ways. The crocodile's life-style, its ecology, in the water and on land provides an uncommonly good protection against change.

We hired a rickety metal motorboat and headed for the crocodiles. Our motor conked out and we steered toward one of the richest crocodile sandbanks in the Victoria Nile. We beached so near a five-meter-long crocodile that the evening shadow cast by our boat fell upon its rough left side. I sized up our party. There were 29 crocodiles, lots of hippos, 2 buffaloes and an elephant family a short distance away in the papyrus reeds.

It was thrilling. Reports state unanimously that the crocodile is one of Africa's most dangerous creatures. Studies have been made of the contents of stomachs from a number of crocodiles shot in this district. They were found to contain the remains of many Nile perch and birds, half-digested bits of a mamba, various baby crocodiles (these animals are cannibals), fragments of six hippos—and four humans.

The crocodile spends most of the day apparently snoozing. Around noon, during the worst heat, it glides out into the water for a few hours. Crocodiles don't really need much food. They economize their energy and thus their food supply. Their stomachs contain mainly stones.

It is thought that the stones serve as ballast. Without stones, the crocodile would capsize when it launches out into the water; it also wouldn't be able to lie still on the riverbed. Young crocodiles that haven't learned to eat stones yet and live mostly off grasshoppers have to steady themselves with their feet when they are underwater.

It has been found that the crocodile eats 50 meals a year at most. But who knows when a crocodile just might need a shot of energy? I thought about this on the Victoria Nile, where several hundred crocodiles hide in a 15-kilometer stretch of river. A careless stroll along the shore could easily turn me into one of the crocodile's 50 meals. Two methods of attack seem to be practiced by crocodiles lying in wait in the grass. One has been called "the deadly tail-stroke" and the other "the sledgehammer head-blow." Cautiously, they open one red eye (younger individuals' eyes are light green), then they lash out with their heads, or, if it seems more appropriate, with their tails. Either way, life is over for whoever is in the way.

But this doesn't happen in the daytime. Crocodiles hunt at night.

December is the crocodiles' mating season. Then they are said to be particularly vigilant, perhaps even downright aggressive. Not much is known. In the literature, only a few brief descriptions are given of how crocodiles mate. A forest warden in Rhodesia managed to see two crocodiles in a loving union. Unfortunately, he had no time to give a more detailed description of the matter before he was dragged underwater a couple of days later by one of the crocodiles, drowned and eaten.

Around the New Year, they start laying eggs, 75 of them, in holes they dig in the sand, layering their eggs like packed herring: one layer of eggs, one layer of muddy sand, one layer of eggs, a layer of muddy sand, etc. The female crocodile packs the mud over her nest and then places her ton of weight on top. Then she won't budge (unless she gets a beer bottle on her head) before March, when the young start peeping to be unearthed. For three months, the crocodile lies motionless upon her eggs without a bite of food. It is hard to believe such maternal love exists, and this may be an exaggeration. Has anyone ever watched a brooding crocodile for three whole months, day and night?

When the young call her from under the earth, she has to be around to dig them up. Alone, they have no way of getting out of the sand. Many crocodiles die of suffocation right after birth, because the mother has been killed by poachers. Many die in the egg, because when tourist guides and other people frighten a female from her nest, monitor lizards or troops of baboons often come to dig up the eggs and eat them. This is the crocodiles' greatest threat. Out of 197 nests kept under discreet surveillance along the Victoria Nile, 97 (49.2 percent) were completely destroyed. In many cases, humans were indirectly responsible.

But we, who had intruded, pushed our boat off gradually. Getting off from the crocodile bank, we couldn't avoid frightening two sluggards that rose and slid into the water. One lifted his head and belched, hollowly and gruesomely. Later two pairs of eyes and nothing more stared at us as we chugged by.

To drift with the current down the Nile is to be led each instant through hundreds of millions of years of the past. The last strong evening sunlight may fall upon a giraffe eating leaves among the trees by the shore, and then the sun sets. The scent of hot tropical steam rises from the elephant grass; the bee eaters dive into their holes and, when the equatorial darkness closes in, a deafening music is released from crickets, frogs, remarkable crakes and the crocodiles too. They point their noses up and roar at the blank heavens. ∎

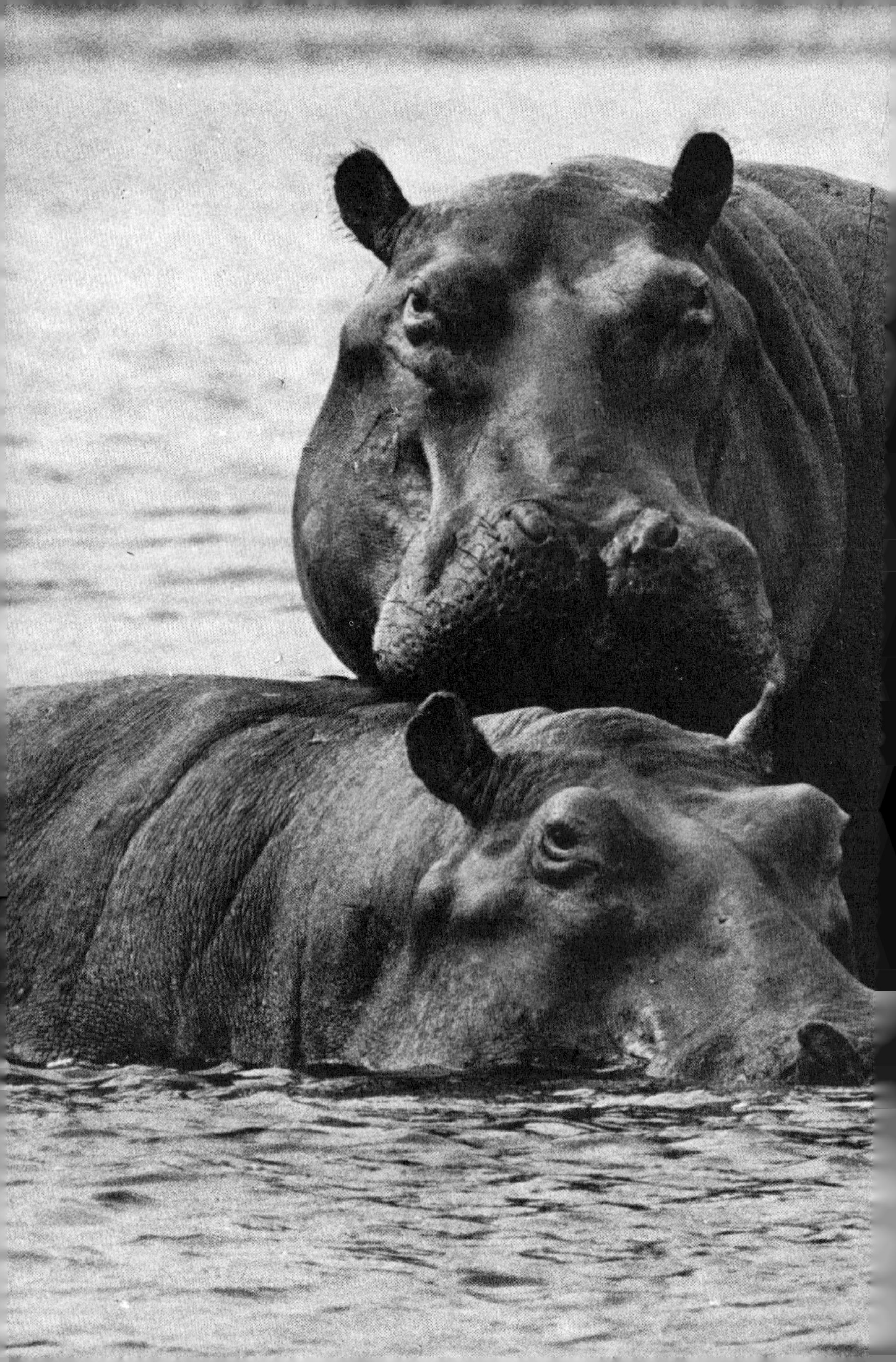

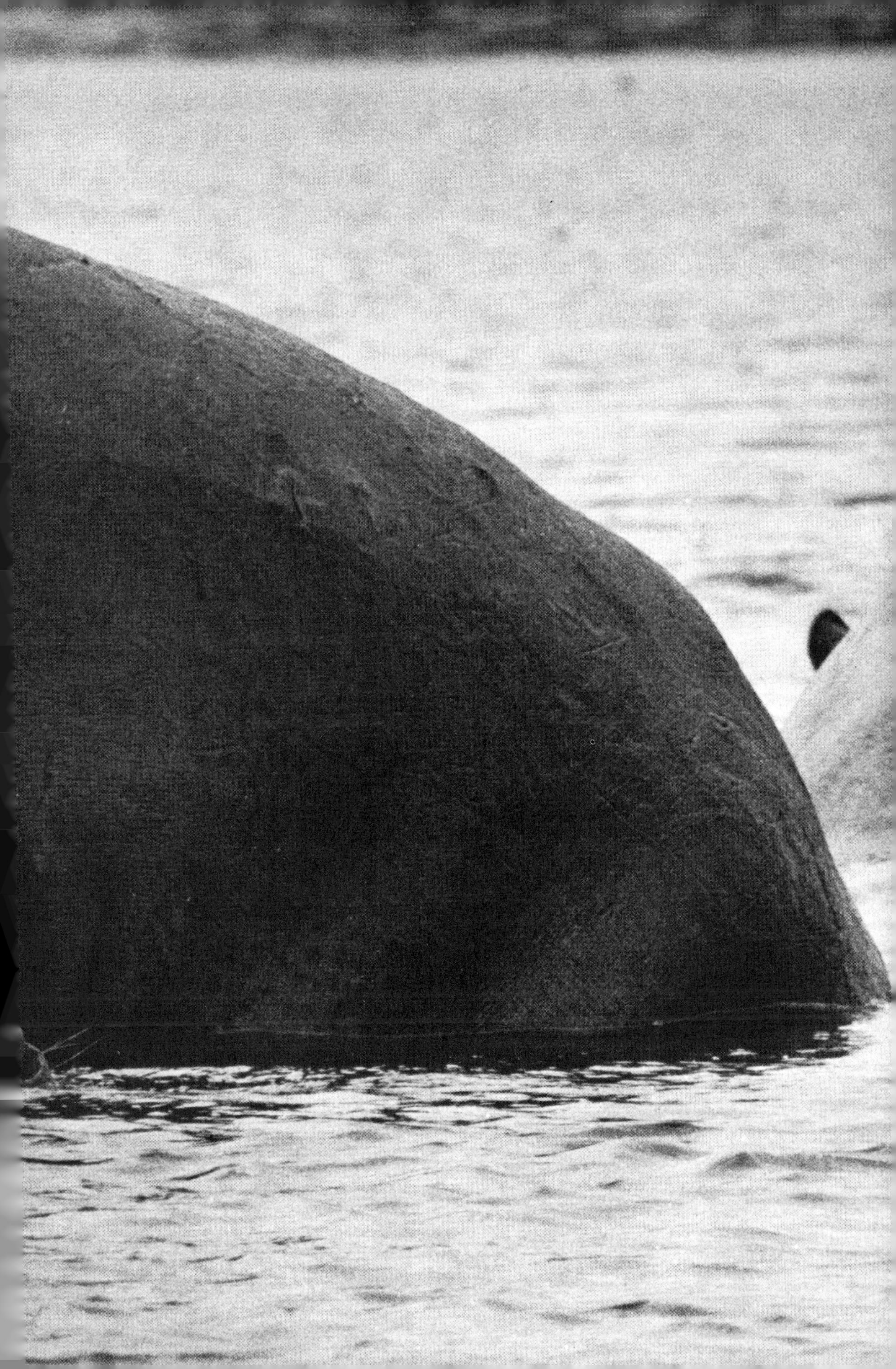

In the evening, the hippos go up on land to eat. They have fasted all day, wallowing in the mild, tepid water. They don't look particularly hungry; their bodies swell out in a prosperous and pleasing way between their stumpy legs. They are actually half-full even when they haven't eaten for 12 hours. Their stomachs are very large and they digest very slowly. You could say that a hippo's morning stomach contains food for two nights. We know this because a British research station in Ruwenzori National Park in Uganda had occasion to study up to 1,000 hippo stomachs annually over many years. (Because there were too many hippos in the park, a comprehensive slaughter was carried out to prevent the grazing land from being totally destroyed by their appetite.) They eat only grass, never bushes and seldom water plants. On the other hand, they leave their droppings in the water. A substantial quantity of masticated straw lies in deep drifts on the lake bottoms, making life pleasant for the numerous fish. Each hippo carries 150–200 kilos of grass in its stomach at dawn. Each animal weighs an average of 2,000 kilos and the median age is 45. When the researchers in Ruwenzori have finished their studies, we will know the implications of the hippos' very considerable transportation of nourishment from the grasslands into the water. The hippo seems to function like a city without sewage treatment facilities.

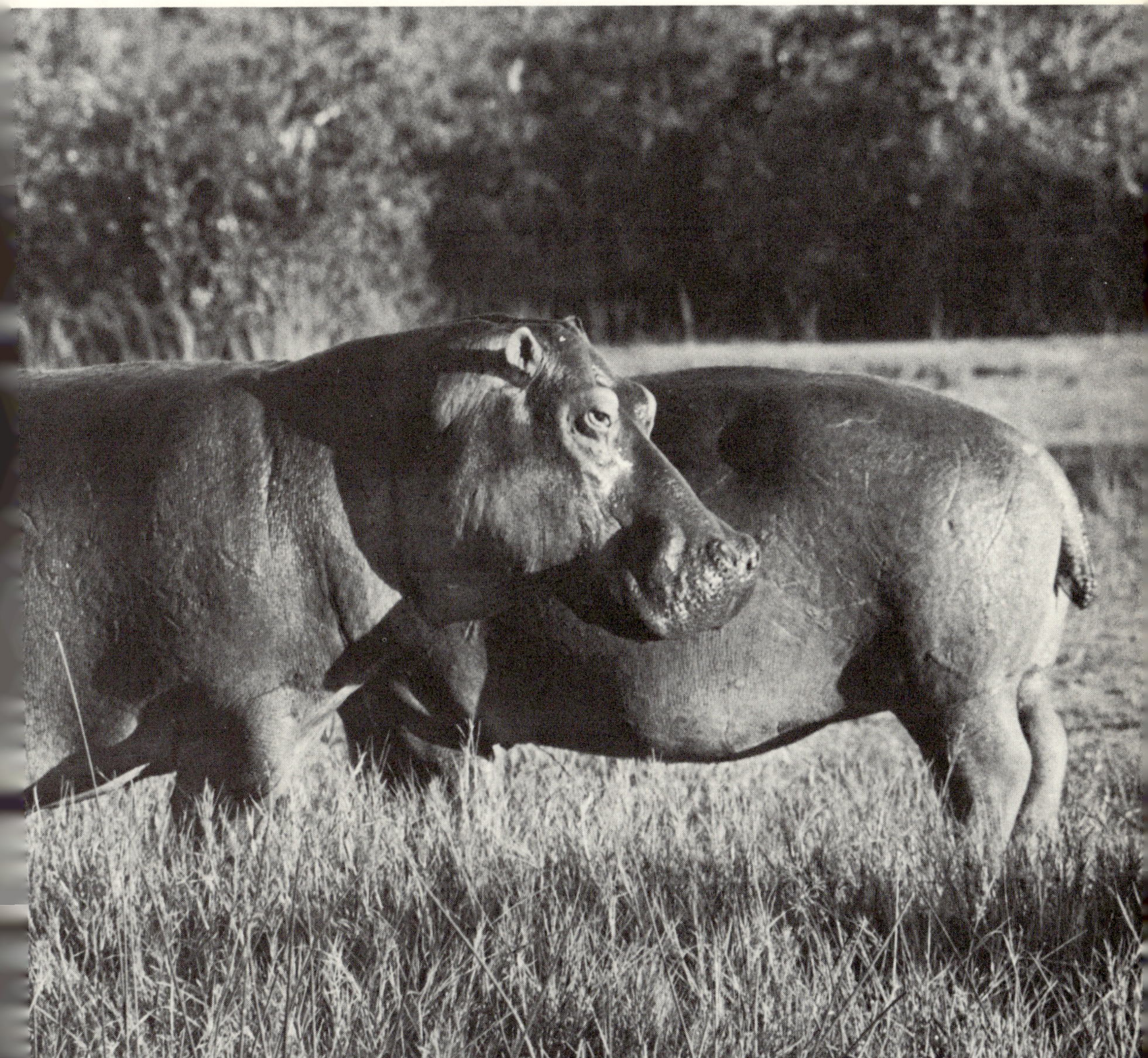

Hippos compete with crocodiles in dangerousness. Most accidents occur at night, in the evening or the morning, when the hippos are up on land to graze. Of the ten Africans killed in game reserves in a number of years, five were victims of hippos. These were women out collecting wood in the dense bush. They met hippos that found their escape routes to the water holes blocked. Of the other five, four were butted to death by buffaloes and one was killed by an elephant.

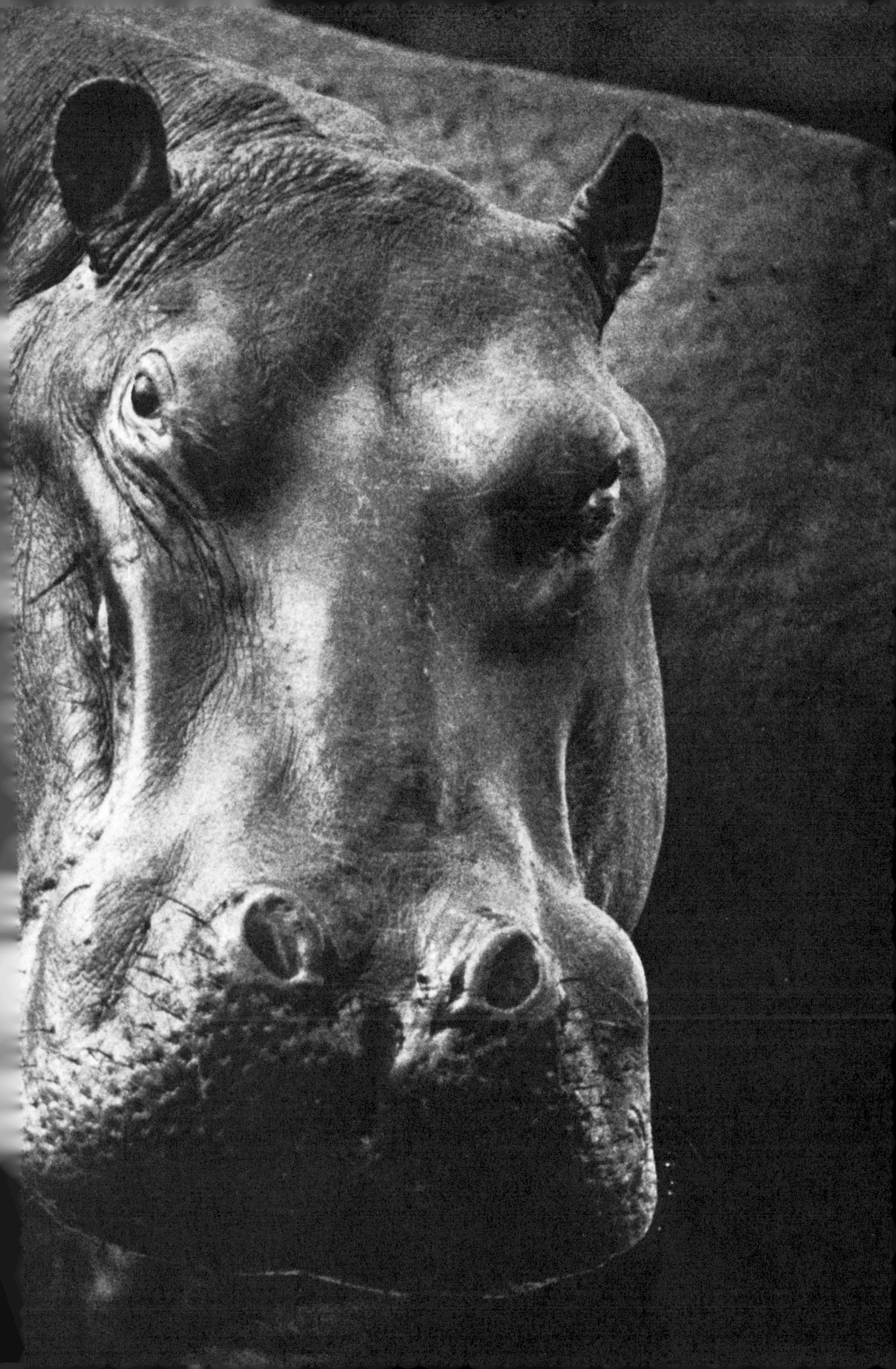

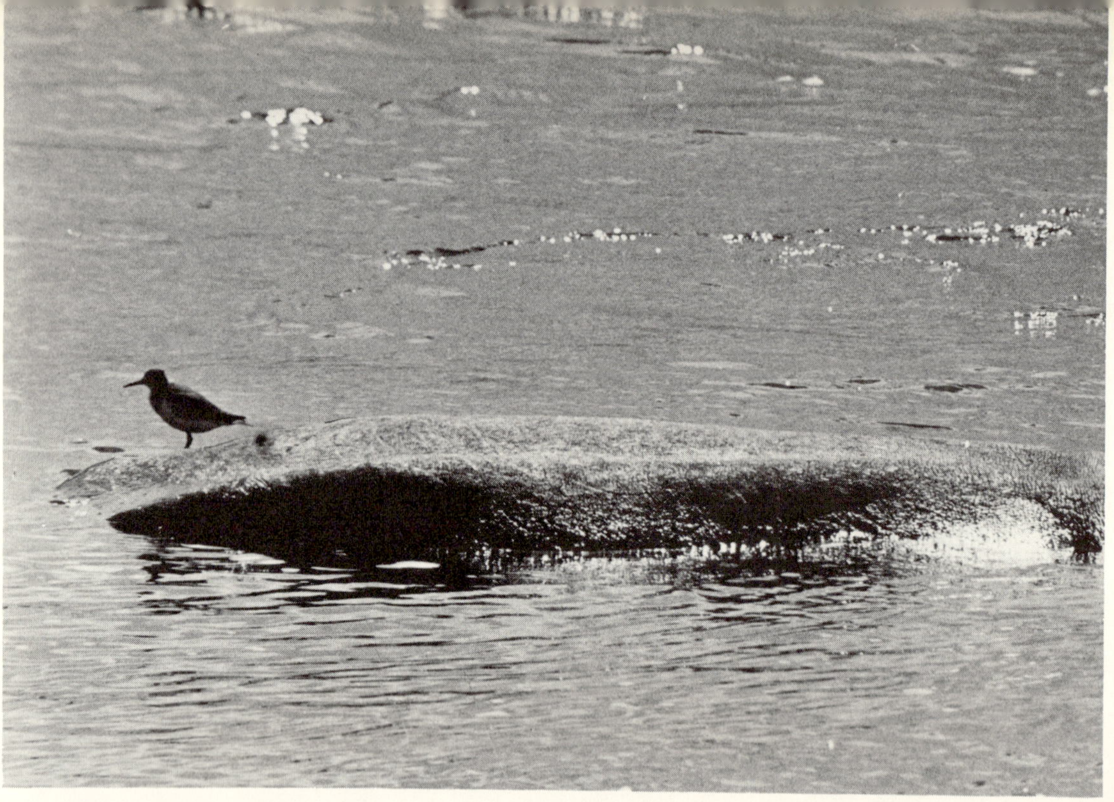

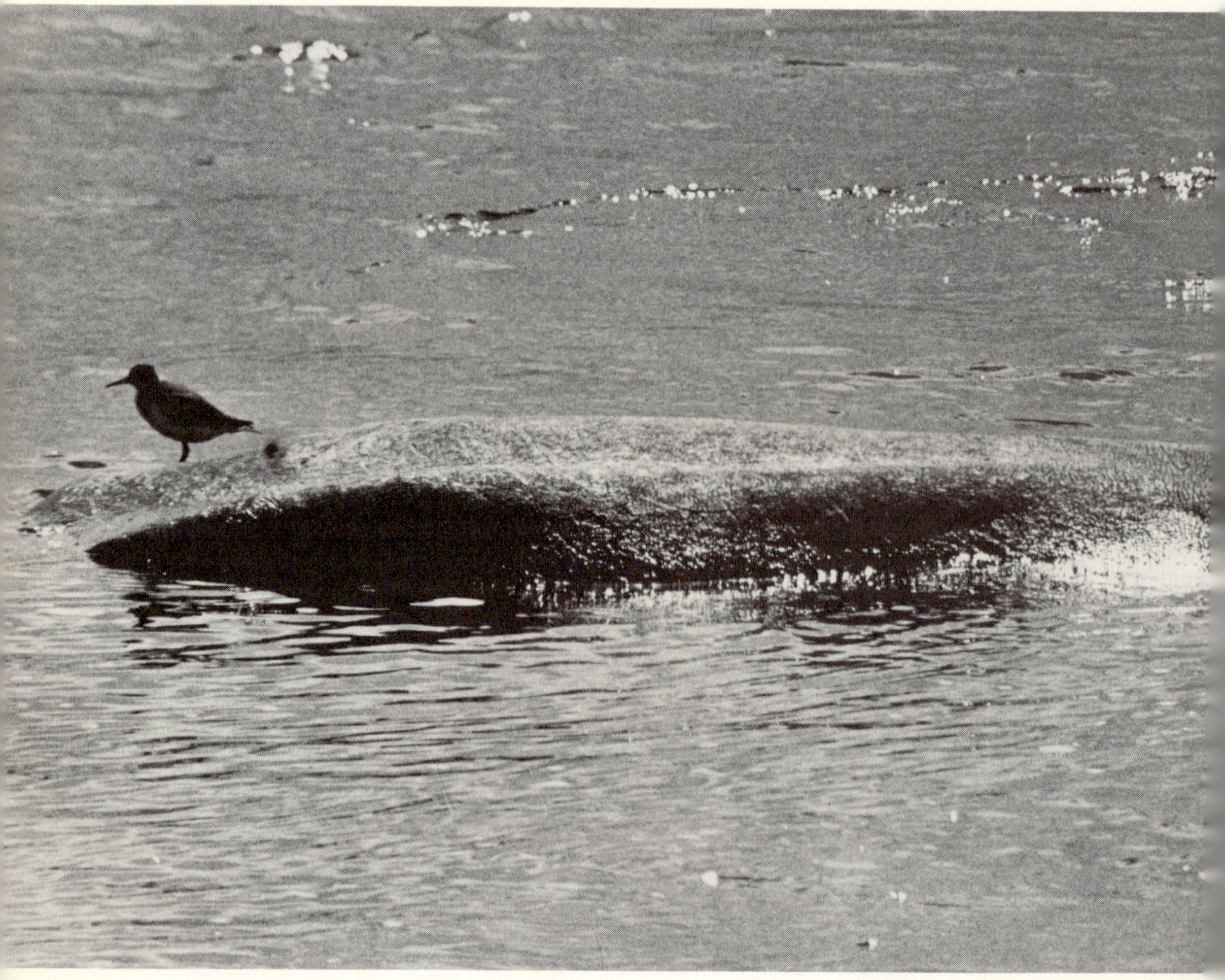

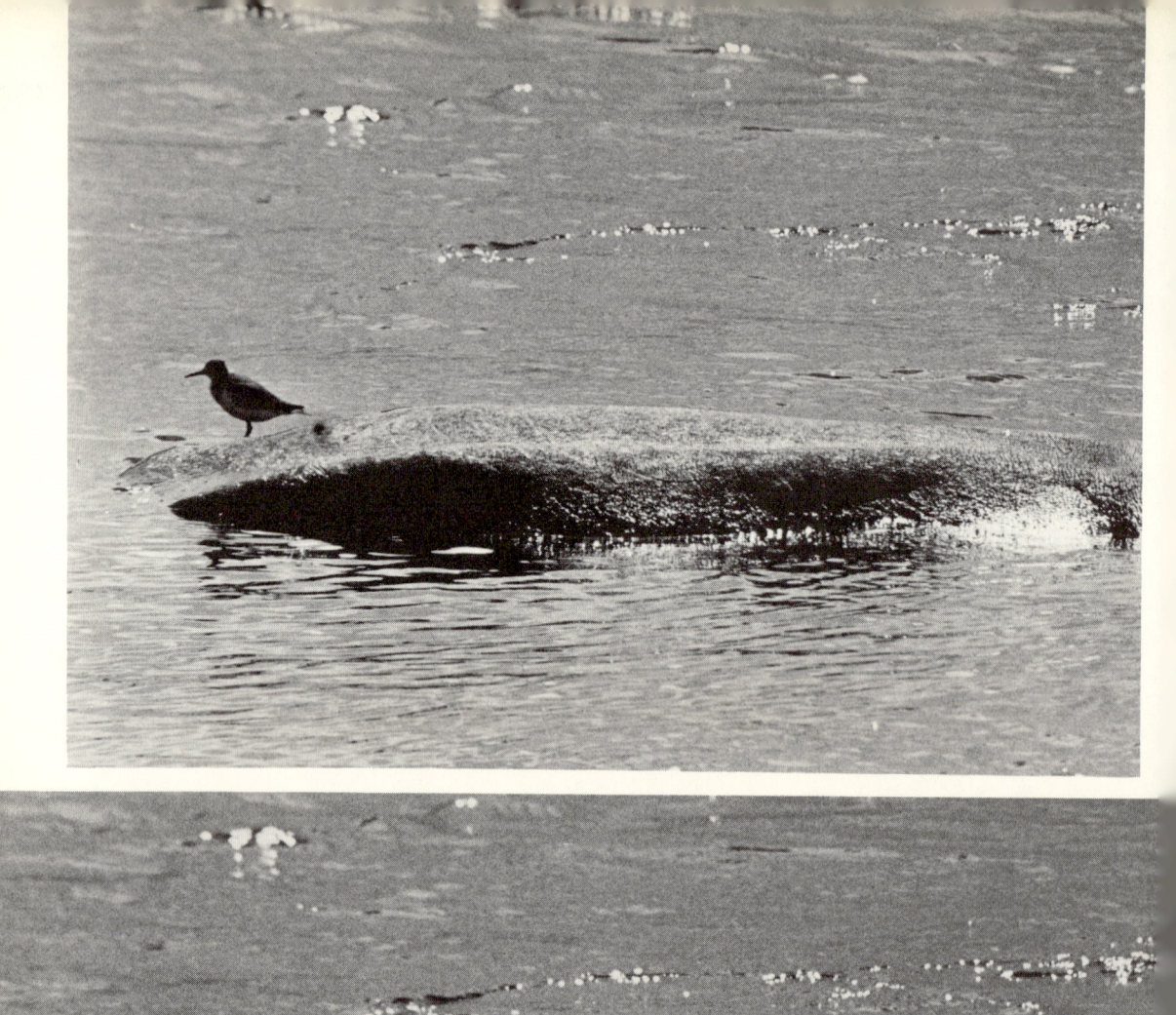

A common sandpiper, resting. This is the same happy little bird that we see on islands and beaches along most European shores in the summer.

But this sandpiper is on a hippo's back in Africa. They don't fancy hopping about in the grass and bushes. For a sandpiper, the hippo is a safe place to take a break. Someone else feels secure with the hippo in this photo: the hippo's calf has lain down to sleep across its mother's face.

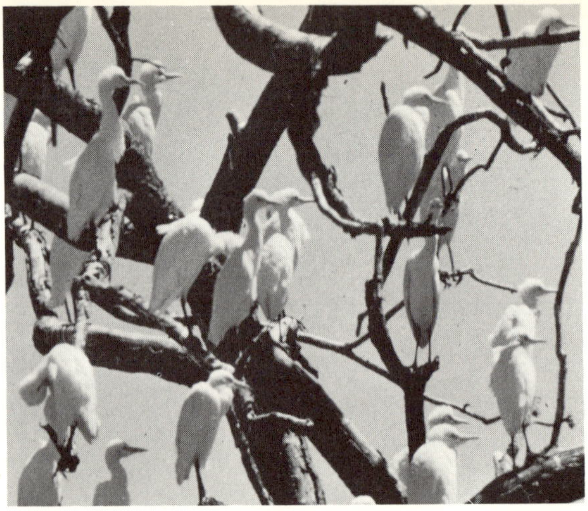

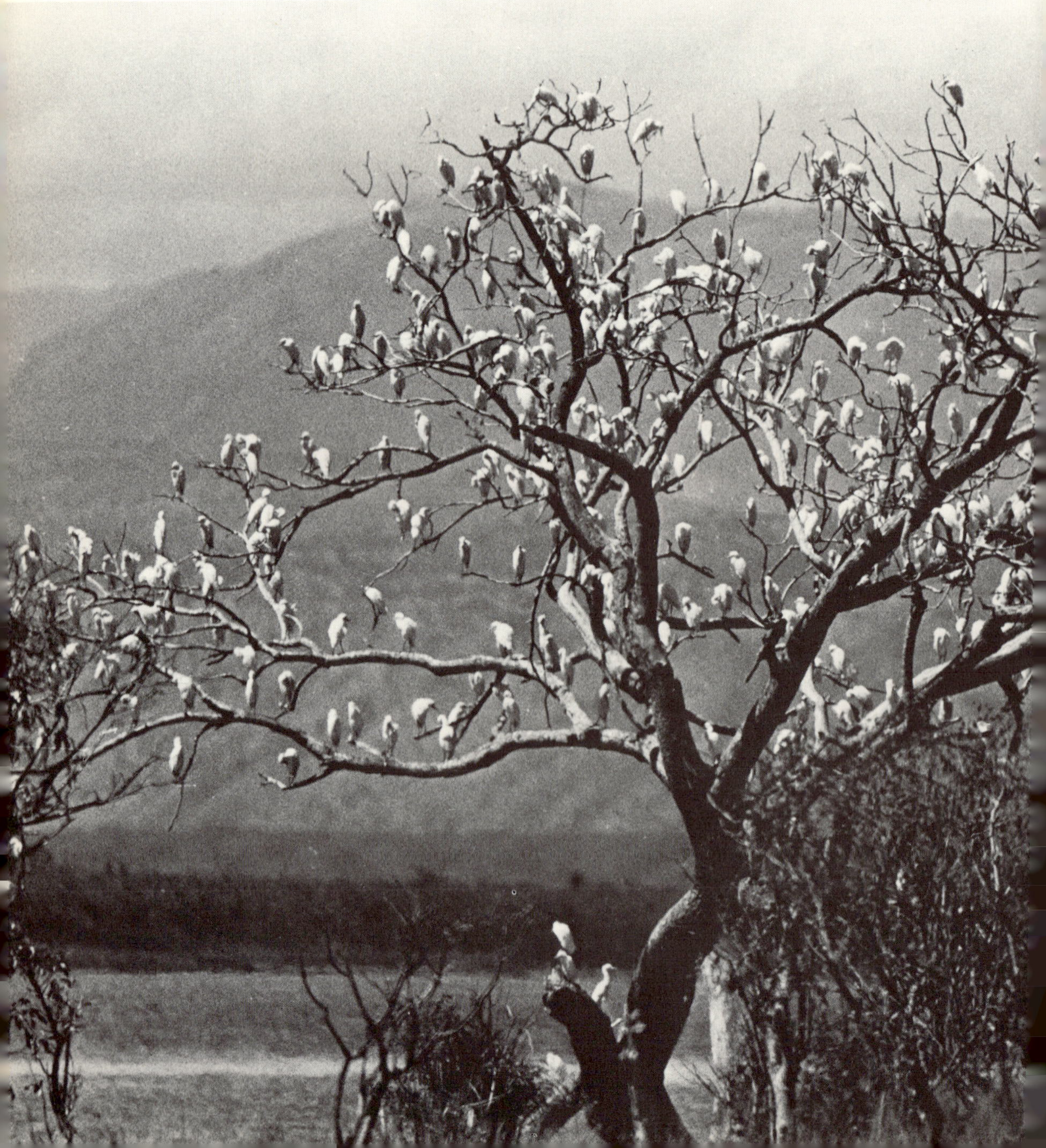

A VERY BIG PROBLEM

It's impossible to compare people and elephants. There are enormous differences, e.g., people don't have trunks. People also have a more developed brain—reason and morals—which can help them get out of the dilemma of their existence which closely resembles that of the elephants.

From a distance, this looks like a blossoming cherry tree. But the tree is full of cattle egrets, taking a siesta during the hottest hours of the day, while the elephants and other animals these herons live with are dozing in the shade or in a water hole.

In a forest of mahogany, the elephant tiptoes silently. It feels sober today; it hasn't eaten any overripe fruit of the Borassus palm.

It's good for the elephant to come to this lovely forest. Its condition isn't what it should be. It has arteriosclerosis. Damn this environmental destruction! The British Heart Foundation has actually shown now that a damaged environment causes arteriosclerosis among elephants. Now, finally, something has to be done about the environment!

Good God, the elephants are starving! Didn't 1,000, both young and old, die in Tsavo Park the other year! Family planning is needed there. The population explosion is to blame for it all.

In the forest, it is really difficult to find an elephant. They prowl around so quietly. We drove along the winding road under the eastern slopes of the Aberdare Mountains in Kenya. The car bumped over elephant droppings, some so fresh that they were still steaming. But when we stopped to listen to the forest, we heard only birdcalls.

Now we stood on the outskirts of Budongo Forest in Uganda. We knew that elephants were very near, among the mahogany trees. Hornbills rocked in the treetops and huge butterflies fluttered back and forth across the road. The forest air was steamy, thick as Granny's famous stewed fruit and just as fragrant. Something hairy tumbled between two leafy branches. It was a guereza, the black-and-white colobus monkey.

The elephant walks on its toes, but this isn't noticeable because its feet are encased in a sack of skin. Under each heel, inside the sack, the elephant's soft tissue acts as a shock absorber, distributing pressure and weight evenly as the animal moves. The elephant doesn't become flat-footed even though it weighs up to six tons, nor does it pound heavily when it runs. A herd of zebras makes a good deal more noise.

Some more facts about the elephant:

- Carried in its mother's stomach for 22 months.
- Weighs 120 kilos at birth.
- Sometimes twins are born.
- Has two beautiful teeth that keep growing throughout its life. It's a good thing they wear down on the other end, otherwise a stylish old elephant of 60 would have two prongs each about ten meters long.
- Reaches puberty between 8 and 14 years old. At that age, the elephant usually weighs 2.4 tons.
- When it grows up, it fans itself with ears weighing 50 kilos each.
- It swishes off flies with a tail that weighs 10 kilos. Its tongue weighs 14 kilos.
- Its heart weighs 24 kilos.
- The penis of a 60-year-old male weighs 57 kilos.
- The cattle egret likes to ride on its back three meters above the ground.
- In Uganda, 60,000 registered scientific observers of elephant behavior conclude that elephants like to remain standing during the day. On only four occasions were elephants

observed lying on their sides in daytime. This occurred between March 7 and 9, 1964, in Kabalega National Park.
· You can see elephants sit down in the circus.
· They defecate 17 times a day.
· The record for one bargain-sized, all-in-one-go pile of droppings is 23 kilos. In Kibale Forest Reserve in Uganda at the foot of Ruwenzori, 413 elephants made 62,000 kilos of droppings—a day. As the saying goes, it's a good thing elephants can't fly.
· In that forest alone, 22,612,000 kilos of elephant droppings were deposited annually. (Those who doubt this can contact L. D. Wing and I. O. Buss, who presented this calculation in *Elephants and forests*, Wildlife monographs number 19, February, 1970. I have been unable to check the information personally.)

It's an advantage that so much comes out an elephant's backside, but these days it is a disadvantage for so much to have to go in the front end. Elephants have become the humans' main competitor in environmental exploitation in many parts of East Africa. Humans and elephants consume land at each other's expense.

The human population increases. Ninety percent of Kenya's people wrest their livelihood directly from the earth. Every rural Kenyan had .89 hectares of arable land at his disposal in 1970. But as the demand for earth increases with the population, by the year 2000, every person in Kenya's countryside will have only .29 hectares. From this he will have to make a living. How can increasing numbers harvest ever greater prosperity out of less and less? A program is formulated so optimistically: the yield will be increased with the help of advanced agricultural techniques, artificial fertilizers, new high-yielding types of seeds and insecticides. With the aid of birth control, the mounting human population will be slowed down. Increasingly, the human surplus will be channeled toward industrial occupations. If possible, land ownership will be reformed to benefit the hungry majority.

Until such happy days when making a living will be measured in quality, increasing land shortage in the country is bound to wreak havoc. Space for elephants, natural areas not yet definitely claimed by humans, decreased by 75 percent in Uganda between 1929 and 1959. People or elephants—the battle over resources concerns how the whole earth provides for every living thing.

In 1929, there were elephants over 70 percent of Uganda; in 1972, they were found in less than 10 percent. At the same time, the number of elephants in this steadily shrinking area increased. From all directions, they crashed into banana plantations and timberland. They became destructive animals in Uganda. The authorities handed out free guns and ammunition to farmers so that they could remedy the nuisance. During the twenties, they shot 1,000 elephants a year. There were 30,000 in Uganda at that time. In the thirties, the war against the elephants was intensified. In certain years, more than 2,000 elephants were destroyed. Between 1926 and 1958, 40,000 were killed.

For all that, there are roughly 37,000 elephants in Uganda. The elephant control continues because space in the human world for these huge creatures is constantly shrinking. The trend is the same in other East African nations. In Kenya, it has been estimated that uncontrolled shooting of elephants yields between two and three thousand animals a year. This elephant harvest is said to increase 3 to 4 percent annually. Perhaps never before—even during the great ivory boom—have more elephants been killed than in these times. According to the export registries, the ivory export from Kenya increased 4 percent annually during the sixties, 6 percent from Uganda and 8 percent from Tanzania. Sooner or later, not a single elephant will be left outside the national parks. That's inconceivable.

The Budongo mahogany forest is magnificent. It is an orderly tropical rain forest. Some areas are still unaffected by forest wardens or elephants (this is near Busingiro, 40 kilometers from Masindi). There you can walk into the jungle, if you're willing to hunch over and wade in the streams. Lianas try to wrap around your neck. All over the ground and on the tree trunks, there are plants that look like our common houseplant varieties.

But large parts of Budongo Forest are the targets of clearing and spraying campaigns using the herbicides 2·4-D and 2·4·5-T to weed out those species of trees that are not as economically valuable as mahogany. The regeneration of mahogany is promoted at the expense of the other trees. Into this reconstructed ecosystem of young mahogany come the elephants. In this simplified nature, the elephants seem to love to eat the mahogany. They are not half as delighted by "weedy woods."

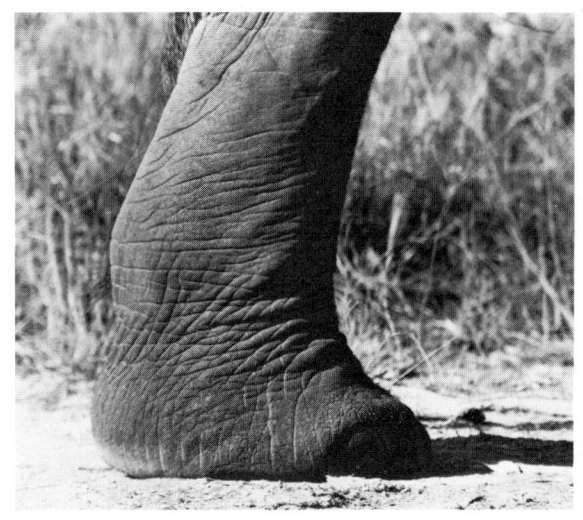

It's during the dry season that elephants come lumbering out of Kabalega National Park so far away. About 800 elephants from there take refuge in this forest every year. In addition, 400 elephants live in Budongo Forest all the time.

Each elephant eats between 100 and 300 kilos of grass, leaves and bushes a day (depending on the animal's size). For a herd of 800 animals, this amounts to a daily ration

Elephants walk quietly and softly because their feet are well-furnished with shock absorbers of rubber-hard tissue under their heels.

of between 80,000 and 240,000 kilos, to which should be added the 400 resident elephants' consumption of between 40,000 and 120,000 kilos a day. A good portion of this consists of prime mahogany.

"Elephants are incompatible with the forestry department's objectives," emphasize these mahogany growers in despair, and we have to believe them.

Now it's a question of choice. Perhaps like good animal conservationists, we should boycott desks and liquor cabinets made of mahogany. We take comfort in the fact that there are national parks. At least elephants can live there the way they and their forefathers used to live in a changing Africa for perhaps 50,000,000 years. Or so we thought!

And then, leaving the forest, we crossed the savanna to Kabalega National Park. From the slopes of Zaire on the other side of Lake Albert rose the smoke of grassfires, and between the small attractive villages, grass was also burning along the roadside so that the zebus would have more nourishing grazing land.

Flocks of European sand martins and other martins that live here throughout the year were catching insects in the smoke. Like us, the grassfires were heading for the national park, but we got there first. There by the road we came upon a silver white heron, cleaning itself on a large rock in an ocean of dry, golden grass, where each grass stalk was two, almost three meters high. The stone that the heron was perched on began to move and then we saw that it was an elephant walking along, scything the grass with its trunk.

Elephants eat a lot of grass. There's ample grass for the more than 10,000 elephants living in this national park about the size of Glacier Park in Montana. Fresh grass is nourishing, but in the dry season grass becomes mostly fiber. It can no longer provide sufficiently invigorating proteins. Then, especially, the elephants have to eat a lot of leaves, twigs and bark from trees and bushes.

At least 10,000 elephants have been eating trees for so long now in Kabalega that large areas of the park are treeless and no unbroken forests remain standing. That is why some elephants migrate now and then into Uganda's mahogany plantations.

The savanna's ecosystem, like all others, is based on the well-balanced interaction of climate, soil, vegetation, animals and men. When any one factor is radically altered, the whole system changes as a consequence. The equilibrium is said to be dynamic. Giraffes, rhinos and browsing antelopes probably have a harder time because the elephants have felled the forests. Forty out of four hundred species of birds are said to have become extinct. The leopards have fewer trees to rest in during the day. Shade is even scantier for the buffaloes, which otherwise are favored by more grass, just as the sinister Egyptian cobra may thrive with all that grass to hide in. This last is pure speculation, but it irritated me every time I set my foot down at the side of a road, because the books state in such a threatening way that "the Egyptian cobra is common in Kabalega Park." It seems to be seen most often right after nightfall when the tourists retreat into one of the park's two hotels.

As for the elephants, the alteration of their landscape presents a grave problem. It is generally thought that in a national park

This is what an angry elephant looks like. The photographer took this picture at the instant the elephant noticed him. The tree in the background is dead. It has been ringed by elephants.

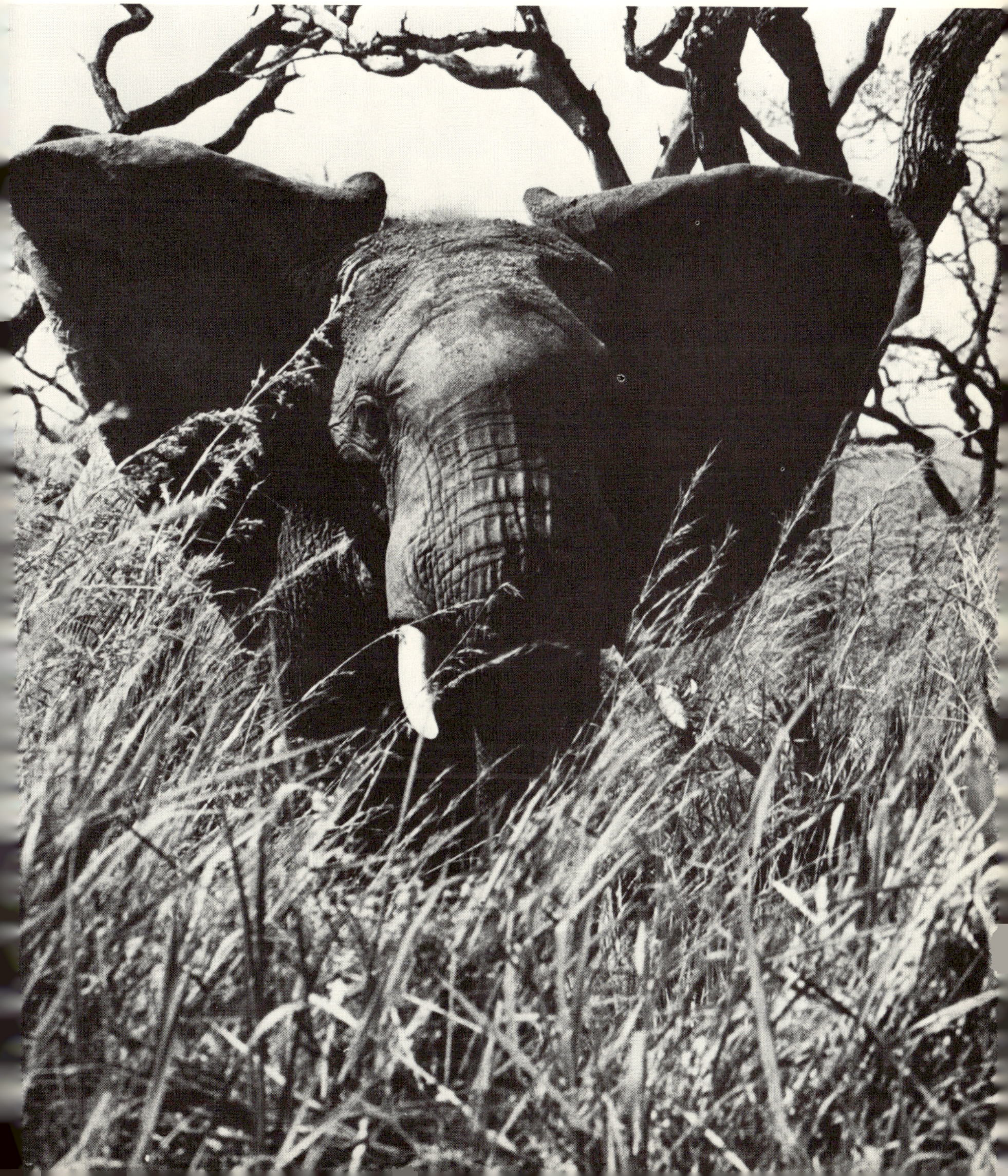

A big pile of elephant droppings can weigh 23 kilos. This would be enough to fertilize a whole garden. Dung beetles, scarabs, are responsible for the distribution of elephant droppings to various parts of the savanna. They can spread a huge pile in a short time. They pat the droppings into round balls and bury them to feed their larvae. Mushrooms sprout quickly in the dung piles. Soon some francolins, which eat the fungi, pass by.

Dung beetles roll their well-made dung balls very fast. They rush backwards with their noses to the ground, steadying the balls with their back legs.

animals can look after themselves. There they can live in peace, while the world beyond struggles with forestry rationalization, agricultural expansion and human society's increased intrusion in nature.

Perhaps the national parks are sufficiently large, if we accept that their ecosystems follow a rhythm of cycles, dictated by the elephants, in which a cycle is 50, 100 or conceivably several hundred years.

This cycle can include dramatic environmental alterations, as well as famine, mass death and uncertain migrations of elephants. A hundred years ago, the area around Lake Rudolf in northern Kenya was a savanna landscape where so many elephants were able to live that expeditions went out from Mombasa to harvest ivory. Today hardly any elephants are left there. The landscape is a treeless semidesert.

If it is true, as some believe, that the forest was eaten up by elephants trapped for some reason in those areas, then bush and tree savannas will eventually return (if other ecological factors don't get the upper hand). Then we will have—in an unknown future at an unknown future time—an understanding of how long-term a cyclical pattern can be in the natural kingdom ruled by the elephant.

Perhaps elephants were also responsible for eating the good, green part of Somalia that once extended a long way inland from the ocean. Now the people of that land are forced to stay by the shore of the Indian Ocean while the rest of the country is semidesert. But in both cases it seems likely that, before the time of the elephants, decisive changes of another kind resulted in the trees not growing back.

Two interesting photographs published in the South African periodical *Zoologica Africana* (number 1, 1965, page 200) capture the elephants' ability to alter their environment in as short a time as 25 years. The photos were taken in 1934 and 1959, in the same place with the same view, over the Rwindi-Rutshuru plain in what is now the Parc des Virunga in Zaire. When the first picture was taken, there were 150 elephants on the plain, a rich, tree-covered savanna stretching as far as the eye and the camera could see. By 1959, the number of elephants in the area had increased to 3,923. The second photo showed very clearly that the plain had become a grassland with only a few trees left standing.

On that savanna, we know that man's encroachment was unimportant. Much too long a time passed between grass burnings for the restoration of the forests to have been decisively influenced. Eight hundred and sixty-three millimeters of rainfall annually is perfectly adequate to sustain the trees on the savanna.

In the Serengeti, extensive landscape alterations can also be predicted in the wake of the elephants. In Seronera Valley, inhabited mostly by tourists and lions, 170 elephants shove over tall fever trees and umbrella acacias at a rate of 2.5 percent of the trees annually. In one area there were an estimated 2,900 fever trees. Of these, 836 were uprooted and killed by elephants.

In Kenya's Tsavo Park, the elephants are rapidly eating up the trees and changing the landscape to grass savanna and bush, especially around the few watercourses where they concentrate in the dry season—where several hundred, perhaps a thousand, thirsty, starving elephants died together in the last severe drought of 1970–71.

We idealistic nature lovers, who have learned to fight for the survival of as many as possible of the last animals of each species, are forced to accept that there is a limit to the number of animals as large as elephants that our last paradise can support. There are very few paradises, they are limited and they also have to be the habitat of many other animals that are at least equally dependent upon the trees. Therefore, attempts are being made now in many areas to regulate the size of the elephant population by shooting, but no definite positive effect of this necessary slaughter has yet been registered.

The ideal elephant family consists of six animals, led by an elderly female, often more than 50 years old. She no longer bears any children; her job for the rest of her life is to escort the herd of daughters and grandchildren and great-grandchildren on a safe course from water holes to pasturage. The adult males stay on their own. They don't belong to any family; they move around in bachelor gangs.

The elephant population in the national parks is on the rise. In the southern part of Kabalega, the average family is no longer six animals. It has grown to 22 members that must be satisfied with a diminishing number of bushes and trees. This population explosion cannot be met by increased resources. The animals are closed into their reserve just as people are closed into a limited plot of land and forced to conserve their resources economically to avoid a catastrophe.

Elephants, unlike people, cannot perceive that the earth's resources are limited. They cannot learn to conserve today for the future, nor can a favored population in some part of an extended area share its supply with those who are more in need. Catastrophe approaches. They continue to consume the limited fever trees in Seronera Valley at a rate of 2.5 percent a year.

Imagine if people behaved as stupidly as elephants with our limited resources of earth, food, minerals and energy...

Slowly catastrophe approaches for the elephants in Kabalega and for the people on earth. The destroyed environment strikes back. The lack of resources is mirrored in the animals' debilitated bodies. We know that similar damage occurs among humans. In the elephant, it appears in diminished fertility and later with increased infant mortality. These are self-regulating factors in an overly-large population. The high rate of infant mortality cannot be regulated by anything less than an improved standard of living for the elephants.

Their aorta walls calcify. It is not known for sure what produces the arteriosclerosis among elephants in Kabalega, but we do know that Mt. Kenya's elephants, still living well in a lush forest environment, do not suffer this complaint.

Perhaps the lack of tree fibers, bark and leaves leads to an insufficient supply of mineral substances or vitamins, which in turn affects the body's calcium balance. Perhaps the chronic shortage of shade leads to regeneration disturbances and resultant calcification in the blood vessels. Both theories appear to be scientifically tenable.

An old fellow stood stamping in a water hole. There was no water but at least the elephant got together a little mud porridge. It sucked up a trunkful and blew the mud over its back. This is a way of preventing its dark skin from drying and cracking in the sun. We watched two elephants attack a red termite mound from two directions. They sucked up great chunks of the termite dwelling and sprayed the crawling contents behind their ears.

The elephant's most important heat-regulating points are located behind its ears. It fans its ears at a speed determined by its need for ventilation. Its ears are like safety valves in a steam machine. When the heat pressure builds within its body, the elephant flaps its ears for relief, or it stands with its ears stretched out to catch cooling breezes. Sometimes there's no wind. Then it needs the help of shade, but its other need—hunger—has destroyed the shade.

When danger is near, the elephant also uses his ears to signal to other family members and people nearby. An elephant was grazing under a desiccated dead tree on a rise. Our road passed next to this spot in such a way that we could turn off the engine and coast along until we stopped close to the elephant without it seeing or hearing us. Then the photographer crept out, clambered on the car hood and then ventured higher onto the roof. There he stood, preparing his camera.

Then there was a bang. I saw a cloud of dust at the same instant, and the photographer was back inside the car shouting at me to start driving (I already was). The elephant had flapped its ears when it suddenly discovered a human several meters away. This is what furious elephants do. A close call. What if the creature had jumped onto our car roof?

This is how a person can drive around, enjoying himself among the elephants and other animals. The opportunity is not wasted if we try to understand how they live at the same time. My enjoyment of this undisturbed nature is based upon an illusion. No person, no animal and no flower can live and play in a game reserve, forever undisturbed. They are all dependent upon

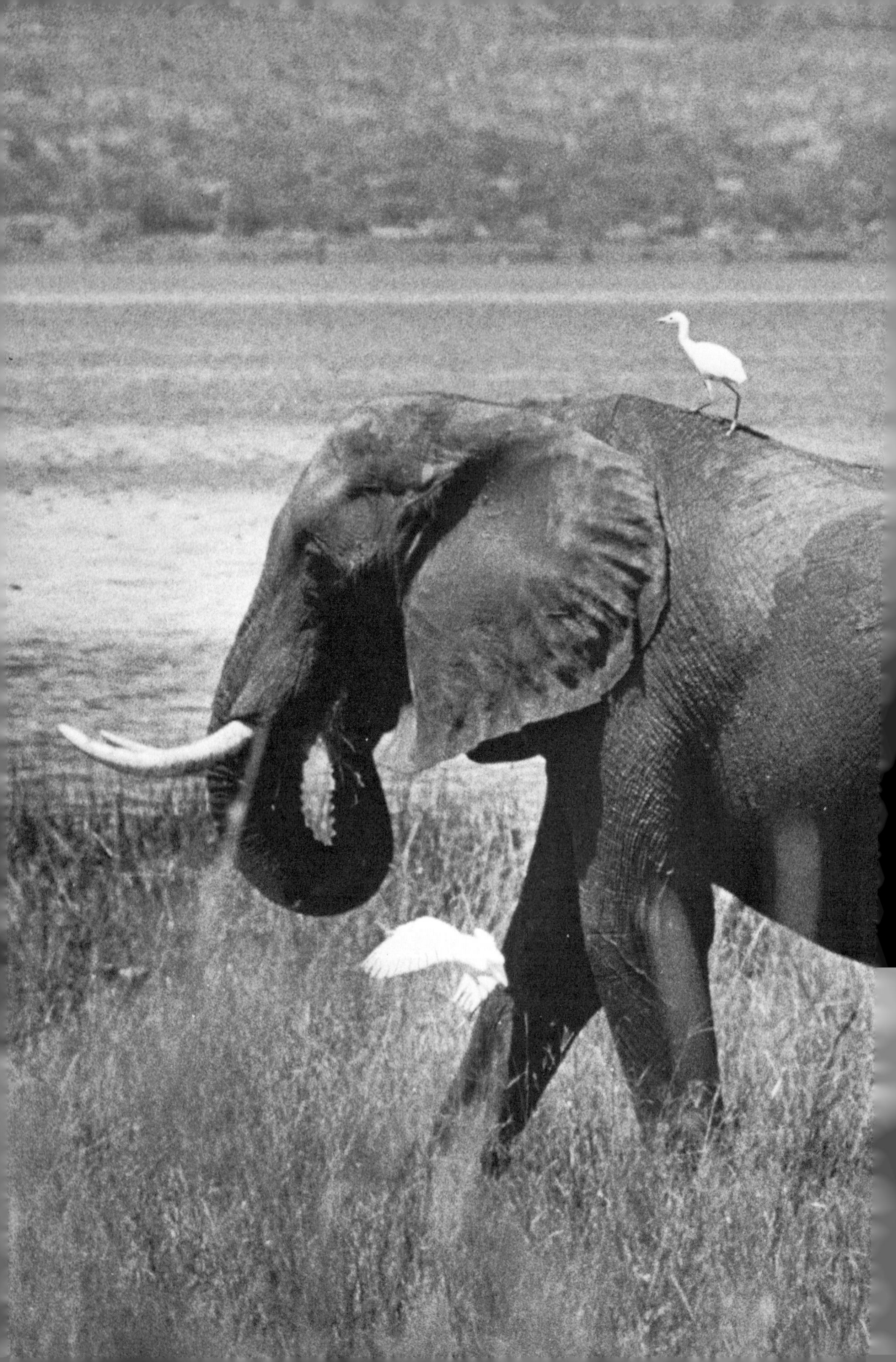

An elephant wanders along the shore of Lake Albert in Uganda with a cattle egret strutting on its back. Several egrets follow in the elephant's tracks. Egrets learned long ago what scientists can now affirm after hard work—birds can catch many more insects in the company of big animals than if they forage on their own. These egrets are apt to hunt alone at noon when the big animals seek out shade and stay still. Egrets are not interested in the elephants' parasites. They eat insects, grasshoppers in particular, stirred up by the elephants' movements through the grass.

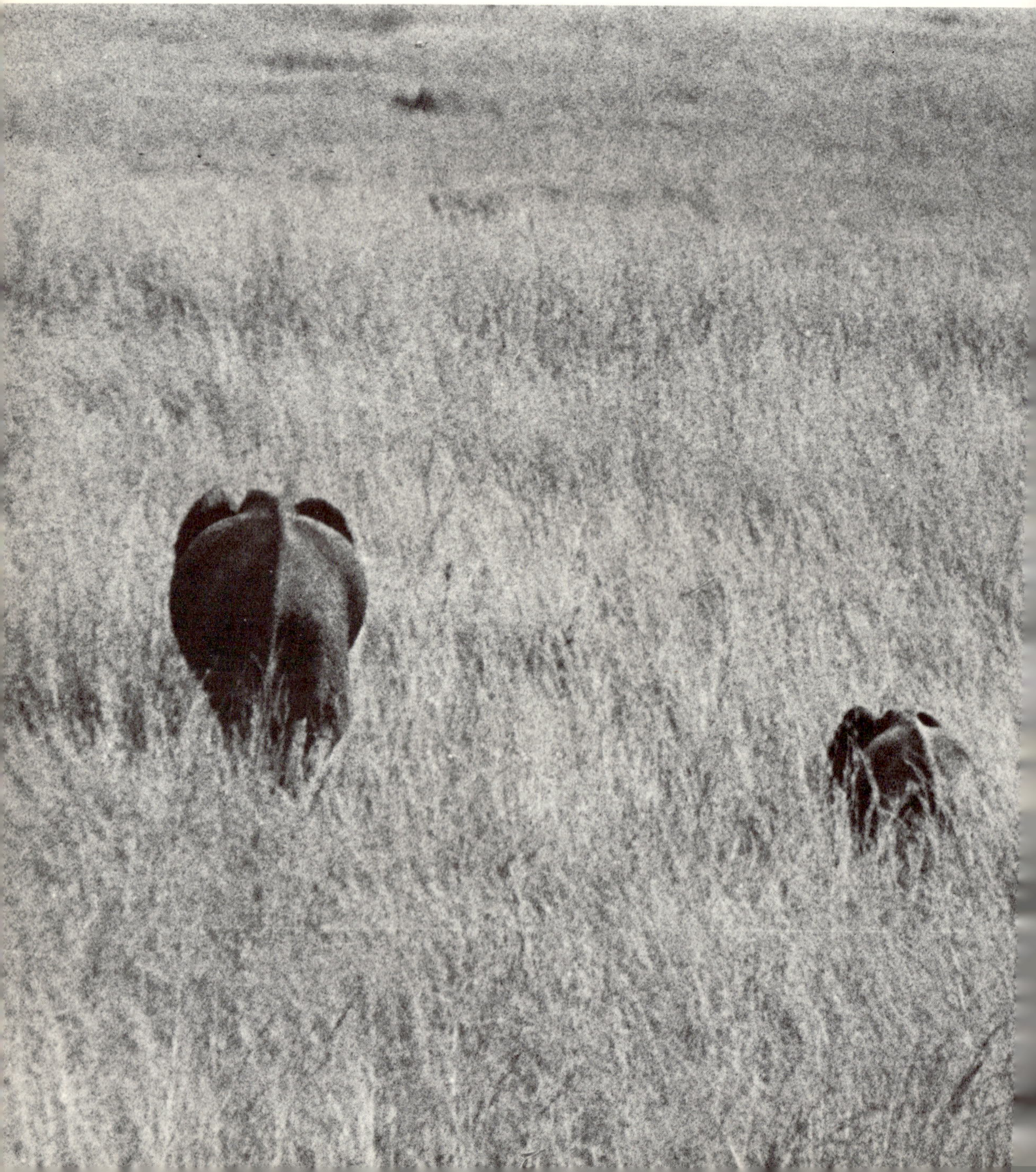

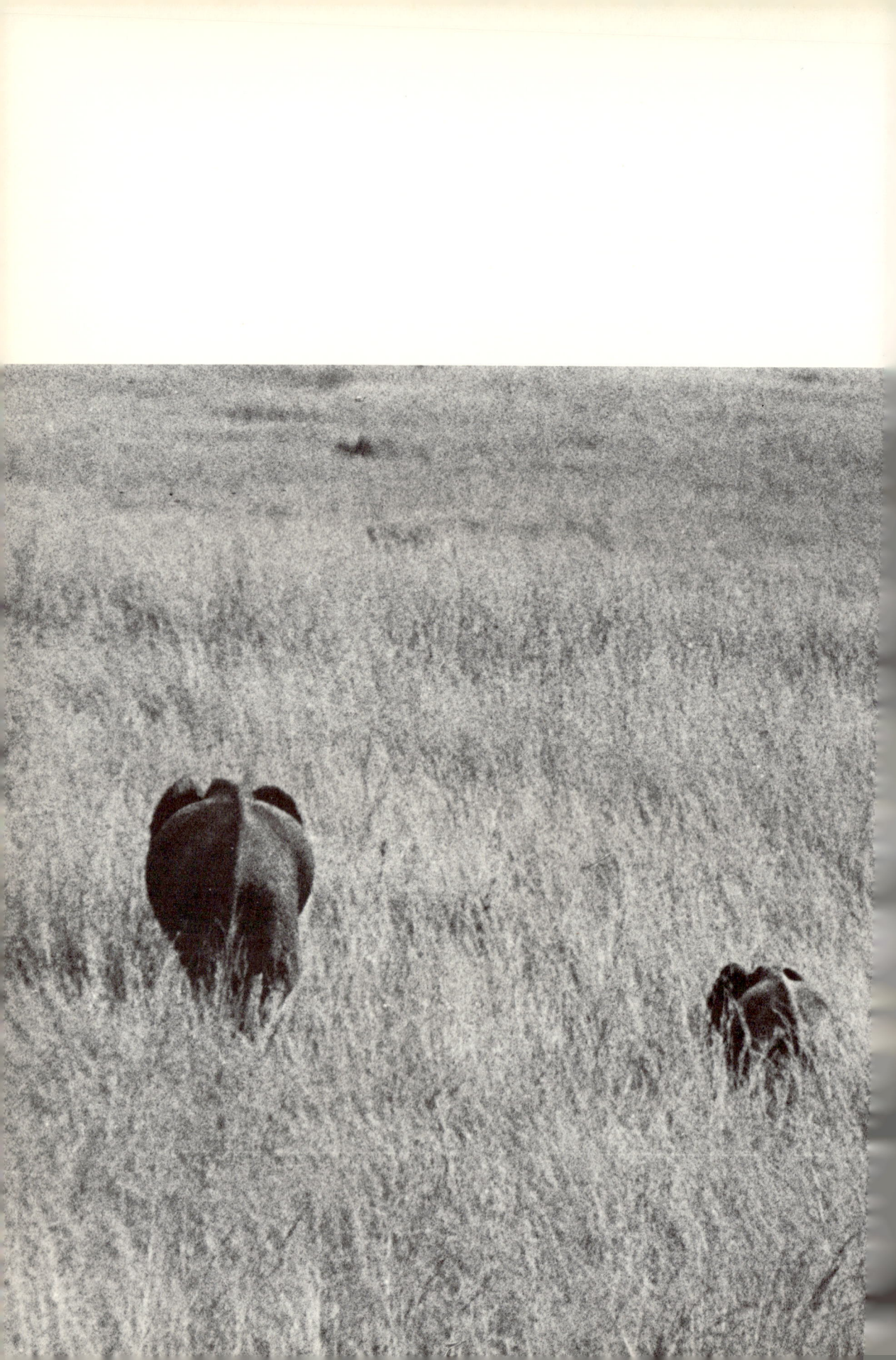

In a sea of grass in Kabalega Park, two elephants grab each other's trunks. Or so it appears. Elephants are loving creatures. They caress and scrub each other with their trunks. Female elephants spray water on their calves. When mothers stroll along with their young, they can sometimes be seen resting their trunks on the calves, a tender gesture. But look at the landscape! Only one solitary tree is standing, a Borassus palm. Elephants love the fruit of this palm and spread its seeds with their droppings. This type of tree depends on the elephants. All other trees here have disappeared, destroyed by the elephants which have become too numerous. Now the elephants are experiencing real hardship in this sea of grass, because they depend on the trees' leaves, twigs, bark and shade.

the evolution that is going on outside its borders. It is not possible for the rich half of the world to indulge itself in excessive luxury for long if the other half suffers from want.

What happened to the national parks in the high mountains of Sweden? They were demolished by an uncontrolled craving for energy that used the virgin lakes and rivers for hydraulic power plants. This craving could not be stopped by pointing out to people how beautiful the flowers are in a mountain valley. The causes for the destruction, of course, lie outside the national parks, where people don't know how to learn wisdom from the flowers.

The primary objectives of the national parks and game reserves must be to serve as sources for the distribution of knowledge about how nature functions, so that people on the outside can understand how to live in their own community on earth. If mankind fails in this, the last paradise will also fall. Elephant or human, it's the same story. They both have big appetites. There's not enough land for both of them. Prognoses have been made indicating when the last elephant will disappear—of those living outside the strictly protected and controlled game reserves. It's very easy to make such a prognosis. With a certain density of people cultivating the land—from experience, 100 per square kilometer—the land can no longer support elephants.

At what density are people pushed out by other people? When will it become too crowded for people on earth? Many now living a good life consider that the earth is already overpopulated. But these may not have reflected on the possibility of sharing—which you can expect a human to do, but not an elephant. ∎

Suddenly in the nyika, the inhospitable East Kenyan bush, this antelope stood before us. A lesser kudu, rather rare, very shy. It eats bushes and hides among thorn bushes. The kudu benefits when grassland turns to bush. This also affects another timid, very nice browser, the gerenuk, also known as the giraffe gazelle. The kudu and gerenuk do not thrive when the elephants clear forests and bush.

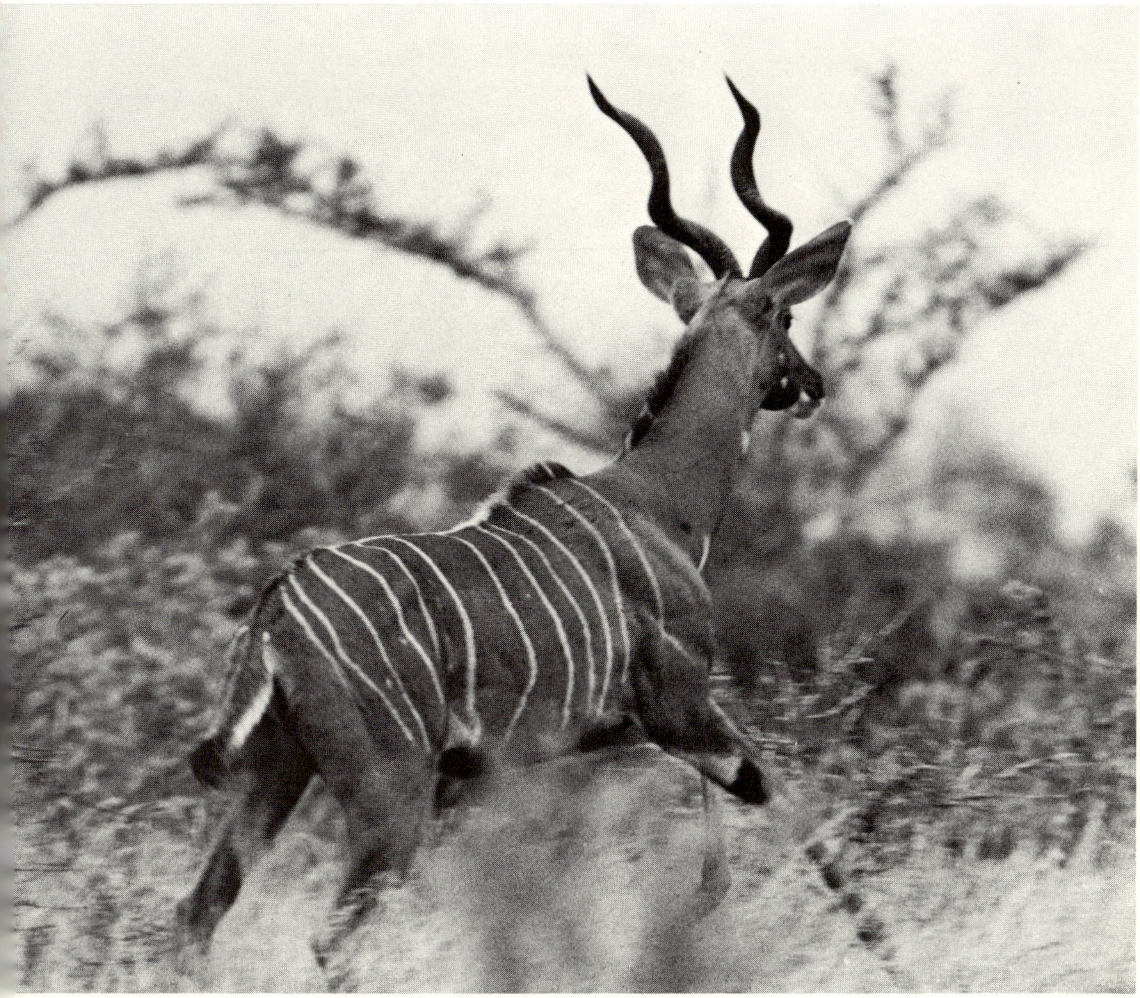

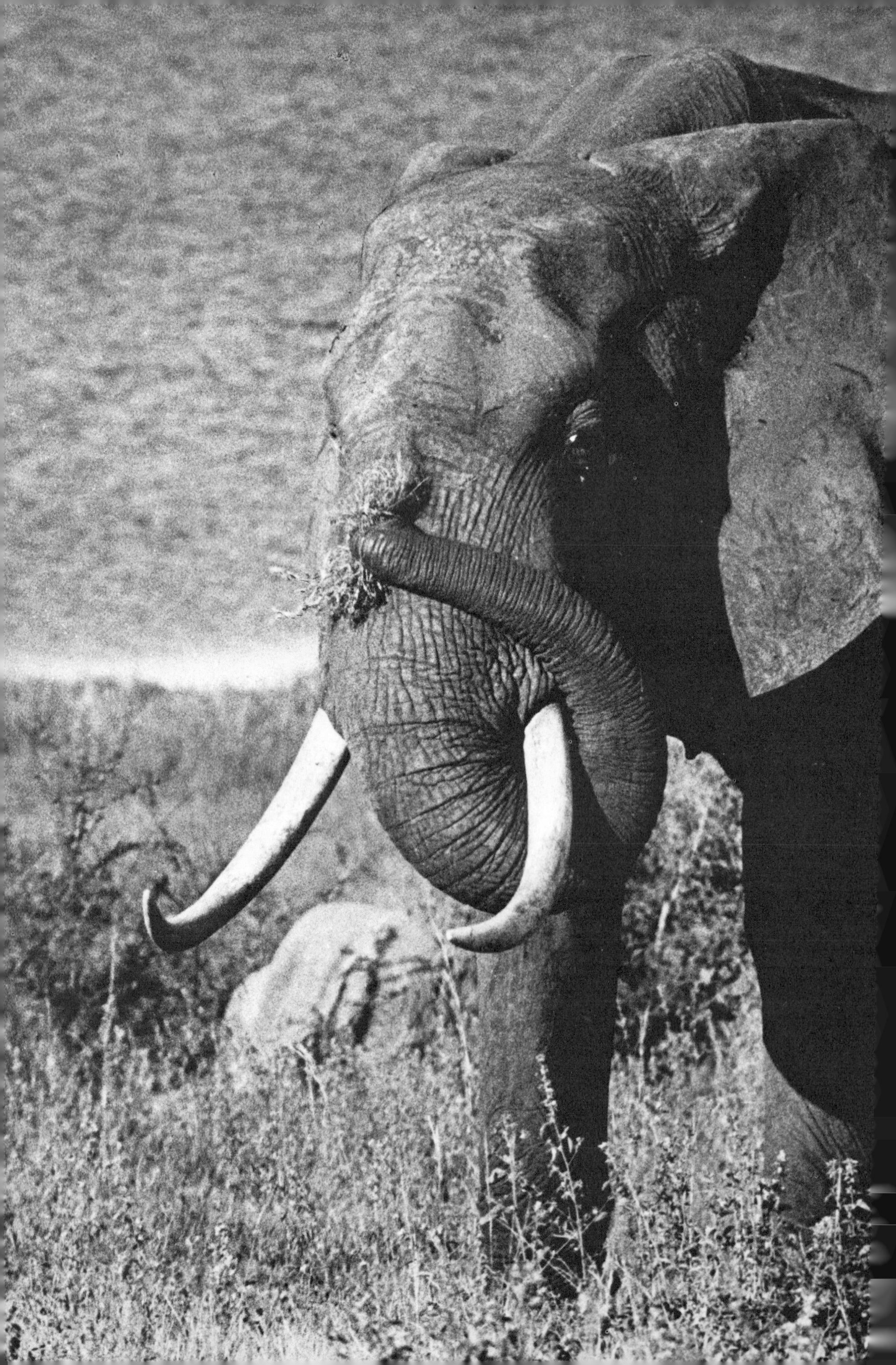

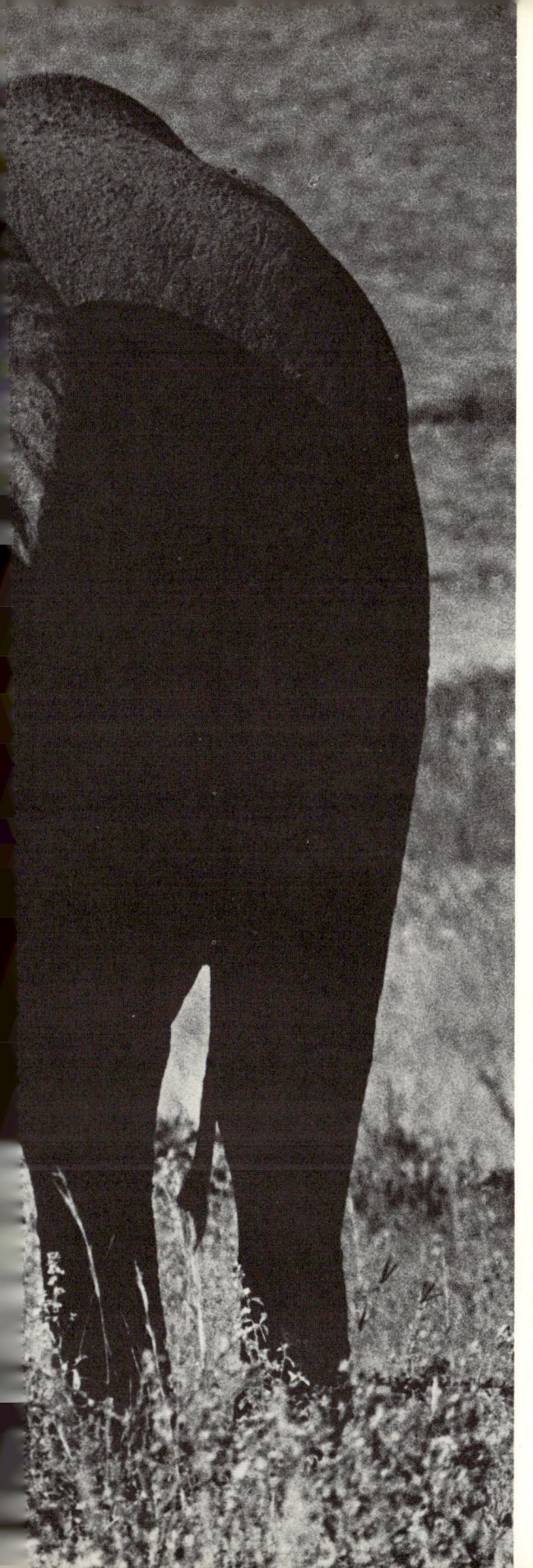

An elephant grabs a bunch of grass in its trunk and appears to dry its forehead. Elephants have well-developed brains indicating a great readiness to learn and an ability to put thoughts together. Maybe its forehead itched and the elephant did this to relieve its discomfort. Maybe it happened—by chance—to have grass in its trunk, since it was going to eat. Often elephants are seen blowing water or sand over their bodies. Elephants scrub themselves against banks of earth and trees. How much awareness is behind this behavior? If they can learn to dry their foreheads with grass, could they also learn to poke their ears with a stick? What potential really lies within the elephant's brain?

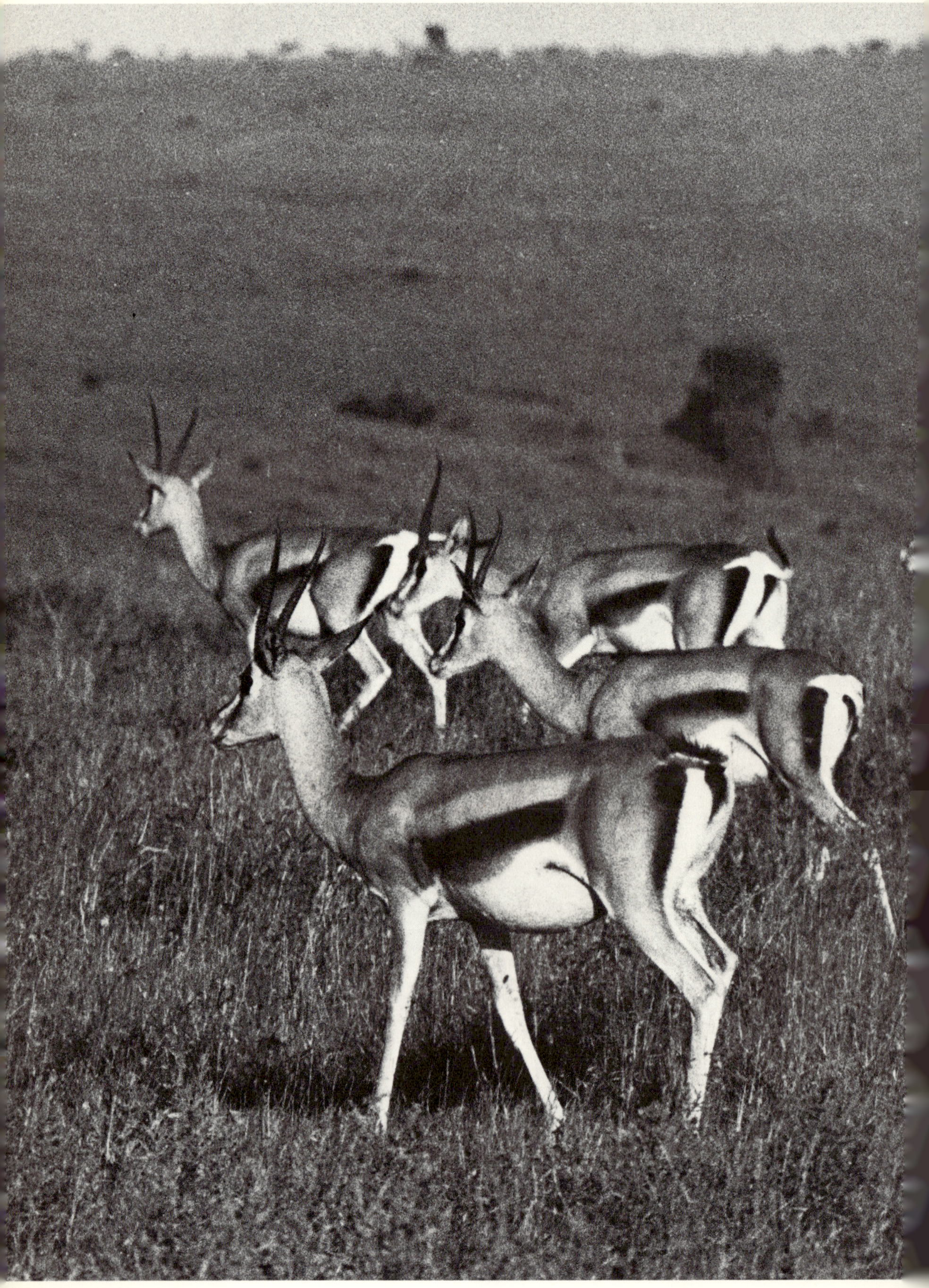

TWO GULPS OF WATER A YEAR

Thomson's gazelles: a picture of endurance. They are shaped for swift escape from hunting jackals. They are shaped for the good life in grasslands that become too poor for other animals. They have evolved an almost closed system of liquid in their bodies. Only humans strive to constantly increase consumption, to increase waste. Humans have contempt for endurance. People in the rich world could learn from the gazelles both the art of economizing and the art of survival.

Research has shown that the distribution of Thomson's gazelles in a given landscape is determined by their proximity to water. How often does the gazelle drink this water that it must be near?

It drinks, in fact, two or three times—a year!

The Grant's gazelle, on the other hand, doesn't have to drink at all. Its range is not dependent upon being near water. Its slender body wanders far out onto the semiarid plains where the only trace of coolness is the gazelle's own fleeting shadow. From the night's dew and from water in the grass it eats, the gazelle absorbs enough moisture.

It makes me think of an aspen's leaves trembling in the breeze, light as the breath from a bluebell.

The Thomson's gazelle and the Grant's gazelle often seek out each other's company. But this is a meeting of two distinct gazelle cultures. The need for two gulps of water a year separates them irrevocably.

Such are the qualitative conditions essential for maintaining life and the community of life for the gazelles, and those which govern human life are no doubt just as subtle. However, we have a hard time discovering these delicate values. The struggle for existence is sometimes undeniably crude and brutal, but at the same time we must be able to hear nuances in the tones of guitar music or what is being told us by the cells in a blade of grass speaking through a gazelle or a cow or a goat.

The need for water is one of the countless clues in that system of adaptations which gives the final shape to plant, animal and human societies. Humans have a greater need than most animals for regular access to drinking water. The first human dwellings must have been built near water. Before people learned to store water and carry it with them, their ability to spread out was limited. Humans, unlike animals, did not regularly appropriate new, extensive territories. They always had to go back to drink. Much later, they learned to make water vessels out of ostrich eggs and watertight flagons of clay or perhaps the hide of a gazelle. Then they could extend their wanderings and expand their area.

Since then, African women have carried water. You meet them constantly, carrying water pots or metal buckets on their heads, trekking long, exhausting distances between the well and home. When we say that the greater part of East Africa's land is scarcely capable of development, this can be understood to mean that much of it is a long way from water and that the people still haven't the technology of sinking wells or constructing water mains.

But the Grant's gazelle reached this stage of evolution long ago. For this and several other wild animals of the savanna, the arid marginal lands of Kenya, Tanzania and Uganda are the most favored territories. Close to three-quarters of East Africa's mammal species live in areas like these. The savanna—defined broadly—is one of the richest in animal species of all the types of land on earth. Its grass can support a larger number of ungulates than any other kind of terrain. Only humans and their animals find the savanna dry and unwelcoming.

A clever person often measures the value of land by the amount of nourishment the earth can yield. Most important are the proteins; the principal source of protein is meat. Protein deficiency is common among humans in Africa's thinly-populated areas. A not insignificant reason for this is that the cattle these people raise for meat and milk are not well-adapted to the savanna. They have a very hard time there and provide a good yield with difficulty. But this is not the same as saying that the meat yield of the savanna is poor. In the Swedish highlands, a person would not be able to survive very well if he depended on cattle grazing, but a perfectly adequate supply of meat is available there from reindeer living for the most part off the miserable lichens.

The vast herds of gnu in the Serengeti alone demonstrate what the savanna can yield—500,000 gnu. An abundance of one single species that looks after itself. But all of vast East Africa can only support 20,000,000 cows. Their pasturage is often drastically damaged by overgrazing and erosion, and the wild ungulates are chased away so that they won't compete with domesticated herds and also so that they won't spread sleeping sickness to the cattle.

But the wild herbivores themselves are seldom ill. They have lived with the tsetse fly for thousands of years; they have managed to develop an immunity to the sleeping sickness parasite that is spread by the fly. The cows might be able to evolve similarly, but it would take thousands of years for them as well.

Perhaps we should oppose owning cows instead of limiting the number of wild animals? Should we promote spreading zebras, antelope and gazelles on land where these animals thrive? East Africa's arid savanna could support hundreds of millions of wild livestock without damaging the land at all. Appropriate solutions to the problem can seem so near to hand. They are weighted with all the common sense we can bring to bear.

> Sixth day. Friday. Lake Manyara—Ngorongoro. The many elephants and bird life by the lake are rewarding camera motifs. With a little luck we will see lions. We will also fit in a dip in the swimming pool before proceeding in the afternoon to Ngorongoro Lodge. [From a travel brochure.]

Sometimes I wish that big signs were posted along tourist routes saying PHOTOGRAPHY FORBIDDEN. The camera hinders contact between humans and also between humans and animals on these hurried safari tours which could be so rewarding for us. We are so anxious to eternalize our experiences and carry them home with us that we

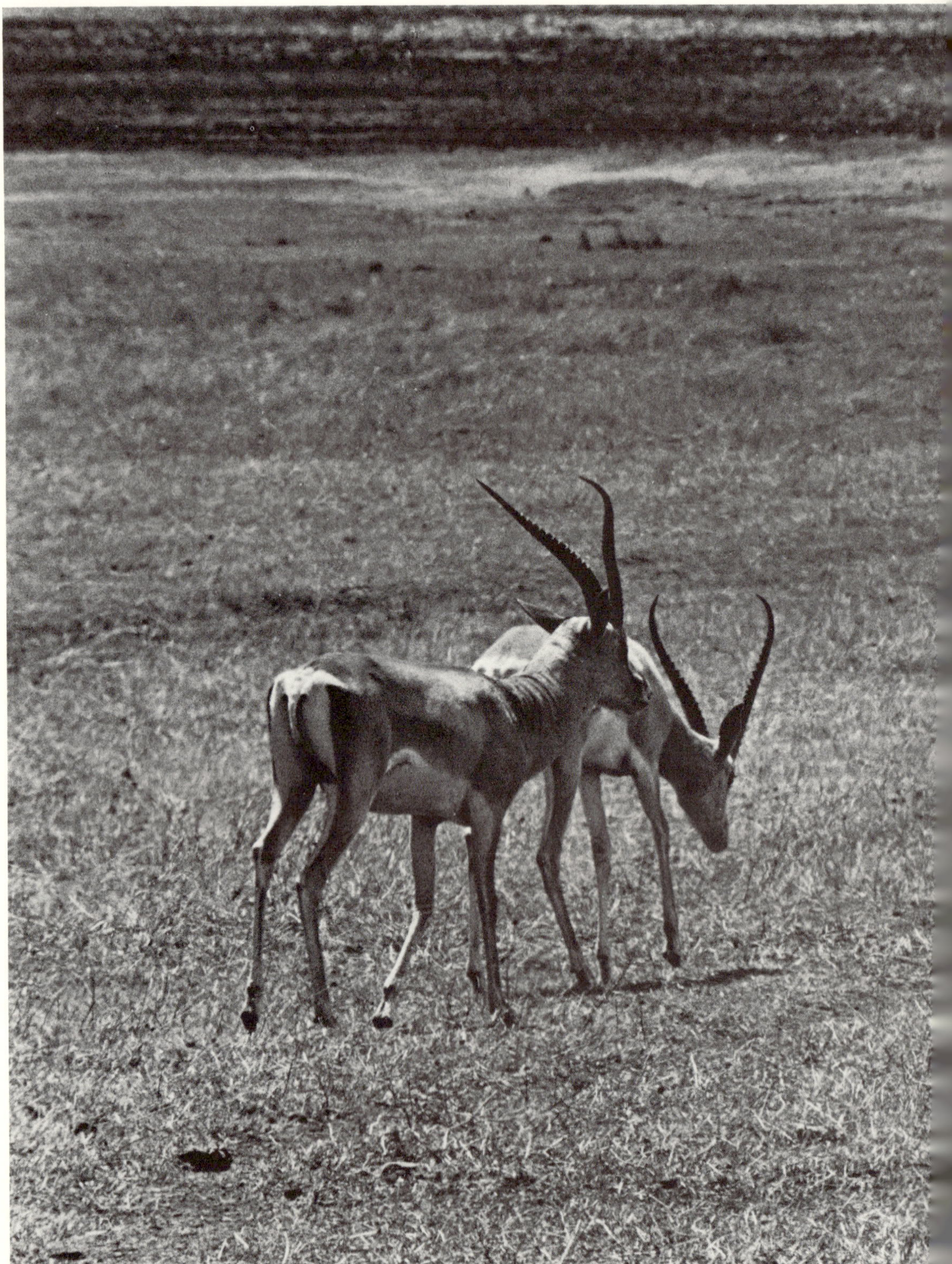

A gnu and two Grant's gazelles meet going different ways on the savanna. The gazelles break their speed and let the gnu proceed with a good margin. Just as there is a ranking order within a herd of the same species, so there is a distribution of roles in a herd of different species. The animals move side by side but also work together. They understand each other's warning signals. Perhaps zebras with their characteristically good hearing contribute to the security of their community when, for example, they are with hartebeests that have a finer sense of smell. Together the various specializations compose an organism, a society.

Gnu and zebras spread over the grassland in Ngorongoro crater in Tanzania. They are free, wild and protected. How long can impoverished land support hundreds of thousands of free-ranging livestock? As long as prosperity is deferred and humans suffer from lack of food, the wild herds are a challenge, yes, an injustice. It has been estimated that the tourist income from Amboseli Park exceeds what a corresponding acreage converted to a coffee plantation would bring in. Game animals are very profitable. But so far the big tourist income has not helped the local populations. The game animals primarily increase the prosperity of a foreign and native elite in the big cities.

Now, especially in Tanzania, plans are being formulated to turn over a larger proportion of the income from national parks to the local population. The understanding that wild animals must be protected obviously increases among those who immediately benefit from them. The possibility of harvesting a surplus from the herds of zebras, gnu and elephants is also being tested in various quarters.

There are close to 200 gnu in this picture. Take away 10 percent. Is there a big difference? This idea is frightening to many. It is an invasion of a natural ecosystem. We are breaking into the last most spectacular natural paradise. The last great wild herds will become a cultivated product. In Ngorongoro, the decision has already been made. Controlled shooting of gnu and other animals takes place and people are allowed to herd their cattle among the wild animals.

often don't take the time to experience what we see.

To a great extent, these photographic safaris have replaced big game hunting and that in itself is a good thing. But we are still seeking hunting trophies, even though the big game doesn't have to die a painful and meaningless death for our selfish gratification. There is an evil in this new commercialized recreation too. It sharpens the feeling of strangeness instead of relieving it.

The proud Masai as well as the lion and buffalo still are not understood, but we have stolen a bit of their dignity and slipped it in among the photos of relatives in our albums at home.

I remember once in Iceland; walking along a country road, I became hungry. I took off my backpack, rested it against a slope, spread out my raincoat on the wet grass and sat down on it. Then a man came up to me with a very determined step. He said, in a language I could hardly understand, "You're sitting on the grass!"

You're sitting on the grass, he said. A while passed before I understood that grass meant something completely different to him than it did to me. I had not read enough of the Icelandic sagas to appreciate what a green plot of pasture could mean in Iceland. With my raincoat and my innocent backside, I was harming a piece of the sacred Icelandic grazing grass. I had simply taken for granted that the customs spawned by my culture also applied in Iceland.

In the same way, the safari tourist or the foreign aid worker can seldom conceive the cultural oppression he or she imposes in African villages and cities. It is all the more hidden from us because it occurs together with gifts, aid and particularly benevolent, rational expert advice.

Half of Kenya's tame livestock is distributed over a savanna that produces poor, uncertain yield. There are 4.5 million cows, 2 million sheep, 3 million goats and a large number of donkeys and camels. There are 1.5 million nomadic and seminomadic peoples living off these animals on the poor, rain-impoverished grassland covering more than 75 percent of Kenya.

What does the grass mean to these people?

Scientists can tell us what grass is. Grass is, for example, a number of essential basic elements. A ton of grass (dried as hay) may consist of 443 kilos of carbon, 420 kilos of oxygen, 61 kilos of hydrogen, 17 kilos of potassium, 16 kilos of nitrogen, 7 kilos of silicon, 5 kilos of phosphorus, as well as a few kilos each of sodium, magnesium and sulphur besides chlorine and a half kilo of iron.

The Masais' zebus must be driven regularly to the few water holes on the steppes to drink. The animals are more numerous than the fragile grass cover can tolerate. They wear out the grass where they walk. The earth is laid bare and trampled hard. It swirls away in the wind. When the rains come, the animal tracks become ditches.

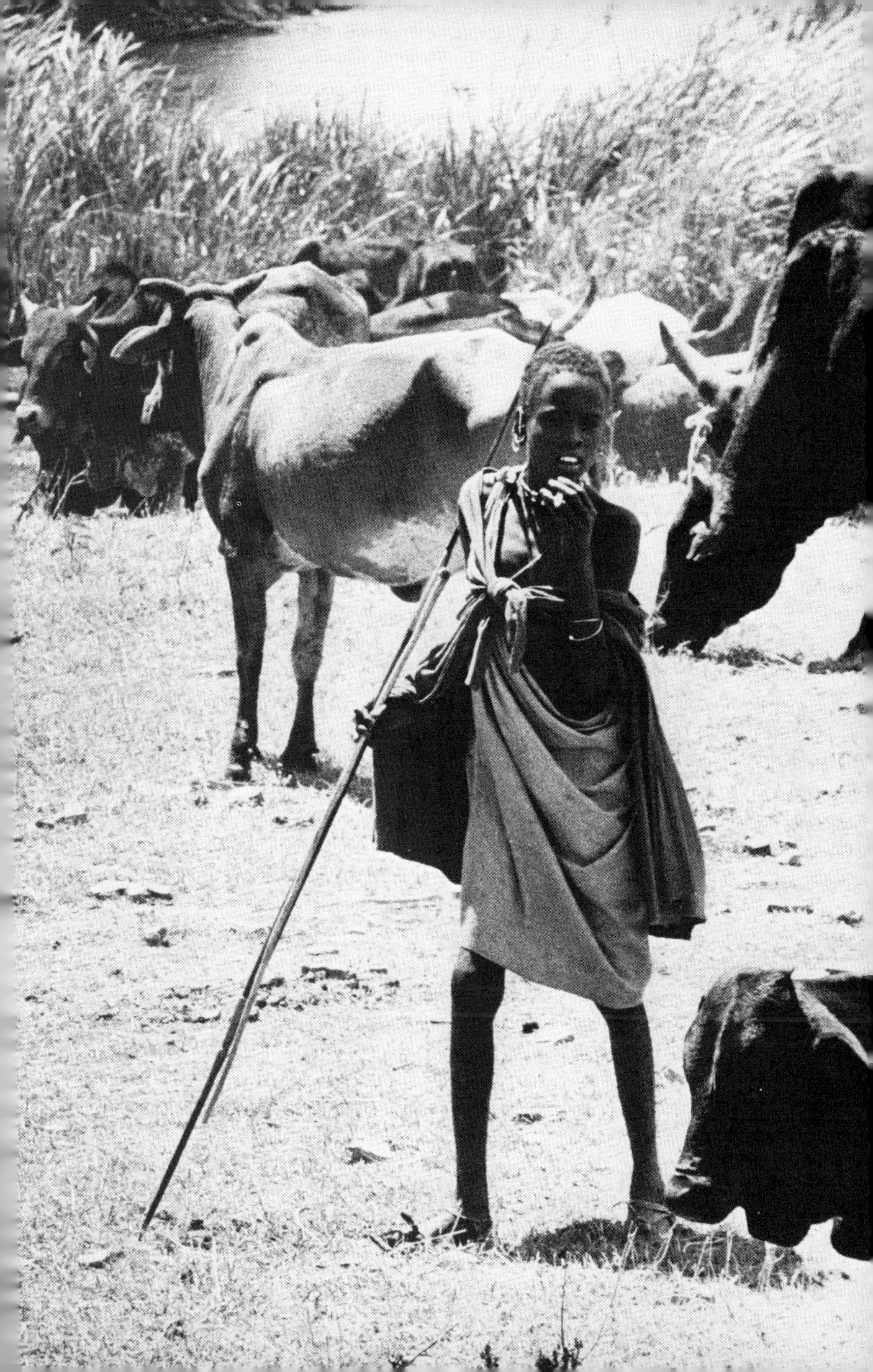

These are topis (a warthog in the background). They are common in the Serengeti where one also finds the closely-related hartebeest. It can be difficult to tell them apart. Compare the shape of their horns.

Nitrogen, for example, is a particularly important basic element in grass since, through various transformations, it becomes a crucial component in the amino acids combined by the grass into proteins. Animals eating the grass break down these proteins and rebuild the amino acids from them, which in turn are combined with the proteins that form the animals' bodies. These are the proteins that we humans basically want when we eat meat.

In this regard, there is absolutely no difference between us and, for example, the lion lazing on a branch in Tanzania's Lake Manyara Park while he digests some buffalo meat that he recently ate. Otherwise, the differences are indeed striking. On the level of elementary nutritional needs, there's no important difference between the grass and the animal that eats the grass. But they also represent two widely disparate cultures. Nutritional deficiency is only cured within the terms stipulated by each culture.

But now try to stop and study the herbivores! This is difficult; it's quite impossible to see much difference at all in the choice of grass. To my eyes, it looks as if zebra and gnu, kob and topi, impala, oryx, buffalo and gazelle all eat the same grass that clothes the savanna—green or golden, chewed short or growing tall, on mountains, in valleys and down dry riverbeds.

They do often eat the same grass. But notice how the grass changes seasonally. It is green and fresh, but most often yellow and dry. It's short, but also long. And there are several different varieties. The grassland is a mosaic. Although we humans don't usually notice, the grassland is just as varied as the adaptations of the animals that live on it.

Take, for example, the determining factor between the topi and the gnu's choice of a blade of grass. They both focus primarily on the grass blade, but they have evolved small differences in the structure of their teeth and jaws with the result that the topi is more successful in a terrain where most of the grass blades grow upright. Gnus, on the other hand, prefer a grass cover with fewer tall stalks, where the grass blades generally grow horizontally.

Therefore, it would be an advantage for the gnu if the topi went ahead of him through the landscape to thin out the stalks and vertical grass. Then the gnu could reach its horizontal grass more easily.

And that's exactly what often happens.

This is called grazing succession, meaning in this case that one species of animal helps the others, that they complement each other and are dependent upon each other.

In the rainy season on the savanna, the brooks are like rivers; it is almost impossible for people to drive on the roads. We had to load the trunk of the car full of stones so as not to be swept away by the current when we drove across a stream. Around that time, many of the wild herbivores move up to the mountains. Up there the grass never grows

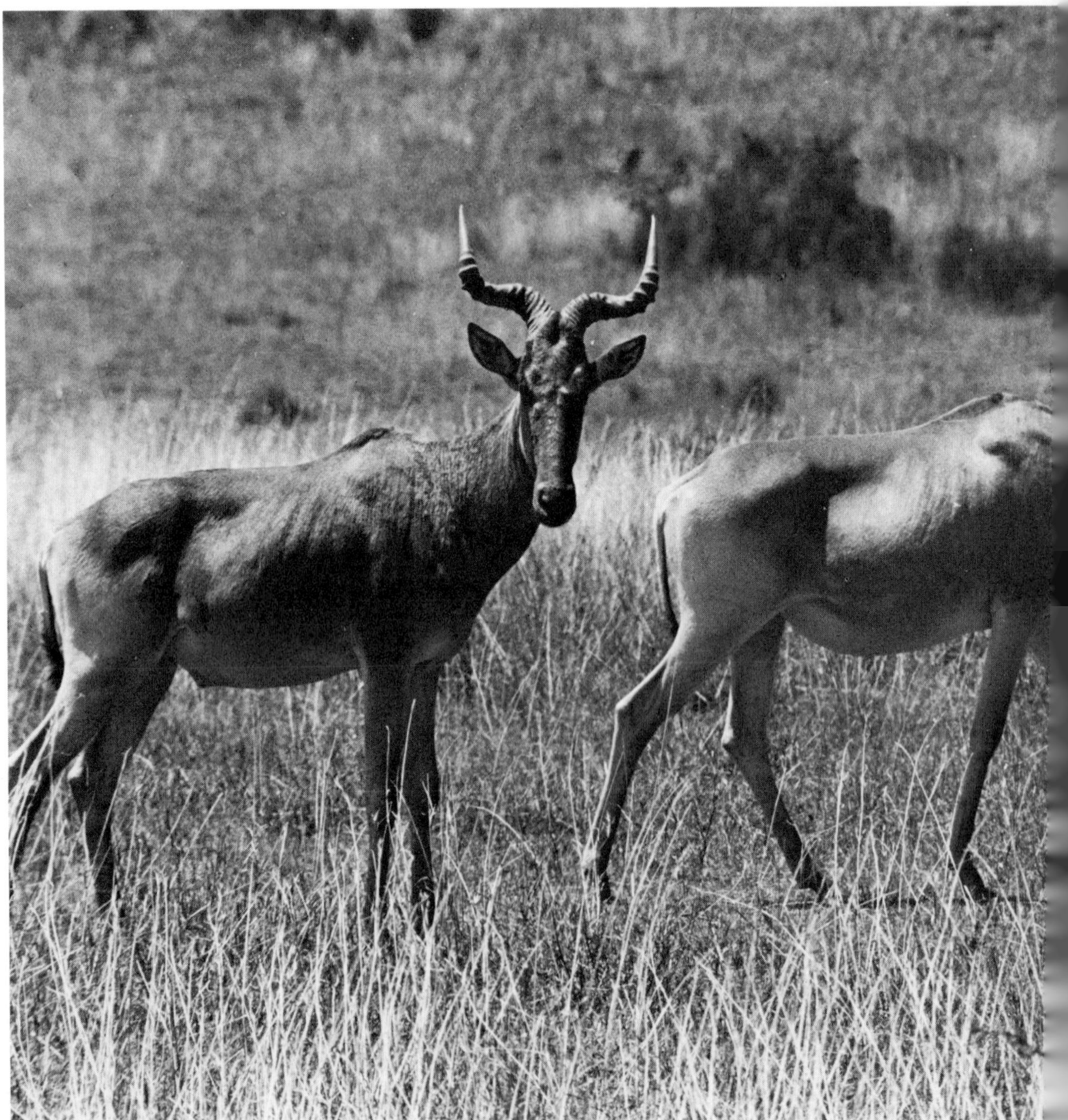

very high; it withers quickly when the dry season comes. But now during the rains, it is lush everywhere and buffalo, zebras, topis and Thomson's gazelles go up to the mountains to graze.

At least that's what happens in the Serengeti, where a field researcher named Bell has studied the grazing succession. When the rains fall, the animals don't have to be as careful about sharing the grass. There is plenty. In situations of need, sharing takes place according to need, following strict rules, because there is a real advantage in everyone profiting equally.

All are dependent on the resources for the good life being distributed so that each and every one gets what he needs. If for some reason the number of one species increases abnormally and takes more than its share, then the whole community would be stricken, even those who had profited unfairly would be hard hit.

They are seeking energy to make their muscles function, to drive their nerve impulses, their behavior and social system. They are looking for proteins most of all—albuminous substances—that build their bodies.

Energy and proteins are present in the

The antelope looking out from under broad forked horns at us in this picture are called Coke's hartebeests. The South African name, hartebeest, is known internationally. This species is called Kongoni in Swahili.

grass cells. When the grass is young and still growing, the cell walls are thin. Proteins in the cells are easily accessible. But the grasses rise up over the ground, striving toward the light and against the wind that will spread its pollen. So that it can stand, the grass develops a skeleton; the cell walls harden and become thicker with the help of a woody tissue called lignin. Dried-out grass consists almost exclusively of cell walls. There isn't much protein left in golden grass, and what exists is difficult for the herbivores to get at through the tough fibers of the cell walls.

They have developed different methods to get the confined proteins out. The gnu and topi are ruminants—they chew and then belch up and work over the grass. That way the cell walls are broken down. These animals work for quality; they extract the proteins from the grass to the last confined drop.

Zebras work for quantity instead. They have small stomachs that can't cope with breaking down the cell walls as effectively as the ruminants' stomachs do. They have to eat twice as much grass as the gnu to get as much protein. Therefore the zebras don't have time to choose; they have to take the most accessible grass. This consists mostly of stalks.

The zebras start the grazing migration down from the mountains when the dry season comes. Already during the rains, the buffalo moved down. They sought refreshment by the water holes and prepared the ground down there for the animals that will come later. The zebras pave the way for the topis. The topis cannot eat as much since they regurgitate and ruminate everything and that takes time. They get to choose the parts of the grass that are richer in protein, which is easier to do after the zebras have taken the stalks and flowers.

Gnu come to this community from the Serengeti's vast, open, high plains, where these antelopes gather by the hundreds of thousands during the rains. The gnu's departure is one of the world's most impressive dramas. They migrate in long lines from mountain to mountain to follow in the tracks of zebras and topis, which have so conveniently prepared a grassland for them in which most of the grass grows horizontally and is fairly rich in proteins.

Such harmonious scenes seem to describe something almost pastoral and ideal. Of course, it is greatly oversimplified. A scientific summary of ecological data would also be a simplification, since nature is so endlessly composite and complex. There's always room for 1,000 reservations in a generalization even if it is correct in principle.

Thomson's gazelles stay up on the mountains longer than the other animals. They never go out into the high grass. Thomson's

Animals on the savanna do a kind of shiftwork. They graze successively, one species succeeding another. Zebras prefer tall grass. Thomson's gazelles require well-grazed short grass. The distance between the Thomson's gazelles on the horizon and the zebras in the tall grass is much greater than it appears. Several months may pass before the gazelles will reach the zebras' present grazing area. First several other species will follow the zebras, harvesting their share of the grass until a suitable stage in the successive grazing has been reached for the gazelles. All this means that the gazelles are dependent on the other species for their sustenance.

gazelles are much smaller than the others. They have smaller bodies to feed and thus have the future before them. On the other hand, their daily protein requirement is relatively greater than that of the larger animals, since a little animal has a faster metabolism. This gazelle must find tender, fresh grass

Zebras, gnu, grass and trees live together in mutual association. From the beginning, man lived on these terms as an organism within the community. Then he put himself over the other organisms. Man thought that he was in contact with heaven instead of earth and that he could live according to his own laws. In our time, we have realized that we, like the other animals, are dependent on the terms set by the earth.

FOLLOWING PAGE:
The Masai are not wild men but cultured people with a highly developed civilization. Like all civilized peoples, the Masai heavily tax their environment. Their way of life is no more in balance with nature than ours. Where they have herded their cattle, the landscape has been changed. When the land has been worked and burnt out, they wander on. Over the several centuries of their history, the Masai have moved slowly southward through East Africa leaving ravished earth behind them. Now they are restricted to certain areas. They have to find completely new paths for their civilization. The same is true for us.

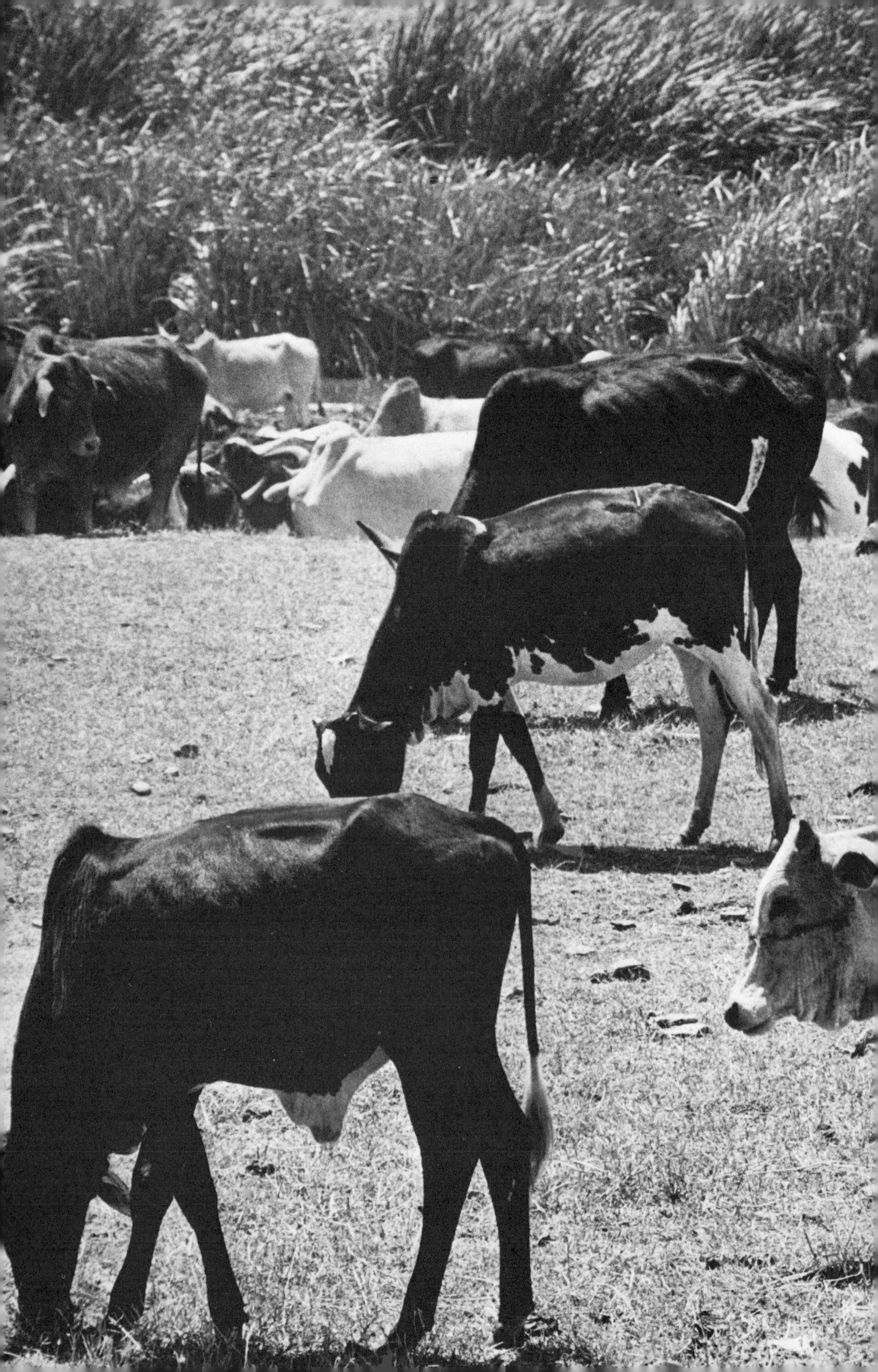

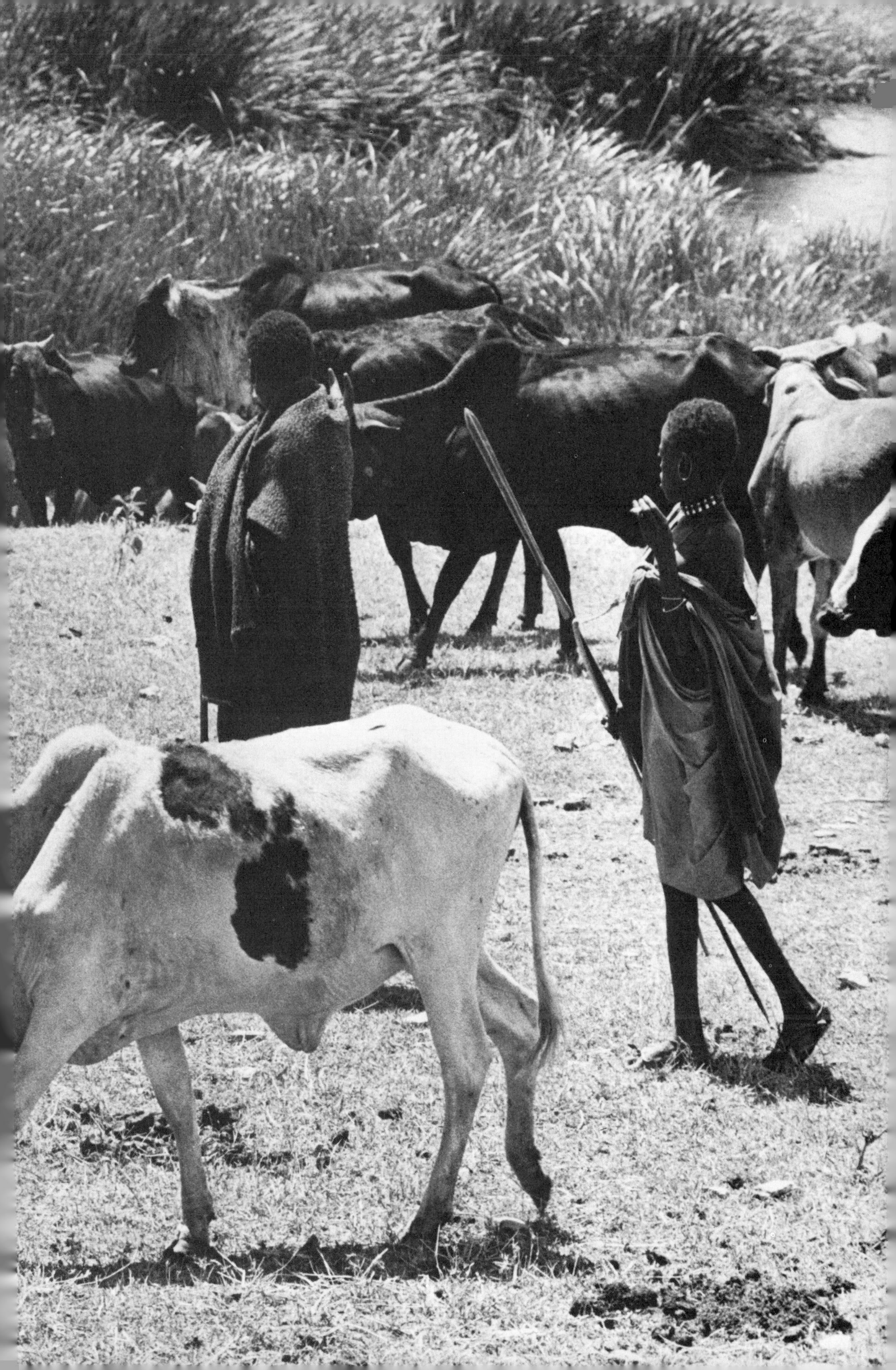

Here zebras and beef cattle are grazing together. Is this a picture of the future? "If the indigenous fauna do not pay their way, they will eventually be forced off the land," wrote Kenya's government in its national report to the U.N.'s World Conference on the Human Environment in Stockholm. "The wildlife must be managed on a businesslike basis" was the opinion of the same government when they, together with two U.N. organs, set up plans for distributing vast privately-owned common lands to the cattle-herding Masai. At best, the future really could be like this picture. The zebra and her foal are allowed to live like domesticated animals with the beef cattle on fenced property of Masai settlers. Other methods discussed in the plans include big game hunting for tourists on the new private lands and the selling of animals to zoos. But for the plans to succeed, the landowners must be able to appreciate that the wild animals can also share in a good life. Otherwise, the uncontrolled evolution that has gone on to date will only be hastened, resulting in zebras, antelope and gazelles being rapidly chased away or killed off everywhere outside the national parks.

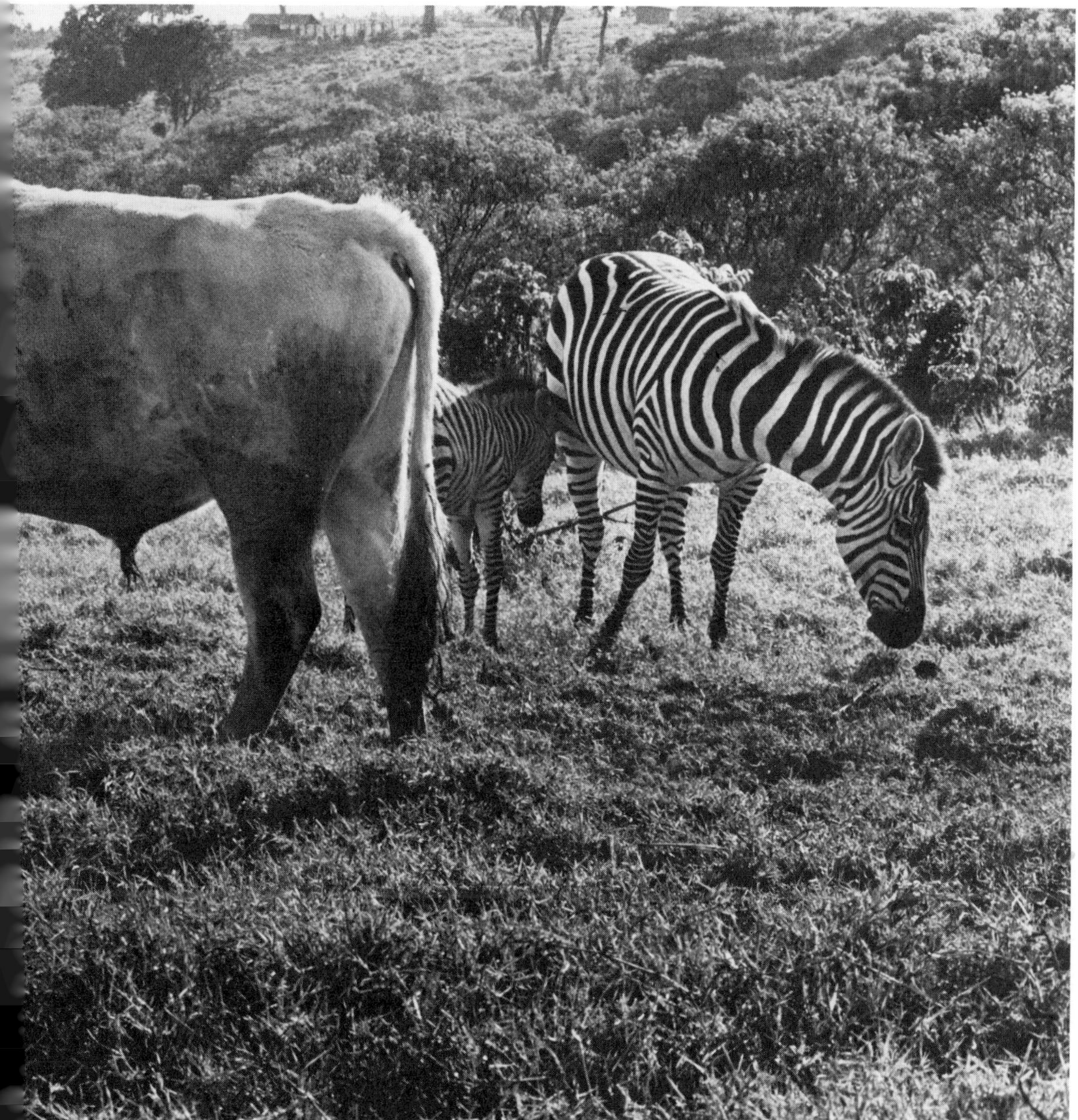

shoots because these are the richest in protein. There aren't many new shoots in the dry season, but some lie close to the roots and the gazelle has time to look. It can stay out on an arid, overgrazed savanna for a long time, and it doesn't come down from the mountains until the other herbivores have cropped a short grass carpet.

Soon enough a path is opened to the water for the gazelle. They drink so incredibly seldom. We don't know what would happen if the gazelles were trapped in an area of half-meter-high grass. Perhaps this would be a devastating, insurmountable obstacle for them.

Once, an unusually heavy rainfall caused prolonged flooding to the marshy grasslands around Lake Rukwa in southern Tanzania. The elephants and buffalo fled. Usually they would have grazed and trampled the particularly high-growing grass by the lake. The hippos would follow them and eat the new shoots of the grass that had been trampled. The hippos came anyway. But the other animals hadn't preceded them or worked over the grass. Some 1,000 hippos stood there and died, surrounded by food that was unsuitable for them.

The zebra recognizes its mother by her stripes. The foal learns to recognize its mother's pattern even from a great distance in a large herd. What does the foal do when separated from the herd at night? It hears its mother's call. It can distinguish her voice from those of the others.

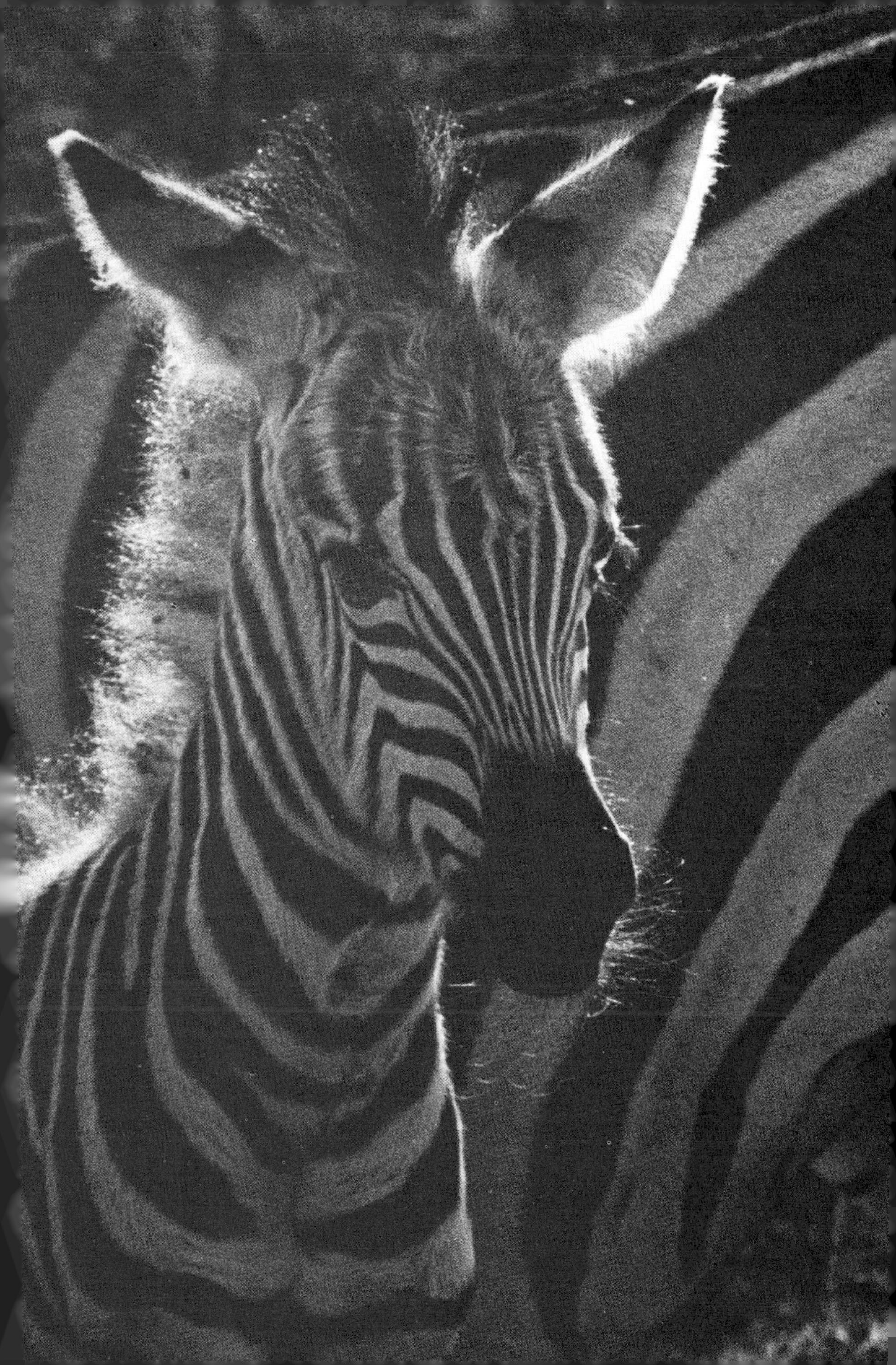

Then the flood waters receded as the dry season advanced and the topis came down from the mountains. In this place in Tanzania, the topis came after the elephants, buffalos and hippos in the grazing succession. But this time the grass was long. The topis milled around in confusion among the proteins that they could not reach. They were seized by panic and rushed in such desperation through the high grass that the sharp tassels of the grass seeds lacerated their eyes and blinded a number of them.

The topis were seized by panic because the social community was not functioning. The grass contained plenty of proteins and everything else in abundance, but it was not suitable for them—it was not their culture. It was, on the contrary, harmful to them, even though it was the very same grass that they usually ate, just grown a little taller, in another form and actually more nourishing.

Historians have asked themselves why the Africans have not domesticated some of the animals native to their home savanna. Several species would appear suited to domestication, in particular the eland, which in recent years has begun to be used as a meat and dairy animal in a number of areas in Africa as well as the Soviet Union.

Cattle-raising was imported from Southwest Asia. Dairy and agricultural cultures were first established in East Africa during the second century before Christ. Until then, the people in these districts lived in their prehistoric settings with their implements for thousands of generations, as participants in the savanna's natural ecosystem, as one of its hunting members, like the lion and the hyena.

Later, the Asiatic zebu came to their aid, and then humans and their domesticated cattle started on their present common path toward the future, our present path, leading who knows where. During its last three or four thousand years on the savanna, the zebu has evolved a meaningful adaptation to this new environment. In the long time perspective of evolution, a few thousand years is a short span. But the pressures of selection operate rigorously in these areas of climatic extremes, evolving a physiological adaptation to economize water. As a result, the zebu has only half the daily water requirement of the beef cattle that have recently been introduced into Africa from England.

What analogous roots formed by which processes of selection have bound humans to the savanna over the 2,000,000 years they have spent in these regions? These roots certainly haven't been eradicated; instead, damage appears in both the humans and the environment. Remarkably enough, we understand the adaptation of the eland and the Grant's gazelle better than that of the human. The animals have learned perfectly how to get the water offered by the grass and how to let this circulate and be reused in an almost closed system within their bodies.

The domesticated animals have not yet managed to enter into this natural ecosystem. They were not part of it from the start, so they do not participate in the grazing succession in a natural way. Even though the Grant's and Thomson's gazelles often follow in the tracks of domesticated cattle over severely grazed land, cows graze alone in their own way, often destroying the pasturage, while a dozen wild relatives of the cows and many other valuable livestock could eat the same grass—and roots, leaves and twigs—in the same field without causing any damage.

Naturally, it would be preferable to substitute such animals for the cows and reap the harvest as meat, thus obtaining much more protein without damaging the land. Numerous studies show that in every conceivable way, wild ungulates are superior to domesticated cattle.

Let us look at an important aspect, the meat yield, since protein deficiency in East Africa causes malnutrition and suffering. The yield is measured in terms of biomass, which means the total weight of living organisms, in this case, beef cattle, per certain acreage. Let us consider a grass and bush savanna in Uganda containing 11 species of wild ungulates. According to an exact reckoning, this can give a biomass of 18,795 kilos per square kilometer. This productivity holds its own on the savanna continuously, a permanent part of the ecosystem. One grass savanna in Kenya contained 18 species of wild ungulates, yielding 13,215 kilos per square kilometer. Dozens of productivity researches reveal that almost no natural grassland anywhere yields as low a biomass of wild ungulates as 5,000 kilos per square kilometer.

But where cattle-raising occurs in East Africa, no grazing lands yield a permanent biomass higher than 5,000 kilos per square kilometer, unless a person is fortunate enough to have artificial irrigation and fertilization. Often the yield is much lower, under 1,000 kilos.

The wild "cattle" are in all respects better than the cows. They grow faster and give more meat per kilo of body weight with a lower fat content. They need much less water or none at all. They don't trample and ruin the earth. Unlike domesticated cattle, they don't have to be constantly dipped in various toxic mixtures to kill their parasites.

There are only advantages. Ecologists outdo each other with examples, and we realize all this must be true, because the savanna animals evolved together in their own environment over millions of years, while the cows that humans introduced behave like newcomers, like foreign colonizers in the ecosystem.

They come crashing in destructively. The nomads' cattle have destroyed—or have accomplished a destruction the farmers began—miles and miles of all the arid grasslands in the world.

But we won't get any further with this.

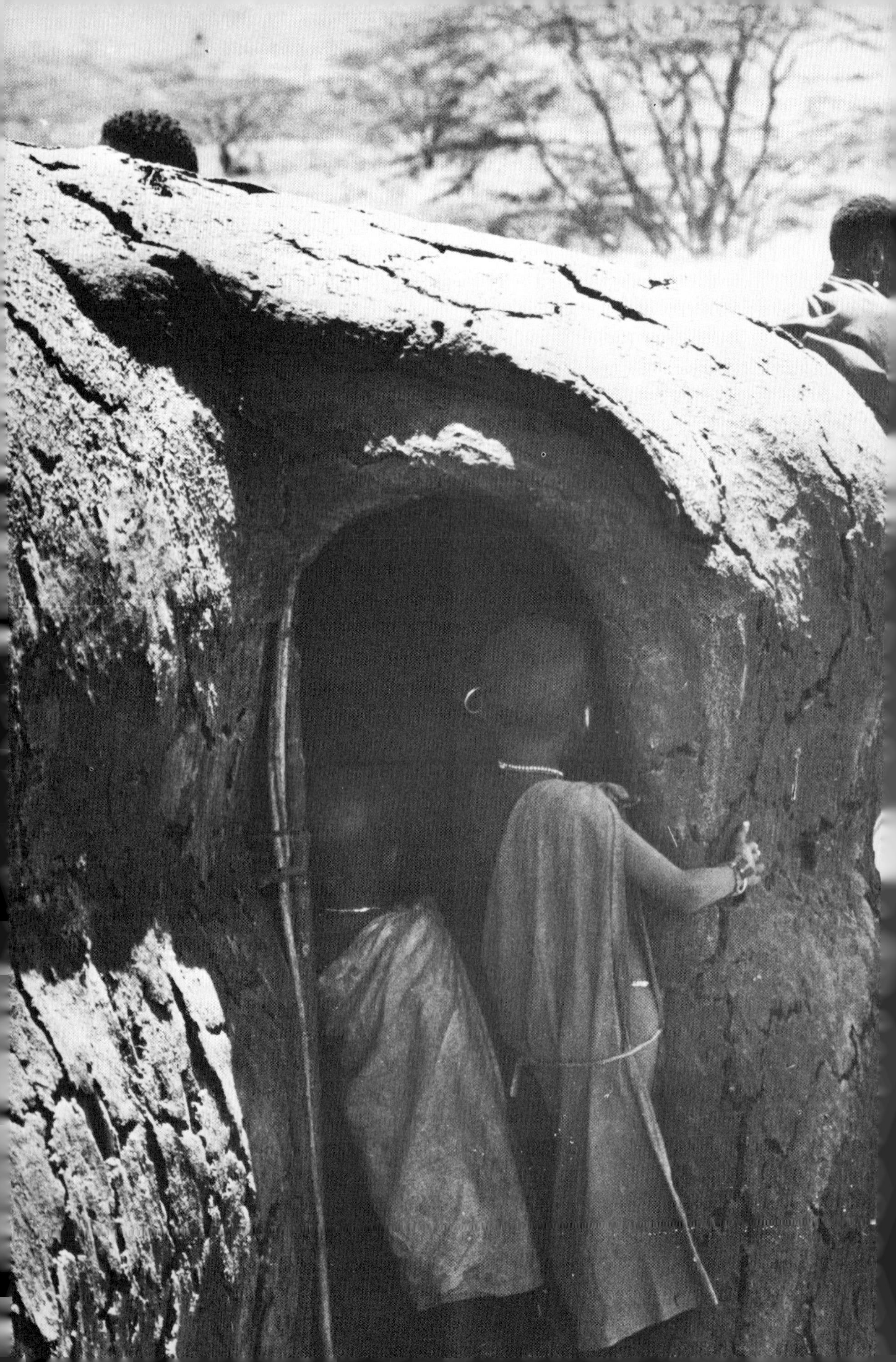

The value of meat, calculations about the maximum yield, the balance of essential elements in the grasslands, ecologically-balanced utilization of primary products, and all the other rational arguments that scientists can summon—none of these will elicit any response from those cattle-raisers most intimately concerned. To them, the grass and the cows that eat the grass mean something completely different from what they mean to the ecologists.

Hardly anywhere outside of South Africa and Rhodesia—where lack of consideration and ruthlessness reign—has it been possible to substitute game-ranching for stock cattle-raising to any appreciable extent. For a nomad, to exchange a cow for an antelope is the same as returning to a hunting culture after several thousand years of cattle-raising.

In the first place, a cow does not represent so many kilos of meat to a nomad. A cow is an article of value, an asset to life, security around which his whole life revolves. With the help of his cows, he acquires a wife. She wouldn't let herself be seduced by gazelles. Cows give prestige just

---

Masai houses are plastered with manure from their cattle. Wild ungulates probably give a higher meat yield than domesticated cattle, which could be seen as poor and destructive users of land in East Africa compared with wild livestock. But the Masai architecture, indeed, their entire culture, is based on living together with their cattle.

163

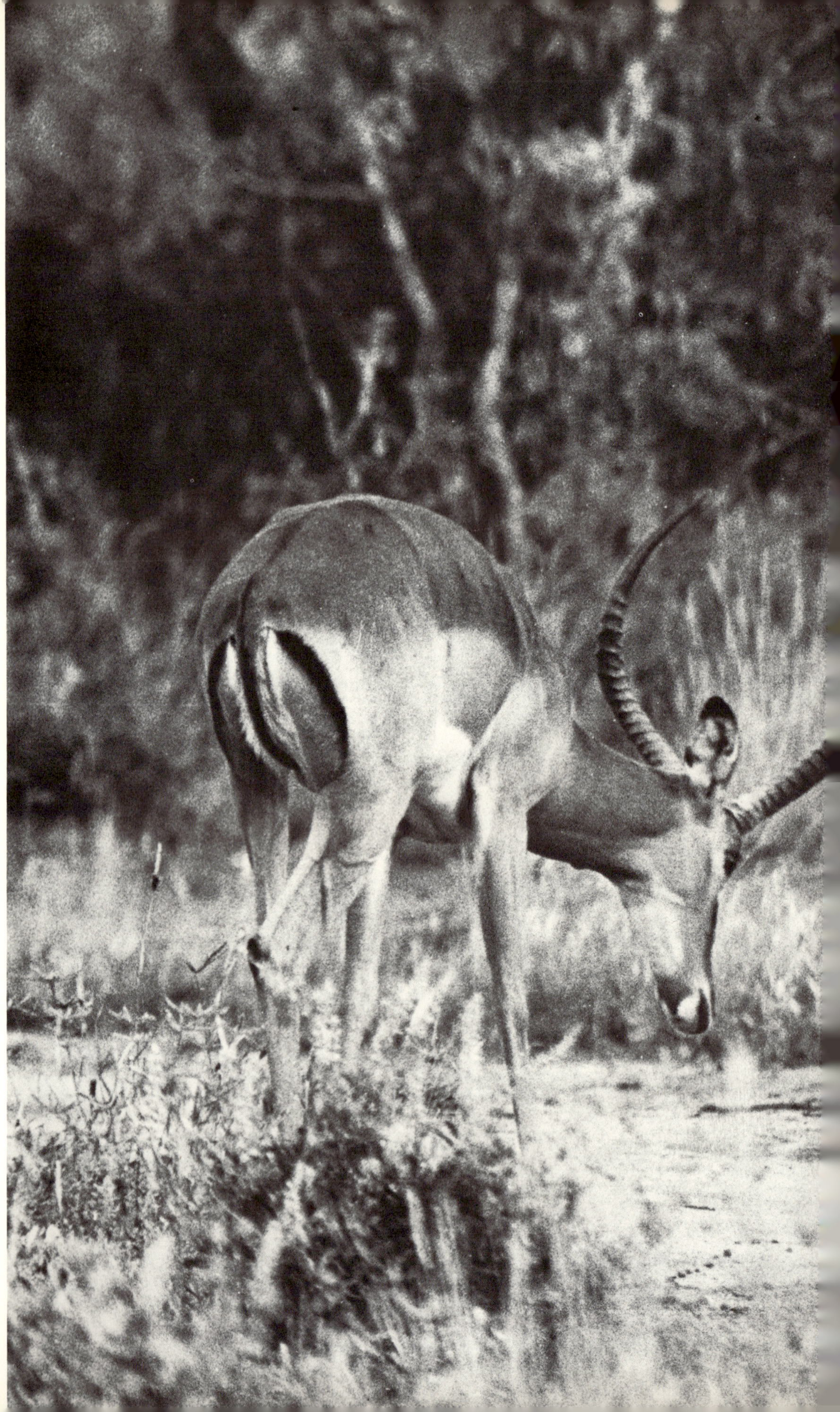

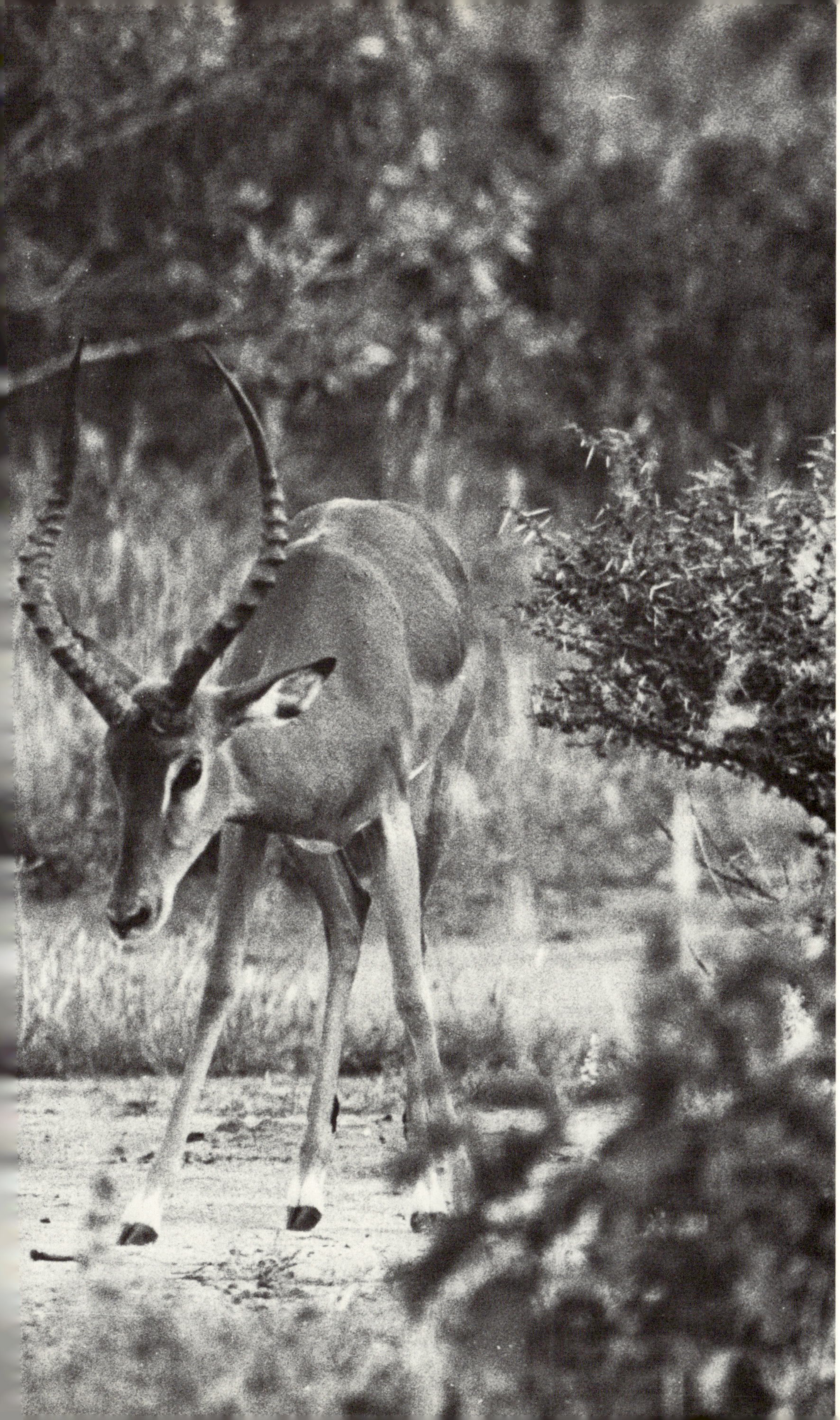

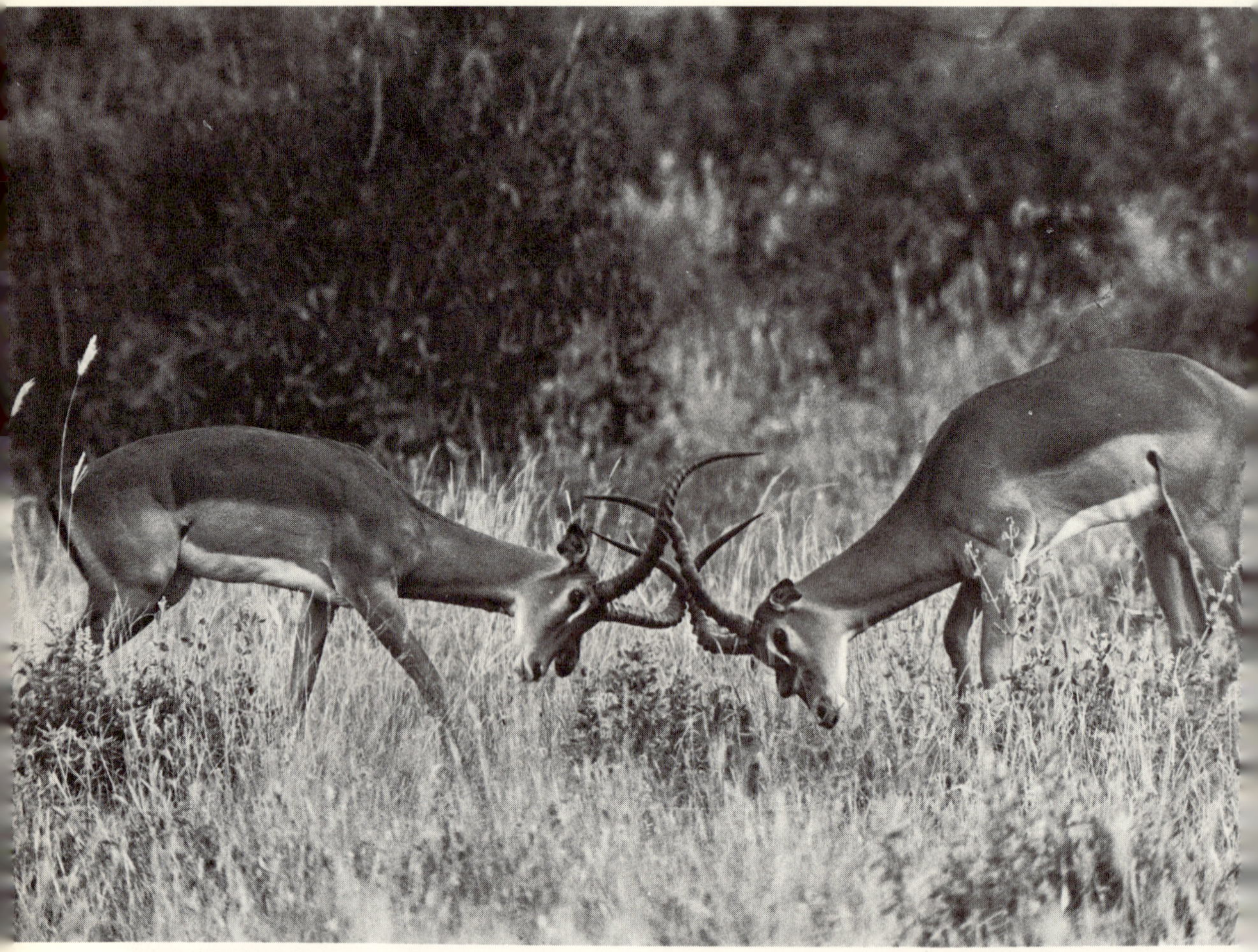

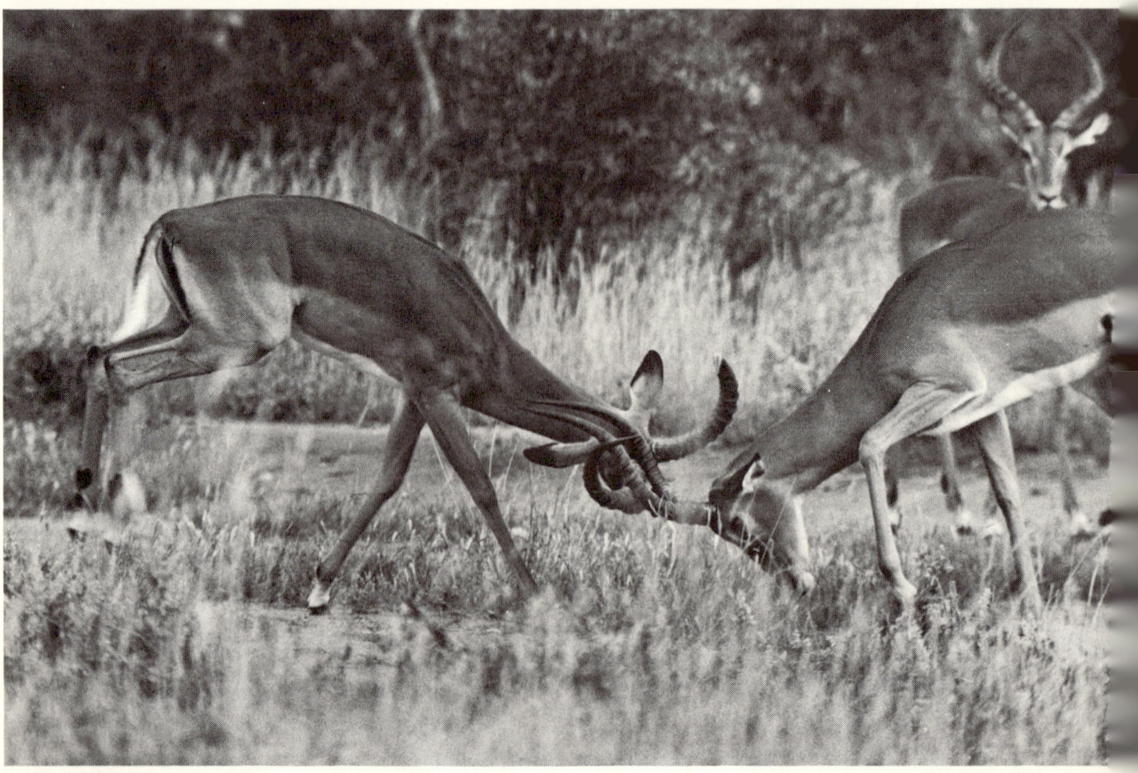

as a car does. With convincing arguments, we can condemn the majority of private cars in the world as uneconomical, environmentally destructive, wasteful of our resources, responsible for fatal accidents—and a very much more effective sabotage against future life on earth than the nomads' cattle, even though these animals are also enormously destructive to the land. But we go on worshiping cars. They are an important part of our culture.

But, we say, the nomadic races in East Africa don't understand their own good—now, when the pressure to convert them to our culture is so great. But we don't know our own good either. Even though all the wise, well-founded advice and most rational arguments also compel our development to change.

Perhaps it is too late for human beings. Perhaps only chaos will prevail. We will never really be able to learn to live like the gazelle. The voices speak to us from the grass in so many different tongues. But it is misguided to believe that any one language is right, for example, the one that speaks for the topis, stating that vertically-growing grass blades give the best life. That is really only partially true. Vertical grass is the best for the topis only if the gnus also live well and can prosper because of plenty of horizontal grass. And both of these animals base their existence on a sufficient number of zebras being able to make the best contribution that the zebra culture can achieve.

Thus, gradually, it becomes apparent to us that underdevelopment cannot be relieved with the tools of overdevelopment. Both stages are wrong. Hope for the future—for rich and poor, hungry and well-fed, nomads and motorists—lies in the balance between two kind of development, and this demands a totally new culture, neither that of the nomads nor that of those who revel in the welfare state, but rather a meeting of cultures. Something in between. Something gentle, something slow, something that is not so all-embracingly effective, but that is well-suited to a pattern of countlessly diverse prerequisites.

We can learn this from the animals of the savanna. ∎

Impalas show what horns are for. Fights are seldom so bad that one of the bucks is injured. For safety, the impala buck has a special reinforcement, a kind of shield, under the skin on his forehead.

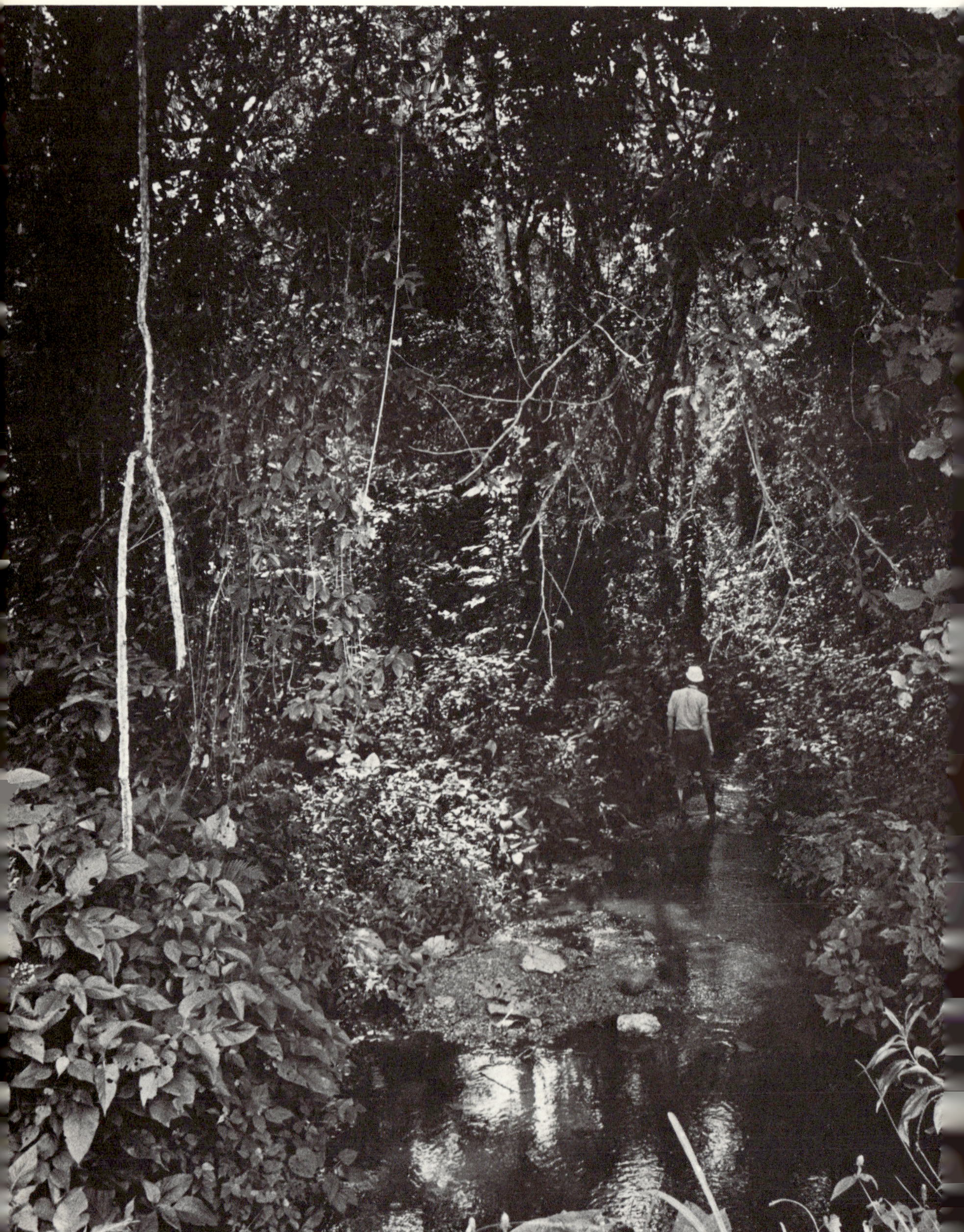

A JUNGLE UTOPIA

When the rain falls, there is a meeting of heaven and earth. Rain can fall violently on trees, bushes and crops, but it passes gently between twigs and foliage, drops from seed tassels and leaves, trickles down branches and trunks, is sucked up by moss and humus, damp earth and porous roots and then, when the roots' thirst has been quenched, slowly trickles through the earth to enrich the subsoil water and fill the brooks, rivers and ocean.

This is a blessed meeting of heaven and earth. Each leaf blesses the rain. But wherever there is land abuse, rain strikes the earth with a curse. Raindrops strike like malevolent rifle shots, bouncing, richocheting bullet-like off the bare earth. Erosion is rainfall's revenge. Rain is the sky's punishment, striking ground that has been abused by humans.

I'm walking in a rain forest. Far, far beneath the treetops, I'm following a recently-cleared path. I walk through the forest's aroma and the earth's breath. The air is stiflingly dense with carbon dioxide. No wind blows down here to swiftly waft away the invisible vapors that animals and plants give off as they breathe and decay. These heavy gases collect at ground level, in the stillness of the forest. I imagine that I can perceive the tremble of a leaf breathing, the last breath drawn by a fallen twig and, simultaneously, a new shoot unfurling somewhere—one of millions—it extends, touched by that recently departed friend.

The forest strains my nerves, fills me with unease. I'm afraid of losing my way. I stretch my head back and look up at the treetops. Do I feel dizzy? Can you feel dizzy in a chasm that's upside down? Every perspective in a rain forest is appallingly, dizzyingly deep. It's clouding over up there; the afternoon rain is coming. Confused, uncomprehending, unable to make normal connections, I stand there forlorn and ineffective, but then I leave the path and clear my way through the vegetation, crawl beneath fallen trees, duck under lianas and roots and twisting plants. Soon I stop. I don't dare go any further. My tracks disappear behind me. Every second my presence is being obliterated—and now the rain is coming.

I can hear the rain come. It is already falling on the treetops high above me. For a second, the forest is breathlessly still. Then the wind comes, lashing, crashing through the treetops. I tell myself that I'm fascinated. Actually I'm afraid. Now thunder rumbles. Probably lightning is flashing over the forest but I can't see it down here. I break out of the tangle back to the path and, with a lump in my throat, run for the hut at the edge of the forest where I'm staying. My clothes are drenched by underbrush weighted down by the rain.

Then I sit there on the verandah, watching the lightning whip long flashes across the sky. These were not, as in Sweden, individual bolts of lightning followed by thunder claps: the lightning was powerful and unceasing. It struck in series. The blue-black sky over the forest was filled with lightning all the time. Then, unexpectedly, it was all over.

Tables and charts from the world meteorological organizations indicate that thunderstorms occur in parts of Uganda 240 days a year. Like the rain, lightning acts as an encounter between sky and earth. Thunderstorms actually fertilize the forests and soil. Lightning strikes with incredible power, forcing some of the nitrogen in the air to react with oxygen or hydrogen. Then, when the rain later falls over the forest, it is enriched with the basic elements for proteins. Lightning contributes to life on earth—with 7.6 million tons of nitrogen a year.

Down there on the forest floor, where only a small percentage of the midday sunshine can penetrate, I can come very close to the origin of life. Here in the darkness was one of its beginnings, the forest and plant life's earliest home. I find no regularity, no uniformity in the forest. I see a mass of individual trees of countless, many-shaped species. It looks chaotic, but it is the order of life.

Something pulses ceaselessly in every cell. A seed that falls to the ground must germinate instantly, because nothing that does not live intensely can survive in a primeval forest. Whatever does not must relinquish its place to something else.

Many trees lose leaves from only a few branches at a time, so that most of the foliage functions constantly and retains its life force. Sometimes leaves sprout so fast that the leaf's vein system cannot keep up. The clustered leaves hang limp and flabby waiting for the vein network to catch up with the surface size.

How long does a leaf live on a tree in the rain forest? Perhaps it pulses in full activity up there for 20 months before its task is accomplished and it is cast to the ground. For a few weeks or months, that twig will remain bare. Then a new leaf will unfurl from an almost invisible bud.

How slowly does this leaf die, when it falls from a twig in the tropical rain forest? Ivan T. Sanderson in his *Book of Great Jungles* describes how he once laid a piece of wire netting over a big fresh green leaf that fell to the ground in front of him one morning in the rain forest. By noon, the leaf was bright yellow. By evening, it was brown and had been nibbled by small creatures. By midnight, only a filigree of leaf veins remained. Next morning, the leaf was gone, except for a few tiny bits of the stem that two large ants tried to carry away. This is how extraordinarily fast decay may occur in a rain forest.

We cannot follow this leaf any further. But soon, very soon, its life forces are restored to the tree. It has not been apart from the forest's communal life for a second. Even as it was falling from the tree's foliage down 30 meters through the rain forest space, it contributed to the energy of microorganisms that found their way into its tissues.

In a West African rain forest, it has been estimated that a full eight tons of leaves fall to the ground over every hectare of earth annually, together with a ton of flowers and fruit and a couple of tons of twigs and branches. The life components in the decaying leaves—the elements that never die, for example the nitrogen compound originally produced by the lightning—are transferred as nourishment to other cells in the forest's cosmos of living organisms.

Here in the forest, it is hard to perceive that death exists. In the stream of life, death is continuously absent. Death is only the comma in a long sentence that tells a true story about the fantastic potential of existence.

Perhaps all plant life started on our globe with the life force in the rain forest. There are strong indications that even our temperate flora originated in tropical rain forests. From the beginning of the Cretaceous period to the end of the Tertiary, the greater part of the earth was covered with rain forests. This forest structure and the composition of flowers that we find in these forests today have presumably remained unaltered in their basic characteristics for millions of years. The rain forest probably still lives and functions as it has since the Tertiary period. As far as we know, those primeval plants resemble the plants that live in today's rain forests. The rest of the world's plants have appeared relatively recently, and they originated in these primeval forests. During the earth's earlier history, the rain forest was the center of evolutionary activity that distributed flowers over all the continents.

What does it mean then that the few remaining rain forests are rapidly being cut down and replaced by uncertain grain crops and pine or cypress monocultures? Among other things, this means that an ancient, fresh source is being dried up. Now future plant evolution must derive its nourishment from an interrupted source. Will it work?

Plant authorities, botanists and everyday romantics can never get to the source to find the basic knowledge of green plant life. We cannot yet break the code that creation wrote in flowers and trees and cultivated plants. Here is an ever-present source: conditions from before Noah's ark still prevail in the forest. But the forest is going to disappear. Perhaps only a few small preserves will remain. The tropical rain forest is exceptionally sensitive to interference. It is very stable, but at the same time this complex web of security and stability is as fragile as a spider's web and can be destroyed very easily.

I think that we should seek out lessons from the rain forest before we turn it all into

---

Ferns rise like tongues of fire from the moss-covered branches; elsewhere, mosses and club mosses hang downwards. There are almost no unused spaces in the rain forest.

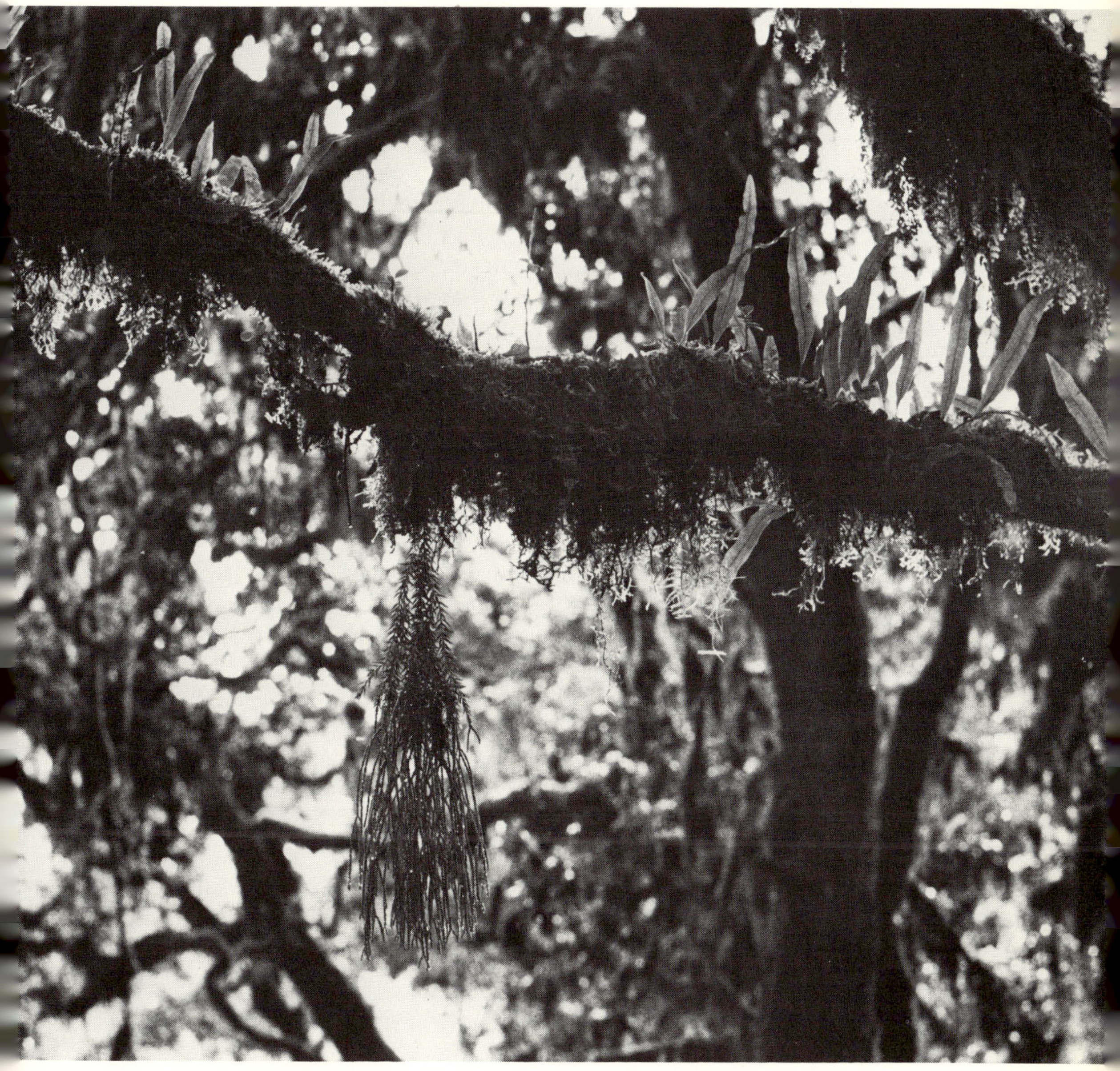

parquet floors for America. We may be able to derive more from these forests to help us order a good life on earth than we can get from stories of creation from Christianity and the other religions. We may not understand these thought constructions, but we have always neglected the stories present in the world of our senses. Now we are erasing, annihilating it.

Everything that is magnificent, both plants and animals, everything that blossoms and is green, lives in the highest dwelling places of the rain forest. It is as if the colors strive and soar upward from the pallor and darkness near the earth in a gradated scale of color intensity that bursts out as sunbirds, butterflies and splendid flowers in the hanging gardens high up in the air. It is the same with sounds in the forest. Down near the ground there is silence; a few flycatchers sing in the intermediate space, but up in the leafy branches the silky monkeys and innumerable birds, hardly visible from the ground, shriek loudly.

Sunlight lures them all. See how lianas hang from the almost naked trees, clad only in scanty ferns and mosses near the ground. Leaves open high up there, interwoven among the trees' foliage. Up there the orchids (epiphytes) and parasitic plants dwell on the branches and trunks. If they happen to fall to the earth, they shrivel up swiftly in the darkness.

The sun provides warmth, an even, intense heat throughout the year with only slight fluctuations. The light is almost constant: at the equator the variation in the length of the days during a year is only a couple of minutes. The humidity is also constantly high. No long dry periods occur; rainfall is plentiful, recurring at least every two or three days.

An environment with such minor climatic variations means that organisms have few adjustment problems. It functions conservatively with species and forms, but at the same time facilitates the evolution of new variations of adaptation. Studies of ten to twenty million-year-old fossilized plant remains in Trinidad reveal that during that period the rain forests had plant complexity not significantly different from today's West Indian forests, which in turn closely resemble African ones even though the plant species are almost always different.

The black-and-white colobus monkeys, or guerezas, are found in the topmost dwellings of the rain forest, in the crowns of the tall trees. It is difficult to catch a glimpse of them. Their black-and-white body contours are erased in the forest's light and shadow play. They are timid, fleeing as soon as a human approaches. One can hear leaves rustling and branches shaking. Through binoculars or a telephoto lens one sees the monkey high above. But there are times when no one within a kilometer can avoid knowing that guerezas are around: at dawn, just before sunrise, when they send out an indescribable, hoarse, trumpeting song through the forest.

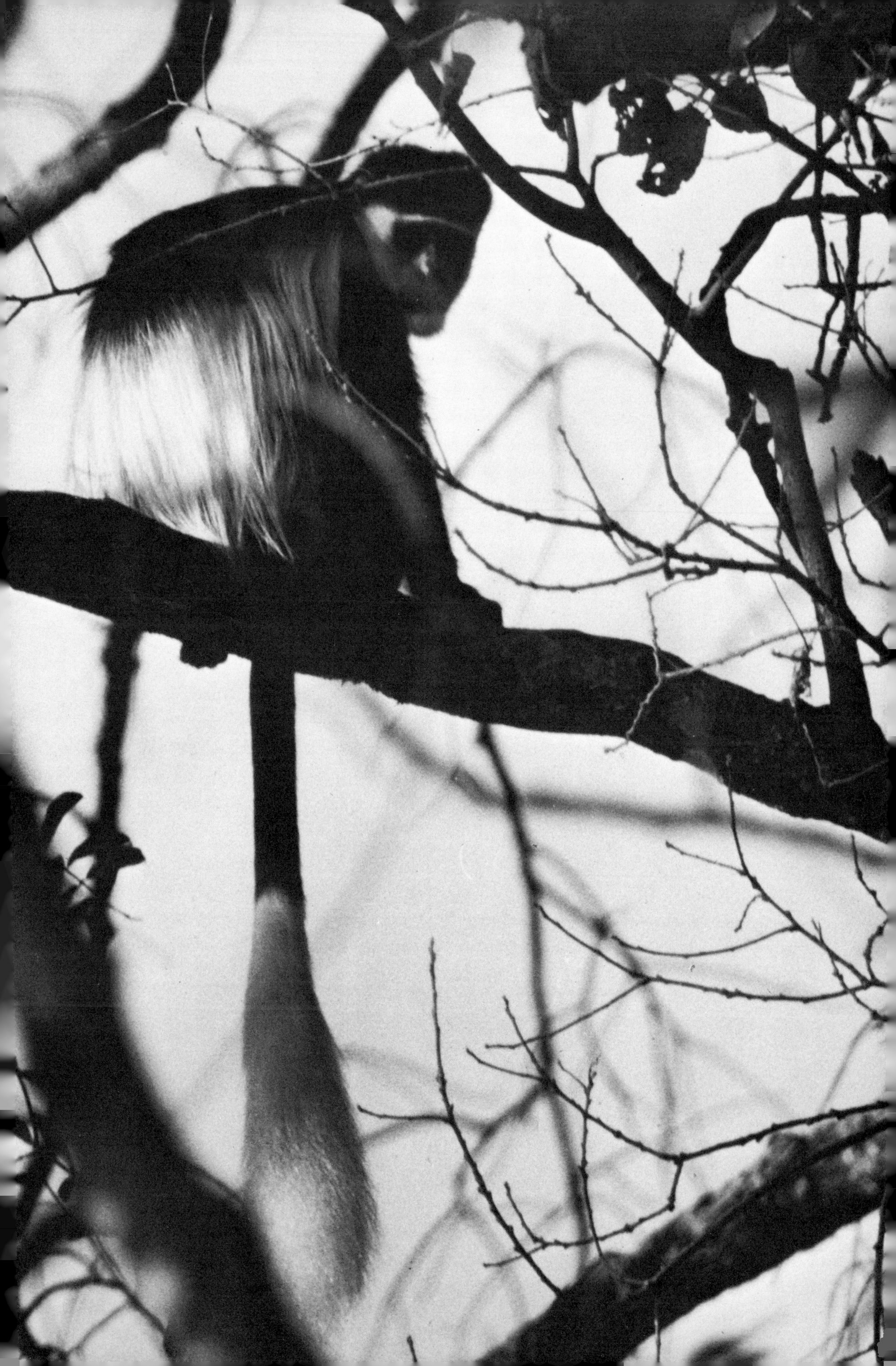

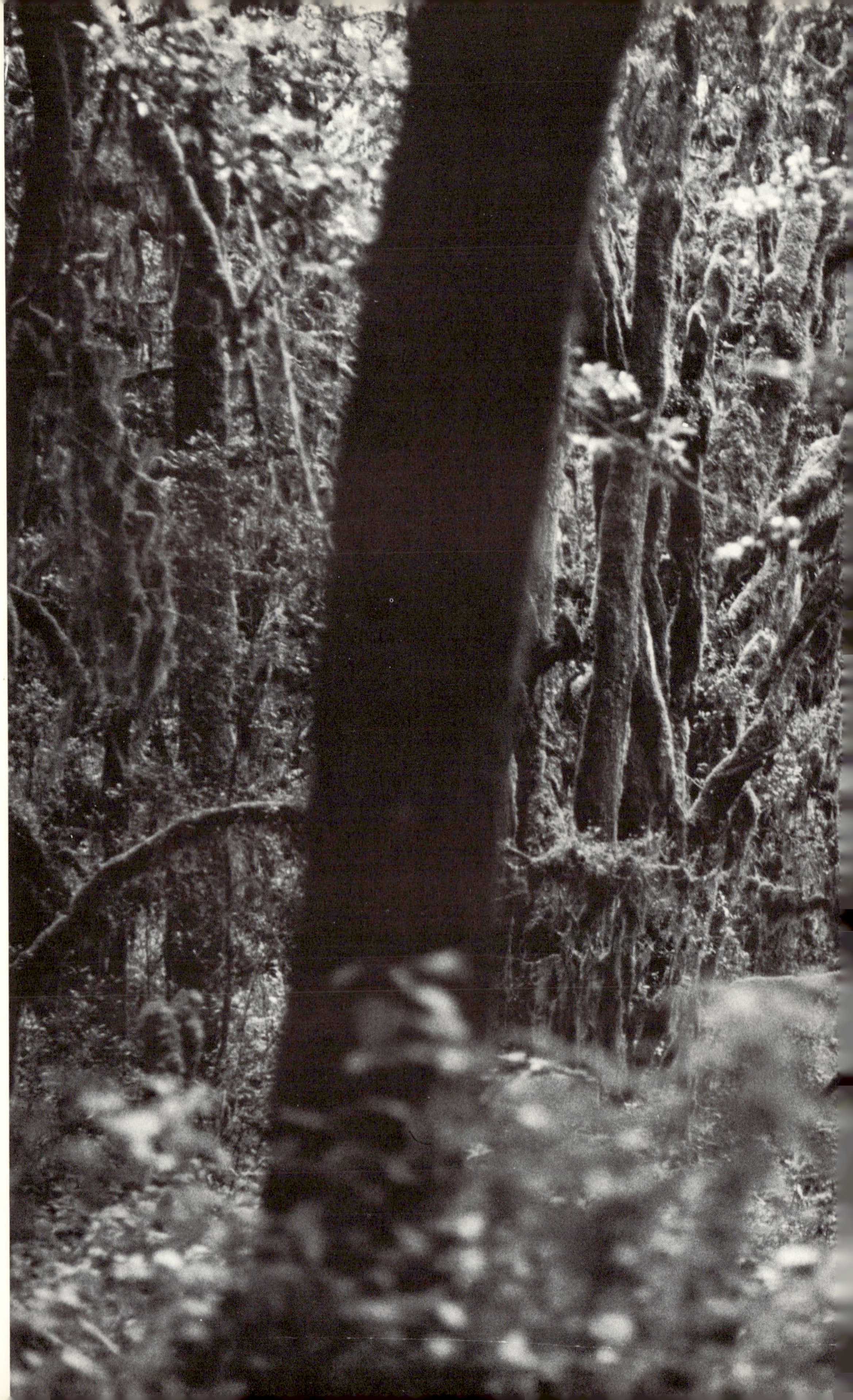

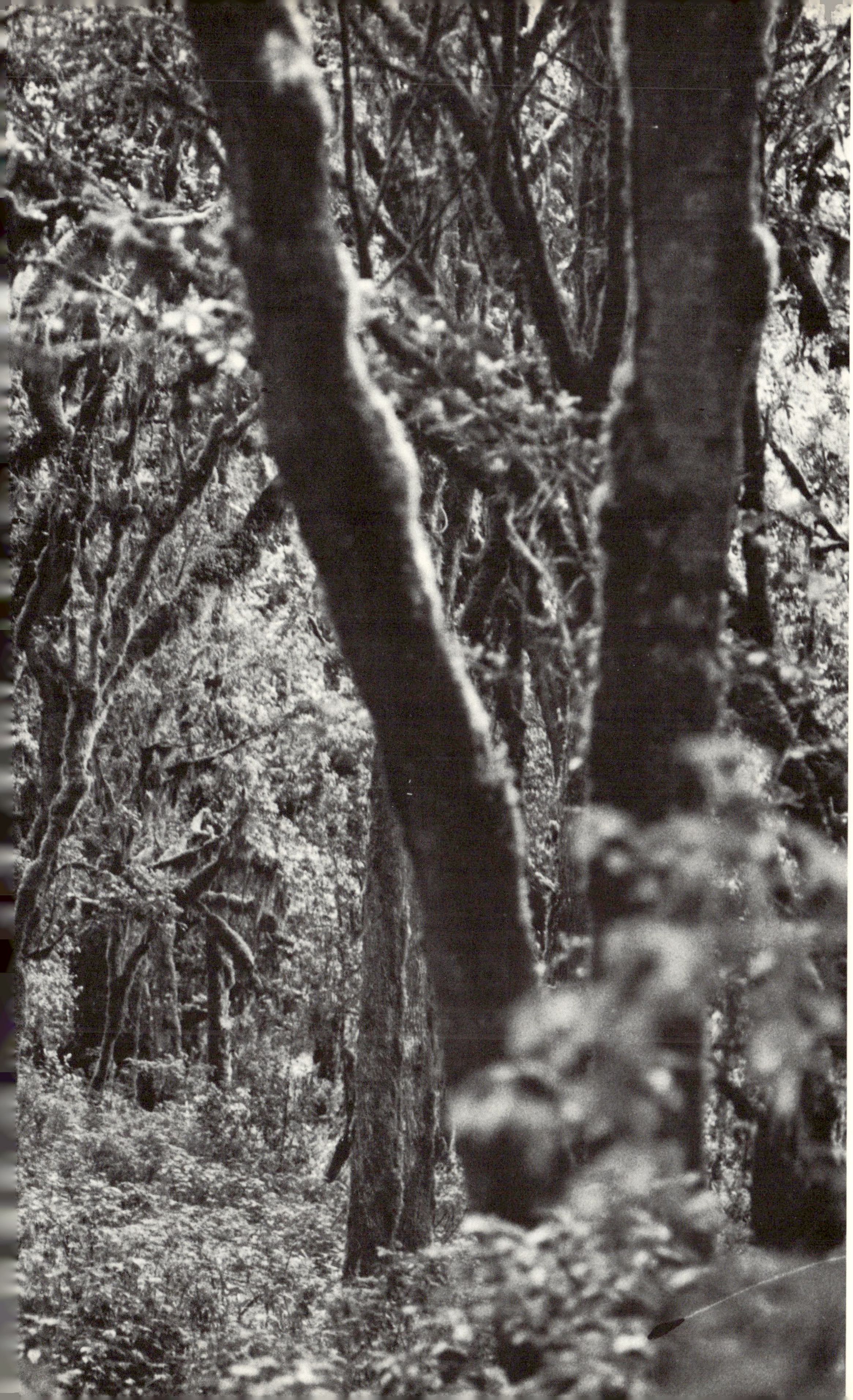

PREVIOUS PAGES:
Like hanging gardens, heavy, dripping with moisture, the trees wind upward toward the sunlight. Can you tell by the photograph how still the jungle is? Why does the forest seem so strange? Maybe because this powerful greenery always appears full grown, complete. You see countless proofs of extraordinary, powerful growth, but you never see growth itself. The collective power is perceptible, like an electrical charge, and yet it is calm, serene. The jungle is an eternal lull before a storm that never comes.

We are far back in time now. The rumble of thunder, the flashes of lightning, rain and sunlight are ancient and reliable gods. Here they have functioned as calm masters, guaranteeing stability to the life they have produced and supported. The evolution of extravagant species and the profusion of forms that we encounter in the rain forest could take place because of this stability. Consequently, the living organisms have been able to share all the potentials provided by stability without having stresses working upon them from without; they have been able to evolve specializations for every niche in the living space. (Doesn't this pattern suggest an ideal democracy?) The totality—stipulated by the external environment—could be preserved all the while consistently in those parts of the world where rain forests have evolved and endured. But within itself, this stability has been restless and fragile. The pieces have been rearranged and exchanged, redistributed, improved and supplemented while the totality continued.

It is only in human society that the laws of the jungle—of Kipling's vintage—exist as a general rule. In the jungle they are secondary. Competition or liberalism that allows a better, more favorably endowed individual to rob and suppress another individual unilaterally is a very primitive phenomenon, Much too primitive to occur in nature. In a well-developed society, such as the rain forest, that stage was superseded millions of years ago by a community based on strictly binding mutual need. "The jungle plant," writes Sanderson, "fights not for itself alone, but for the general welfare." And he points out that the community is just as precisely regulated as the community shared by various parts of the human body. The hand doesn't compete with the foot, the nose isn't allowed to develop at the expense of the ear. Instead, the body's organs work together.

As we saw earlier, the leaves of a tree cannot die. Even as they fall from the tree, they provide sustenance for other organisms. A heavy rain squall rips violently through the foliage. But many of the rain forest trees are so well-fettered by lianas (which with the help of the trees can reach the sunlight) that they cannot be blown over.

An abundance of tree species is very typical of the rain forest. One species is seldom more common than another. As a rule, there are more than 40 different species on every hectare—sometimes 100 different species. Each species is individual, unique, but if the so-called "laws of the jungle" had prevailed, it would have been reasonable in all these years that some of the species would have taken over the whole area and become sort of multinational entrepreneurs of the forest.

Instead, they stand side by side, high trees and low ones, those with narrow crowns and those with broad ones; flat, cone-shaped, shieldlike or sprawling like giant spiders on their backs. They all share the light; they divide up the times and methods of dropping their leaves so that the least possible competition occurs.

The abundance and multiplicity of forms is optimal. The distribution of work is splendid. The rate of production in rain forest society is extraordinarily high. But—and this is paradoxical—the soil is thin, exhausted and very poor in nutrients.

Cut down the forest, plow the earth and sow suitable crops. For a couple of years, there will be good harvests. Then almost nothing. The traditional practice of burning in the rain forest necessitates a fallow time of between 8 to 20 years. This kind of cultivation can yield 700 kilos of rice per hectare annually in the best cases (data from Sierra Leone). But in Japan, 10,000 kilos of rice can be produced on a single hectare that could hardly support as lush vegetation as that of the rain forest. How can the poorest earth support the richest forest?

The path of water from the sky to the earth and on to the oceans slopes downhill. This is a basic rule (in fact, quite obvious). But it has many exceptions. A rain gauge placed at a normal height of 1.5 meters in a rain forest will only catch 33 percent of all the rainfall. After the rain, which is often heavy but brief, you can see steam rising from the forest. Thus, a good part of the rainfall returns directly to the atmosphere. It never reaches the ground. A good deal of the rainfall that does not reach the rain gauge has dripped through the foliage. Leaves in the rain forest are often provided with drop spouts in their shape so that water can quickly drip off them. This diminishes the risk of fungus spores attaching themselves to the leaf. Water is not lacking in this perpetually damp forest. Trees don't have to keep and economize water like most other trees elsewhere.

But orchids and other epiphytes living high up in the trees often have special organs to collect and store the rain water. For these, desiccation is as great a problem as for desert plants. As a matter of fact, it is thought that epiphytes in the rain forest come from desert plants that wandered in and established themselves in the strong sunlight on the rooftops of the very wettest of forests, where there is a prevailing water shortage.

Here we have a substantial population of plants that do not, except indirectly, require fertile soil. They live on the scantiest soil balconies, off insignificant salts released from raindrops up in the trees. All these epiphytes are held up to the sunlight on the trees' shoulders. Is this competition?

Most of the rainfall reaches the ground directly from the sky, or patters through the foliage, or runs down the trunks and lianas on its way to the ocean—46 percent runs and drips down to the ground, 33 percent falls directly. On the earth, the mineral substances (growth nutrients) are released when leaves and twigs, all plants and animals, disintegrate into their chemical components.

This description makes it sound as if a great supply of nutrients should be lying and waiting on the surface of the earth since the forest is dense and overabundant in decomposing greenery. But if you were to make a soil analysis, you would discover very scant nutritional substances for growth.

Though decomposition is rapid (the leaf disappeared in 24 hours), the withdrawal of released nutrients is equally immediate. Most roots in the rain forest lie close to the surface and with the water's help quickly suck up the elements that have been released. The reserves are consequently very meager but the working capital can be very great indeed.

Some of the soluble substances escape despite the roots and accompany the water deeper and deeper. It is said that the earth is wearing out, that it is becoming poorer. This constant depletion is striking in the rain forest. It is compensated by the mineral elements released in the bedrock which the deepest roots of the tree can reach. A big tree functions like a pump. The nutrients that it fetches up from the bedrock are then distributed to the rest of the plants in the forest—those that cannot reach so deep for nourishment—when the tree loses its leaves, when the flowers fade, when fruit falls to the ground and twigs and tree trunks rot. For example, some ten tons of plant material fell over every hectare of one West African forest annually, giving, among other things, 170 kilos of the nitrogen essential for life.

A basic part of the growth nutrients is gathered by a certain type of bacteria that lives extensively throughout the soil and with the trees' roots. These bacteria can take the nitrogen from the air and change it to a chemical form suitable for the tree. Almost half of all the plants in a rain forest receive such nutritional aid from bacteria. This is a further example of the jungle's benign laws.

But the rain forest does not function in such a way as to increase the fertility of the soil. It does not store up any reserves. It utilizes its whole capital all the time and thus becomes a stream exclusively devoted to production. The growth nutrients are there, but they circulate very fast all the time. The stream of life catches the chemical breaths released by shriveling cells and very swiftly the breath becomes active again as part of the cells' renewal of substance.

When people cut down the rain forest and burn dry timber, brush and lianas, the ash makes for a good harvest. Thus, people uti-

---

I stare uncomprehendingly at this picture of the rain forest. I stood staring equally baffled there in the jungle at the foot of Kilimanjaro in Tanzania. I searched desperately for a way to generalize about the implication of the rain forest. But where to begin? It is easy to become metaphysical in a rain forest. What truths take shape from all the questions and answers evoked by the rain forest's composite puzzle? We may never sort them all out because the forest is being cut down and destroyed.

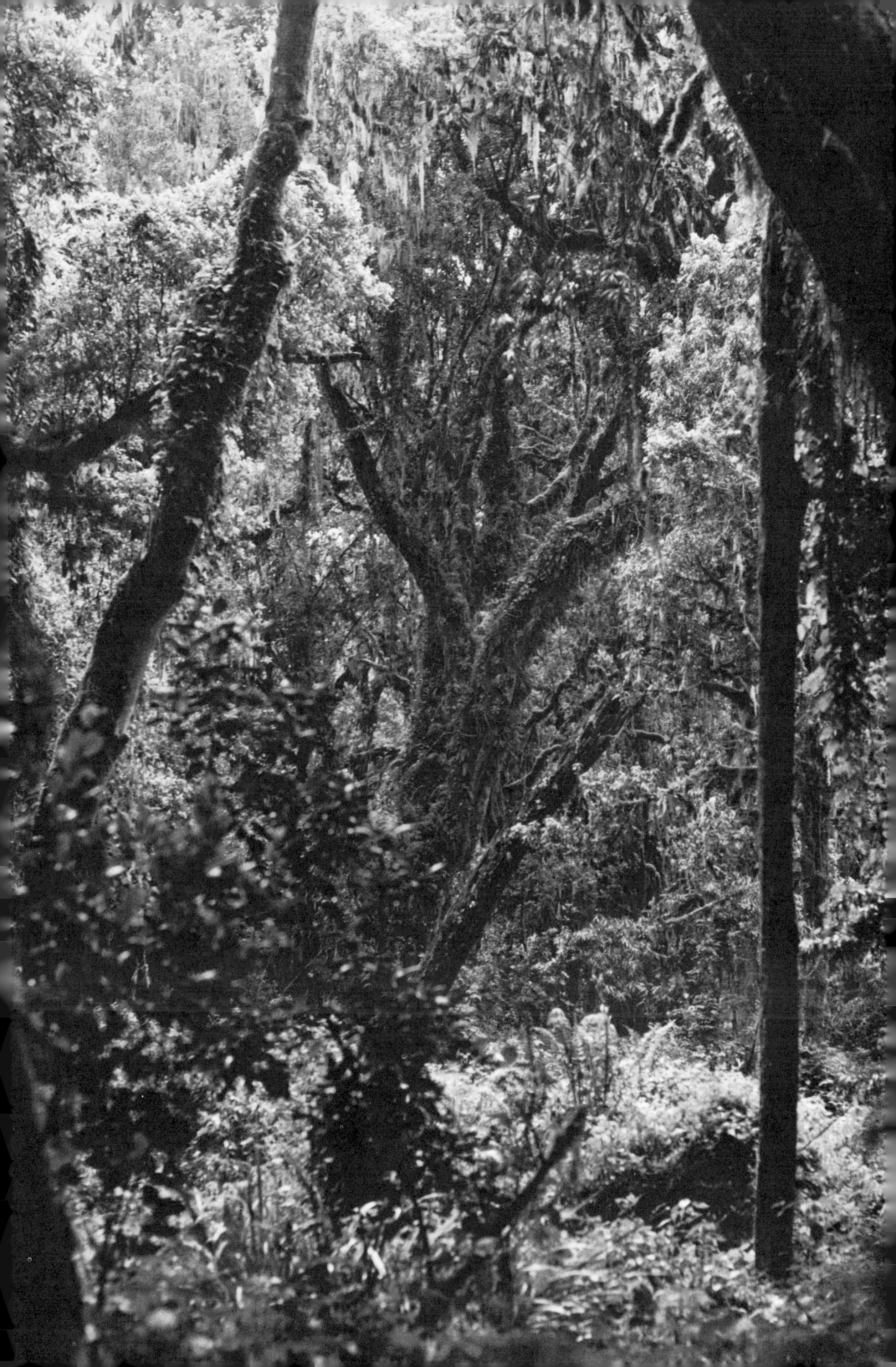

Pines, and nothing but pines in stands all of the same age, are replacing the rain forest. An incomparable natural kingdom is being destroyed because a pine monoculture provides great wealth—counted in money. This Kenyan plantation in Kakamega was planted 19 years ago. In record time, the introduced species of trees reached felling size. The native trees of the rain forest have no chance of competing with intensively cared for cultivated trees.

---

lize the working capital of the living forest. But the soil continues to be just as impoverished. When the meager supply of nourishment has been consumed, there will be no more crops. And tree roots will no longer draw fresh nourishment from the bedrock. Then the earth must rest, so that a new forest can grow, or else people have to supply a great deal of artificial fertilizer. This is possible only if disastrous erosion during the exceptionally heavy rains can be prevented, an erosion that disperses both the artificial fertilizers and the soil if the land is sloping. Low fertility is in itself an erosion factor, since a weak and sparse ground cover increases both the impact of raindrops and the ability of floodwater to scour the earth.

The rain forest does not live beyond its means. It has managed to last for millions of years. But it utilizes available resources in an intense, effective way. The unbelievable abundance is a consequence of the fact that every available space, every conceivable possibility, has been utilized. There are no empty spaces, just as there is no time given to rest.

On this meager base, things grow in such a way that you think you can actually see a leaf uncurl or a stalk shoot up before your very eyes. Pure imagination. And yet, observing bamboo near the mountain rain forests, researchers have noted a growth rate of 22.9 centimeters every 24 hours over a period of 2 months. A single bamboo shoot grew 57 centimeters in 24 hours—that might be called seeing the grass grow!

The poorest soil produces the lushest forest. It wears orchids in its proud crowns. It weaves a variegated web of life, twice as dense as a northern pine forest. According to one estimate, the net primary production was 50 tons annually per hectare, as compared to 28 tons in a temperate pine forest.

It is tragic to have to state that this lush nature can support only about two people per square kilometer as hunters and seldom more than ten per square kilometer—in optimal cases, 100—in an economically-sound system of brush-burning agriculture which includes a fallow period to protect the forest and the soil's potential. No people have been able to evolve a rich civilization in the rain forests, except the Maya, who cultivated the exceptionally well-endowed highland rain forests of Central America. Their civilization, however, gradually collapsed. The profit has been much too low.

People struggling to stave off starvation cannot afford to keep rain forests. The governments of the developing nations allow the forests to be felled. In Kakamega, Kenya's most magnificent primeval forest, people are going about this in two ways. They remove economically worthless trees (the vast majority) and plant unmixed stands of the kinds of trees that produce the most valuable wood. All vegetation is cleared away, the forest is clear-cut, the rain forest totally destroyed and monoculture plantations of imported cypress and pine are substituted. It looks a little gloomy, like spruce acreage. These pine trees grow much faster than the majority of rain forest trees and give a much higher financial return per hectare. But hundreds—thousands—of plant and animal species are threatened with extinction. The lushest nature is killed off; in the future, Tarzan will have to be content swinging from pine branches.

This treatment of the world's oldest forests ought not to appear shocking to us. In Europe, not one single stand of virgin forest remains. We sacrificed them all along the way to our prosperity. Most of the forest land in Europe was changed to farmland several hundred years ago. In the tropics, the shift has only recently begun. There the forest soil is poorer and more fragile, its cleared plots demand greater care and attention, and presumably greater capital of human energy and money to yield viable, continuously good crops. The greatest threat right now is that the forests will be replaced by a type of cultivation lacking in expertise or resources, so that the land which is so sensitive to erosion will be irrevocably damaged. Then we could lose both the forest and the soil.

There is also a deeper loss: the rain forest as a conceptual model, a new utopia to aim for.

Over the centuries, with the help of our philosophical and religious doctrines and the power of our society, we in the West have neglected the natural world we belong to, our true humanism, in favor of an eternity beyond the world. This godly nonchalance was evident during the Renaissance and the Enlightenment and later was completed by the blind scientific-technological phantom that today holds us and our environment in a stranglehold.

We're floundering. Under duress, we run and hide. We dash into the primeval forest and sit down to think. Far off, we hear the huge forest-clearing machines coming ever nearer, driven by corrupt, desperate governments without ideals. Meanwhile, we discover the forest. Or perhaps the forest takes hold of us.

When it has rid us of our anxiety, what do we see? We see a living, effective, functioning order, a community where equality reigns, an efficient community without competition, which economizes its limited resources, and boasts a stability that is millions of years old. The rain forest seems the ideal model for a democracy.

Too bad people are not included in this utopia. But why isn't rain-forest ecology required for sociology students? Why don't philosophers take walks into the forest these days? They would surely stumble onto something. ∎

Charcoal-making is a stage in the rain forest's conversion to pine woods. First the trees that give usable timber are felled. Trees unsuitable for timber are laid in pits in the earth and burned to charcoal. Smaller branches and twigs are collected for firewood. Scrub vegetation is cut and dried, then burned. Then the rain forest becomes agricultural land, and sorghum, various grains and vegetables are planted in the ashes for as long as the poor soil's store of nutrients lasts. After that, cultivation is stopped and pines and cypresses are planted in regular rows. This is what is being done in Kenya's largest lowland forest, Kakamega.

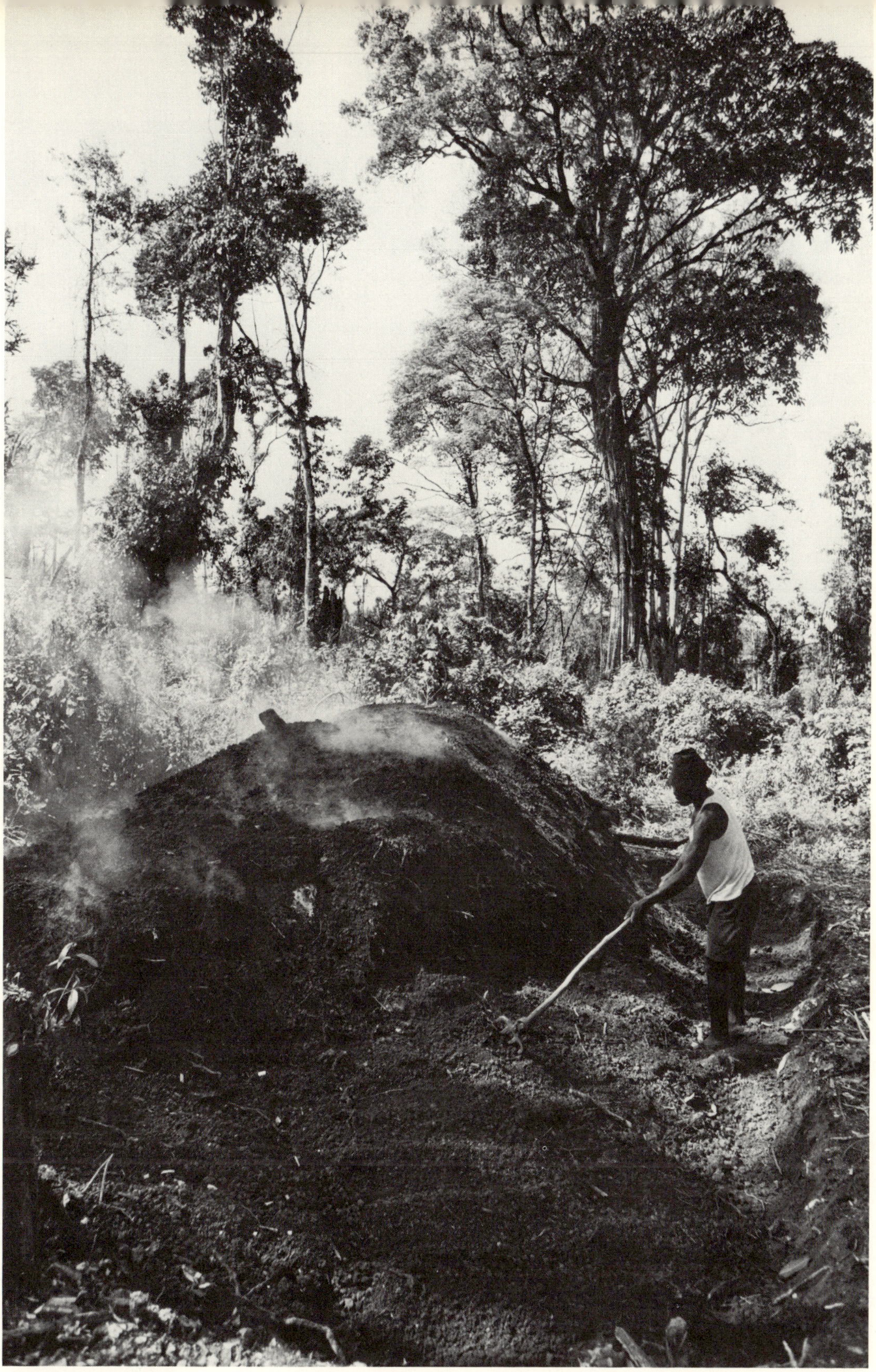

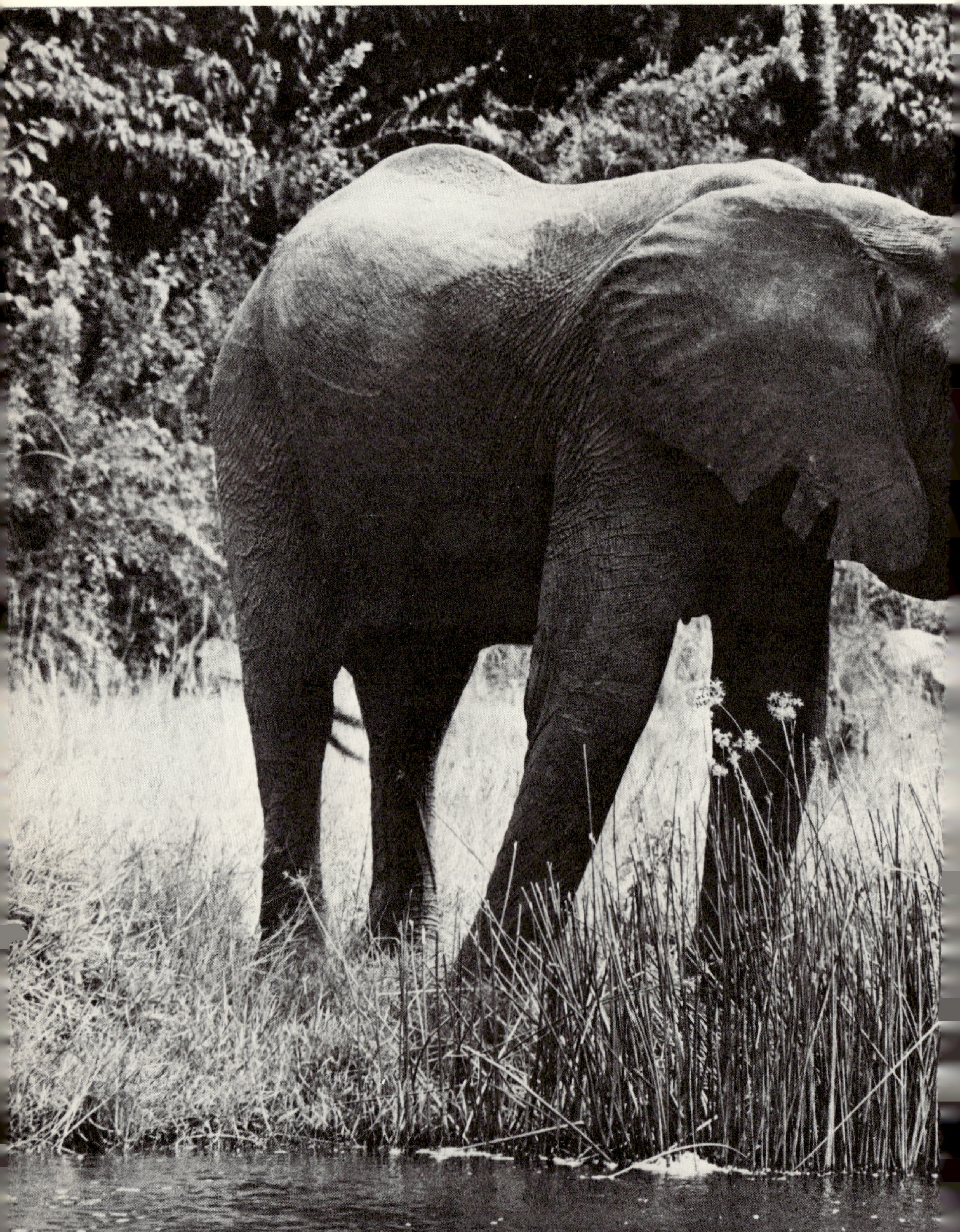

THE EXAMPLE OF LAKE NAKURU

The elephant is enormous, with an appetite to match. It can rearrange the landscape almost as radically as humans do. But the elephant's intervention is not always to its disadvantage. It digs water holes in the savanna. The water is later invaded by water plants. Then the elephant comes to bathe and drink. It also eats the plants. It harvests a crop which, in a way, it has cultivated.

Some elephants dig a water hole. The hippos come and root around messily, making it deeper. It turns into a small pond to which the hippos come back every morning after the night's grazing excursions. Nile lettuce, *Pistia stratiotes*, soon invades the water hole too. Then a large snail, *pila ovata*, wanders in some mysterious way across the dry savanna to live in the water hole. The open-bill stork, which loves snails, soon discovers the place. The stork likes to stand on the hippo's back while scouting for snails.

This description should not be misinterpreted as an observation of hierarchy in nature: the elephant is more powerful than the hippo, the water hole, the snail and the stork. They are all dependent upon the elephant. The elephant can crush the snail and the snail must grovel before the elephant, because after all, it created the water hole.

A hierarchical world image has had a decisive influence on Western civilization ever since Noah's ark was stranded on a desert dune. God ruled over everything and everyone. He gave mankind dominion over all the earth's environments including its plants and animals. The right to exploit was left to man's discretion; he was crowned the all-powerful sovereign of everything on earth. It was a divine virtue, a blessed edict—to subjugate, exploit and fleece the environment. Only man's needs counted. This world view —older than Christianity which gave it moral sanction—laid the basis for our civilizations and led to the expansion of our welfare cultures.

Perhaps it wasn't so strange, wrote John Black in *The Dominion of Man*, that in early Christian times the Hebrews constructed a world view in which nature was subjugated. They lived in a desert environment where humans had always struggled, as they still do today, at a great disadvantage against the powerful forces of nature.

So things went wrong under the influence of this hierarchical philosophy of nature. Humans subjugated nature, but history reveals that nature gradually struck back— witness the ruins of once fertile earth and blossoming regions. It let itself be subjugated exclusively by the needs of human beings. Fertile lands have become deserts because the doctrine that humans are all-powerful rulers of nature is false. Recently we have begun to realize that the opposite is true. We have started a global environmental debate. The lessons of this debate can be summarized as follows:

- Humans are slaves of the environment (of nature, resources).
- Their unparalleled ability to exploit is a threat to their own existence, unless it is subordinated to the laws of ecology.
- Humans must learn to live in harmony with the rest of nature.

The open-bill stork's singular bill is a special adaptation just like the elephant's trunk or the giraffe's neck. Its bill is made to crack the shells of a certain fresh-water snail. The stork is entirely dependent upon these snails for its survival.

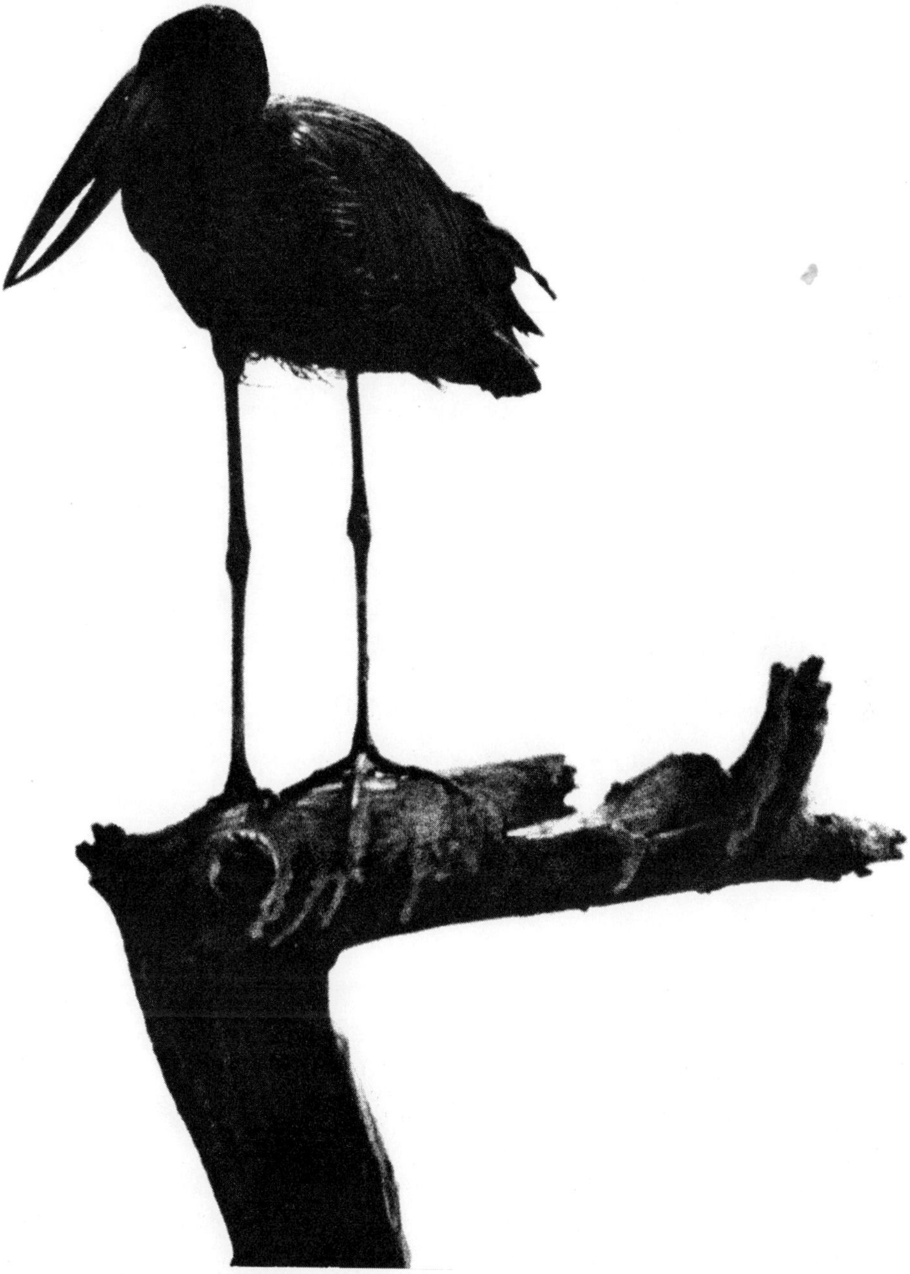

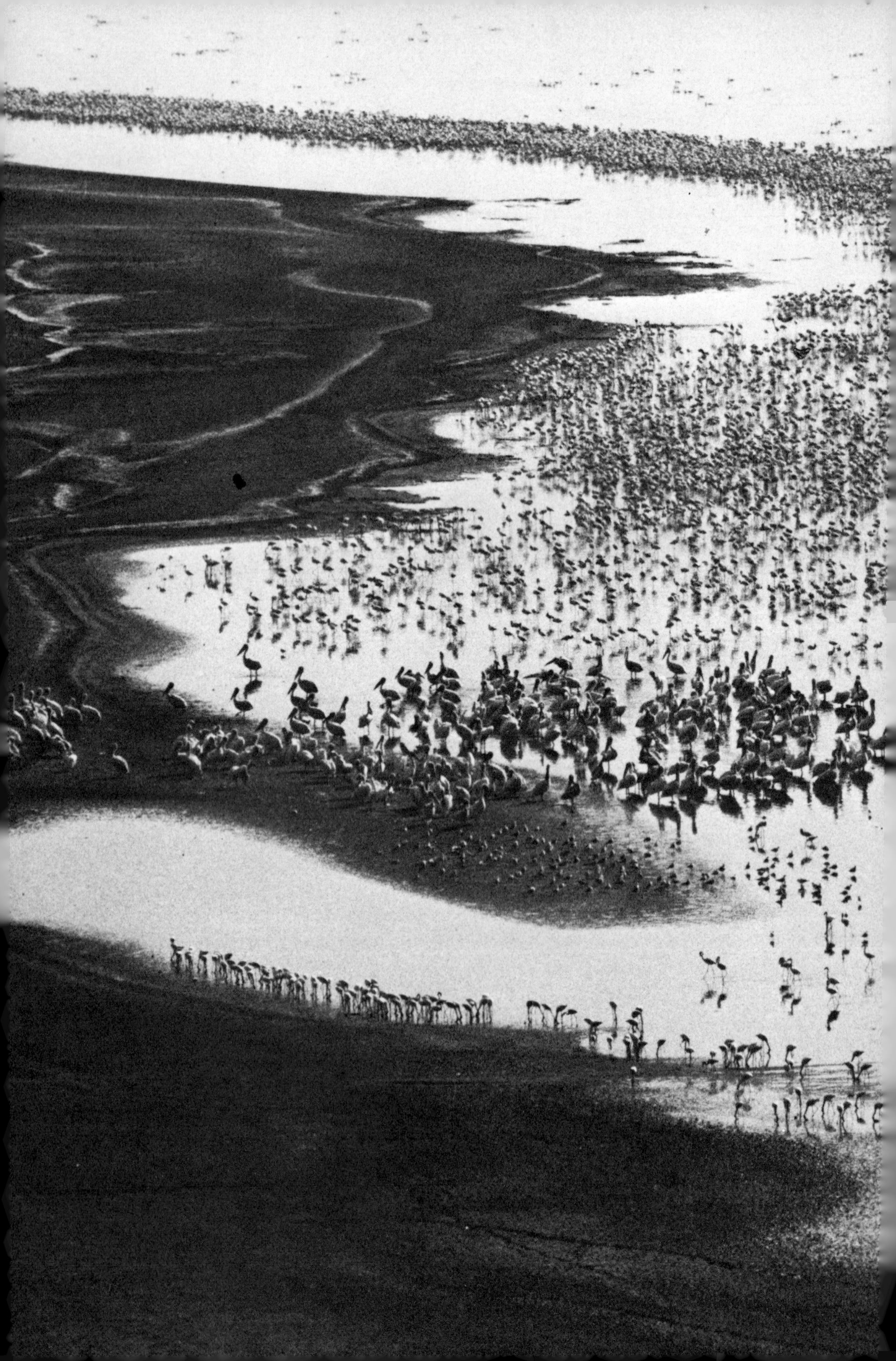

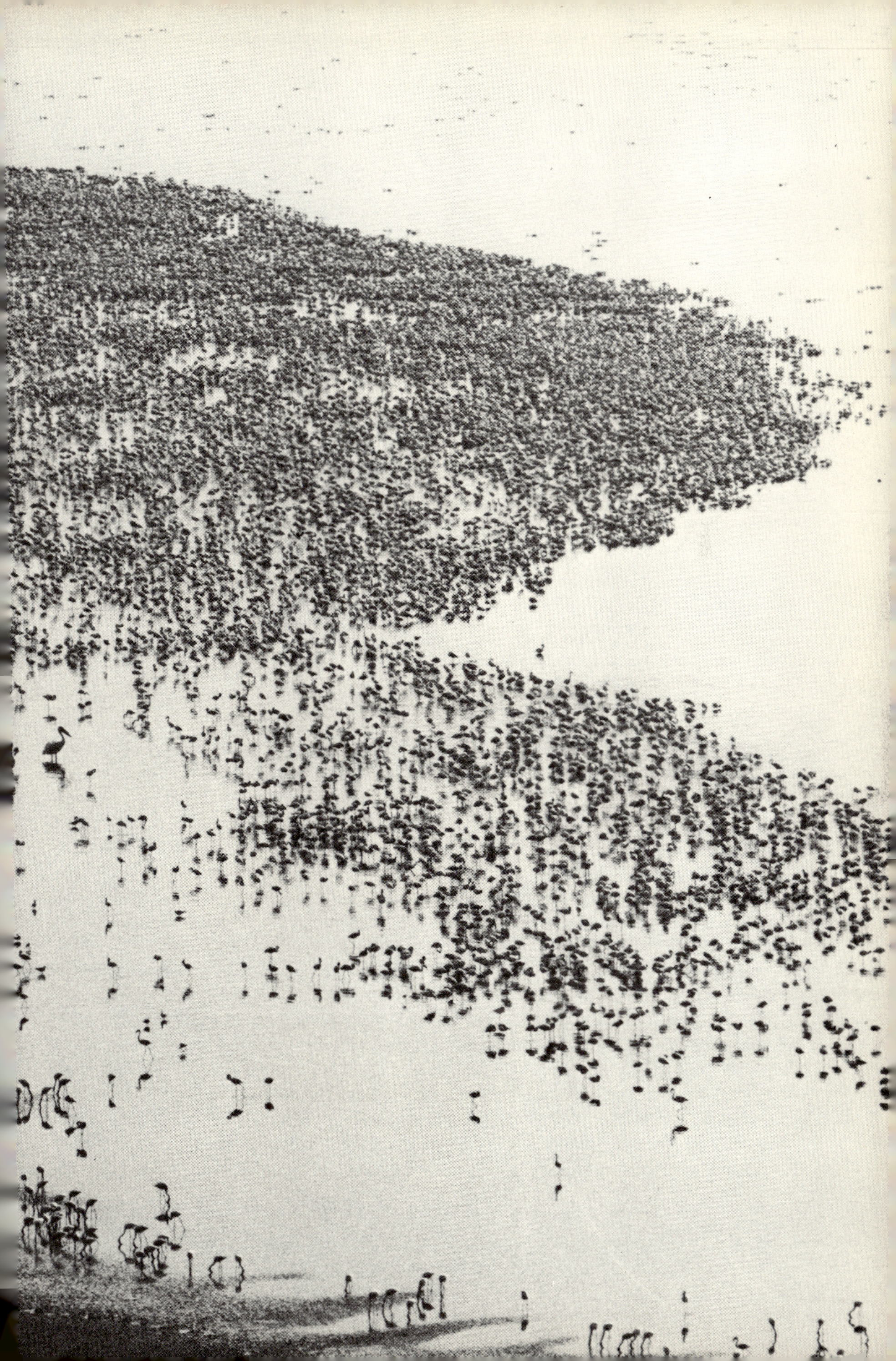

PREVIOUS PAGES:
This is only a small fraction of the nearly 2,000,000 lesser flamingos that as a rule live in Lake Nakuru. There are an estimated 4,000,000 of these flamingos in East Africa. Half that number can be seen at one time in this 35 square kilometer lake. There are also about 1,000 of East Africa's 40,000 greater flamingos. The group of larger birds to the left in this picture is a flock of about 200 pelicans. None of these birds breeds by Lake Nakuru. They come there to eat the lake's riches.

- For better or worse, the effect of humans in the environment is decisively important.
- Yet humans are not the rulers of nature.
- Nature can get on well without humans, but humans cannot survive outside of nature.
- Therefore, biology is the most important of all sciences.
- The world view of those who survive us should be based on the science of life.
- There is no other alternative.

During the rainy season in Kenya, Lake Nakuru covers an area of about 35 square kilometers. By the end of the dry season, the lake sometimes hardly exists at all. It has virtually evaporated away; it has no outlet. Salts remain there, leeched out of the earth and mountains around the lake by the rains. These salts are mostly sodium carbonate. Sometimes the water temperature rises to 37° centigrade.

We don't understand how fish can live in this extreme environment, especially during those periods when the lake is almost dry. But Lake Nakuru is beyond ordinary reality in so many ways. A vast quantity of fish breeds in the lake. Before 1961, however, there were no fish at all. Malaria ravaged the district; mosquitoes that spread the disease hatched in the lake. *Tilapia grahami* is a small fish that relishes malaria mosquitoes. It was decided to release this kind of fish in Lake Nakuru in an attempt to control the malaria. Today the lake contains approximately 40,000,000 offspring of this living weapon against insects. Masses of grebes, terns, cormorants, pelicans, storks, herons and fish eagles have come to feast off the fish.

Don't imagine that all these fish live only off malaria mosquitoes. Things aren't quite that bad. But they do catch a good number and the malaria problem may have been alleviated in Nakuru. The fish have increased in vast numbers because of the quantity of tiny, invisible algae in the lake. This microscopic plankton algae has a delightful name, *Spirulina*. So much *Spirulina* lives in the lake that the water is lime green. No matter how much the fish eat, the color does not get any paler.

Spirulina existed in Lake Nakuru before it was stocked with fish. It gave and continues to give nourishment to the incredible number of flamingos. They have made this lake world famous. Because of them, Lake Nakuru has been designated a national park.

Flamingos move around, tightly packed together along the lake shore. They like to be in dense crowds.

A close-up of the Marabou stork. We watched it catch, kill and eat a flamingo in Lake Nakuru. Usually Marabou storks eat carrion. They are seen everywhere on refuse dumps.

RIGHT:
The Marabou stork takes long deliberate strides by the water's edge. The spoonbill swings its bill under the water. Out of the fog over Lake Nakuru, the contours of two species of flamingos can be distinguished. From the dense crowd of lesser flamingos, the tall, long-legged, long-necked greater flamingos rise.

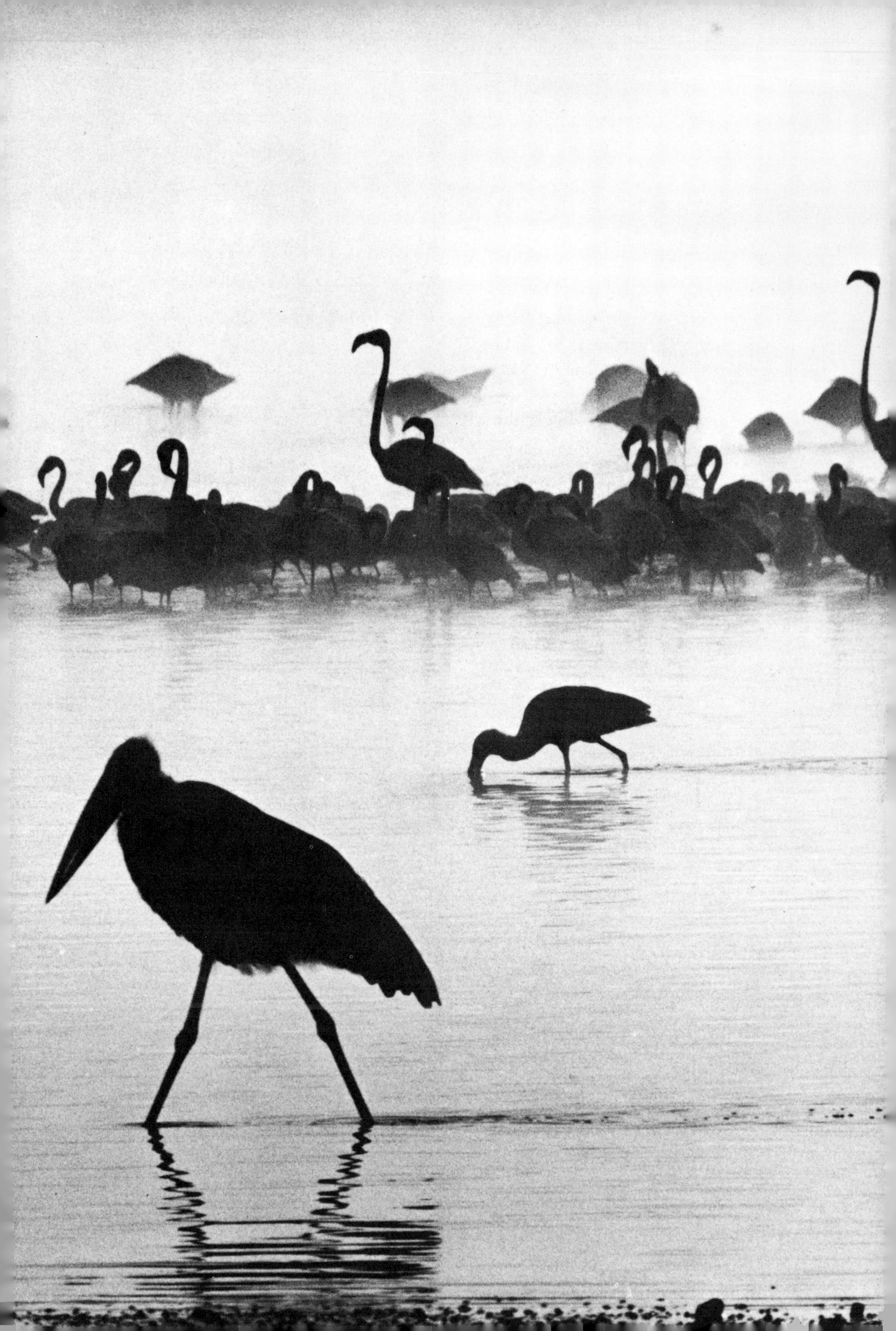

It is now the second most-visited national park in East Africa—only Nairobi National Park has more visitors.

I cannot describe in a few words the experience of seeing these birds. At times, there are between one and two million flamingos crowded into the shallow water. You can hardly see the lake for the birds. We heard them all night long like a powerful roar as we lay awake freezing in our tent (this is the highland and the nights are often cold). We try to figure out what causes this noise among the birds. Was it the clatter of 1,000,000 birds' legs, marching in step, packed tight, in the water by the shore? Or do individual clacking calls blend together into a deafening, toneless music? It is probably a combination of all the sounds made by so many birds moving around. The thunder from the flamingos goes out in waves over the water, through the forests by the lake and over the savanna all night long.

At dawn, we stood there, freezing, staring out as flocks of ten or a hundred thousand of these birds stepped out of the frosty mists, filled with light and color by the rising sun. So abundant and generous can nature be: sun, water and salt blend together into a brew of green cells which in turn give forth millions of rosy bird wings and let a lake glitter with fish.

In the language of ecology, the algae

The wood ibis mopes in the heavy afternoon rain.

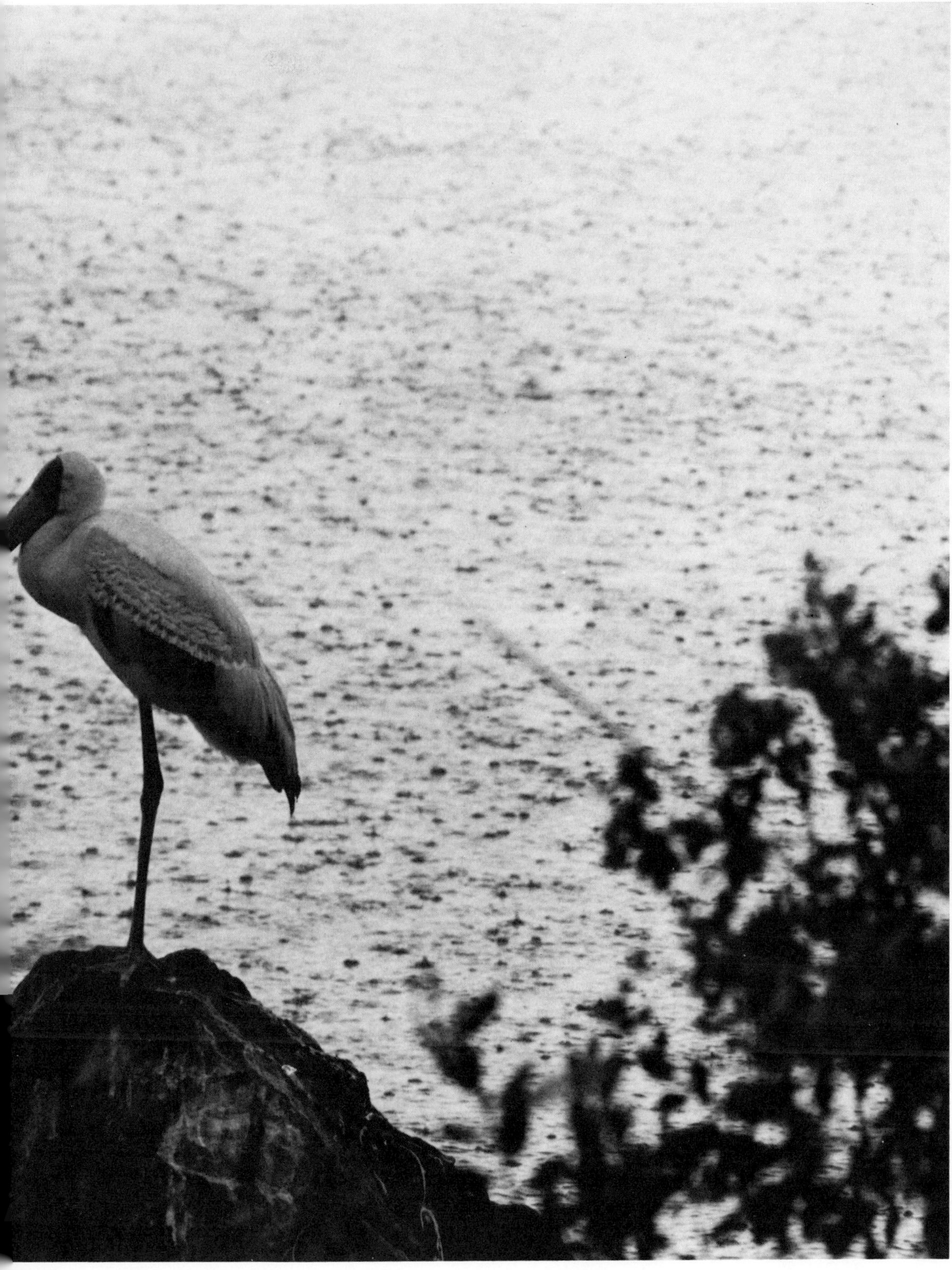

The pelican has a stretchable pouch suspended from its mandible and throat. This functions as a scoop net when the bird fishes. It holds 11 liters, more than twice as much as its stomach. It has been estimated that Lake Nakuru's 3,000 pelicans swallow three tons of fish a day.

Spirulina corresponds to primary production in the lake's ecosystem. The ecosystem is the lake plus the nutritive substances plus all the life that in some way depends on the lake. The secondary production is the 40,000,000 fish and all the flamingos that live off the algae. The flamingos eat 160,000 kilos of algae every day in Lake Nakuru. *Spirulina* replaces this loss in 24 hours.

Birds that eat the fish—pelicans, cormorants, herons, grebes and others—constitute a third link in this ecosystem's nutrient chain. There are other links: the heron, that eats a fish, that eats the algae, gets eaten by a jackal. One of the few leopards in the district eats the jackal. The food chain looks like this: algae-fish-heron-jackal-leopard.

One abundance produces another; nature is generous. Basically, the leopard was nourished by the algae. The tropical sun pours energy down into the lake and starts the production of the algae that everything depends on. The salts provide nourishment for the algae.

A year or so ago, about 750,000 fish died in Lake Nakuru. The cause was not clear. That vast quantity, however, is no more than what the fish-eating birds there eat every three and a half days. They consume 1,700,000 fish a week without in any way diminishing the supply. The 3,000 pelicans, for example, consume three tons of fish a day.

Humans are responsible for a substantial part of the abundance of bird life on this lake, since we stocked it with fish in 1961. We opened a sluice gate leading to that abundance just as the grazing elephant in the preceding example dug a water hole in the savanna that resulted in a motley community of hippos, water plants, snails and storks.

Lake Nakuru is not a unique example of man's contribution to nature, but it is one of the more encouraging among many positive intrusions (at least as many affect the environment negatively). Our contribution of agriculture has transformed almost all the landscapes in the world. Almost every bit of the globe's surface bears the traces of man's struggle for a better life. We talk about a cultural landscape—few areas in the world are not affected by culture, for better or worse.

The example of Lake Nakuru is particularly clear. It must make us become aware that even an insignificant man-made alteration can have great consequences. It might seem that a kind of hierarchical order exists in which humans are more powerful than other animals, just as the elephant could be interpreted as dominating the water hole and the snails. But it is impossible to sort out which creature is the governing organism in each overall system. The malaria mosquito, for example, comes high in one power pyramid and is definitely dominant over the 1,000,000 children who die of malaria each year in Africa alone.

It would be possible to produce more examples to show that humans are actually prisoners of the environment over which we would like to believe we are superior. We are no more powerful than any other organism.

The major acts of human manipulation—the transfer of some fish from one lake to

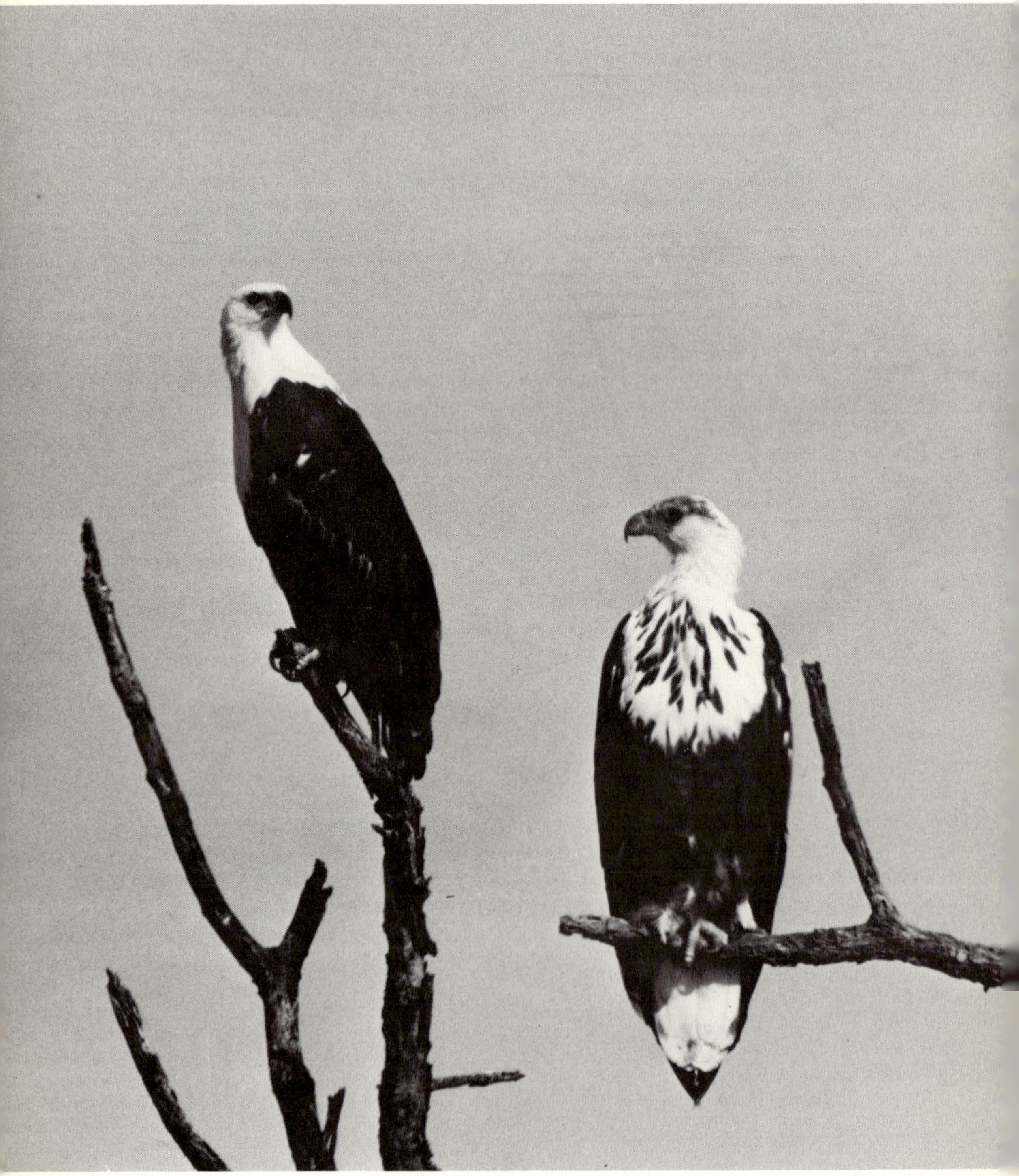

Here are two African fish eagles, one old and the other young, by Lake Nakuru. We know that in snug, well-tended Sweden, white-tailed eagles are doomed to extinction. They have almost no more young, because their fetuses are poisoned in the egg by the agricultural chemicals and industrial poisons that are spread around. The female birds take these into their bodies and pass them on to their young. Since we know that, for example, the dreaded chlorinated hydrocarbons, DDT and dieldrin, are used much more extensively in Africa than in Europe, we might expect that African eagles will be even more threatened than Swedish ones.

But this is not the case. African fish eagles and other birds of prey are, in fact, very common in East Africa and don't appear to be killed by poisons.

On Lake Naivasha, several miles from Nakuru, Leslie Brown, a bird specialist, studied the African fish eagle for many years. There are no fewer of them—on the contrary they have increased from 90 pairs in 1968–69 to over 100 in 1970–71. Scientists can't completely explain why the massive use of biocides in Africa does not (yet) seem to kill the fauna. Perhaps, Leslie Brown suggests, the intense ultra violet light in Kenya's highlands causes a rapid breakdown of the poisons. Other theories propose that more of the poisons evaporate during spraying in hot climates than in the temperate regions so that most of the poisons go up into the atmosphere. The activity of microorganisms is also much greater in tropical soil. These useful workers can function there all year round, whereas the poisons that reach the soil in northern climates lie unworked upon, accumulating throughout the winter. But it is most important to remember that environmental research is drastically neglected in the developing countries. Only a few studies attempt to place the risks of poisoning in an ecological context. The eagles seem to do well, but some of the few analyses carried out reveal that other birds in other areas may have dangerously high amounts in their tissues. Cases of widespread bird deaths are known in which biocides were involved.

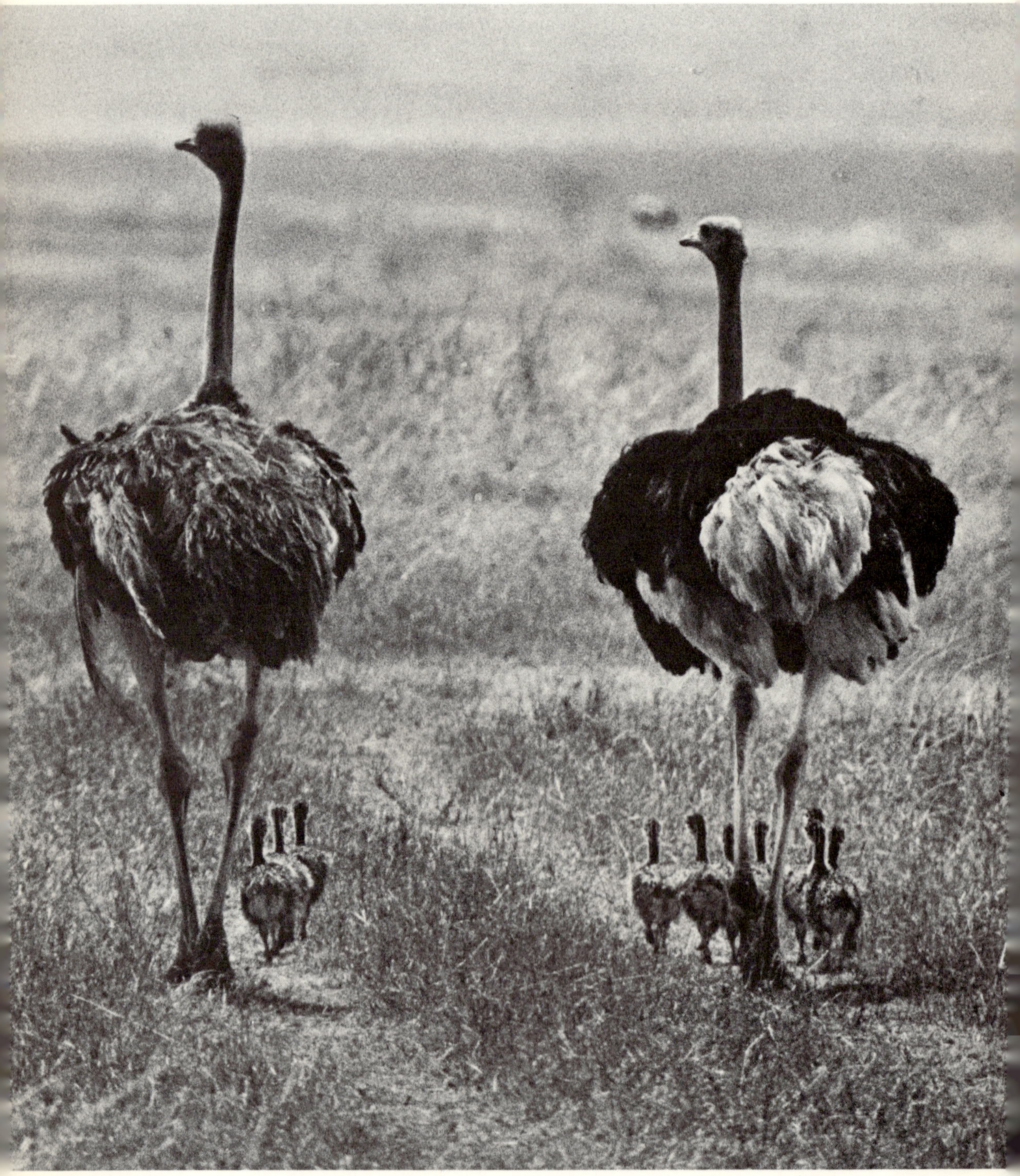

another—do not demonstrate our power over nature but rather, on the contrary, inform us how powerless we are. So very little is needed to start a chain reaction in the environment. Nature, which lets itself be affected, is fragile. Humans, dependent upon the environment, are equally delicate.

I chose a positive example. Let us turn it around and see what we find.

Around Lake Nakuru, corn and many tropical crops are grown. There are extensive grazing lands. One of Kenya's larger cities, Nakuru, is located there with a population which is expected to rise from 50,000 in 1972 to 200,000 by the year 2000. After a biological cleaning process, the city sewers empty out into the lake by a river. Many kinds of contamination and pollution not removed in the cleaning process reach the lake. Almost all the cattle are regularly dipped in insecticides and some of this makes its way into the lake. Large quantities of DDT and dieldrin are used against noxious creatures by farmers along the banks of the rivers that feed into the lake, as well as against malaria in dwellings and swimming pools. Spraying vehicles clean out their tanks in Njoro River that issues into the lake. There is a reeking refuse dump near the beach; the city's crematory is also there.

Lake Nakuru has no outlet. This means that poisons, which break down slowly, undoubtedly stay in the lake for a long time. So this environment is unusually vulnerable to injurious influences. So far it has done well. Despite the plentiful use of chemicals dangerous to the environment, amounts of insecticides are still low in the fish and birds. Percentages of DDE, a product of the decomposition of DDT, do occur in the fish according to careful analyses, but in hundreds of times lower levels than in the severely damaged fishing waters of Europe and the USA. The mean value of DDE in the eggs of fish-eating cormorants is about a hundred times higher in many bird populations of Europe and the States.

But in the very heart of a cormorant on Lake Nakuru, 16.84 milligrams (counted per kilo of tissue) of PCB was found, probably of the brand called Aroclor 1254. This amount is comparable to severe cases in industrialized nations. It is not far-fetched to suspect that the poison came from the

In April, 1973, an ostrich egg was on sale for $225 in a shop in Europe. A baby bird might have hatched from that egg. More and more ostrich eggs are sold as curiosities all over the world. People who purchase them are greater villains than those who plunder the nests and sell the eggs, because if there weren't a demand, the eggs would be left in peace. Then, after a hard 40 days' attentive brooding by both the male and the female ostrich, a batch of handsome chicks hatches, as in this picture, in which a couple are out walking with their brood. When they grow up, they will run as fast as a stallion over the savanna and escape successfully from lions even though they cannot fly.

Legs wide apart, with wings outstretched and a threatening beak, the ostrich takes a stand to face humans or beasts of prey that come too near its young. On this occasion, the threat helped—we fled. More dangerous beasts of prey are lured away by the male, who feigns injury by dragging a wing, pretending to look miserable. While he lures the enemy away, the hen and her young find a safe retreat.

smoke continually belching out over the lake from Nakuru's refuse dump.

Occasionally someone ignites an oil or old paint can or some plastic substance on a dump and that is enough to threaten the fetus of a cormorant that eats only fish and has a nest in a tree a good distance away.

Our smallest actions can affect the environment. Only knowledge and respect for how the environment—nature—functions can solve our dilemmas. It is misguided to believe that environmental problems can be solved by purely technical skill. We can never transform our society into so tight a closed system as to be independent of our surroundings.

We must accept that we function within an environment. We have put ourselves into solitary confinement in our ecological ignorance. So great is our confusion and our self-righteousness that we believe that we live independently.

But look how wide open the doors are to the flowers and birds. See how they live; live as they do. They are our equal co-workers. Their prosperity depends on our enterprise, and our prosperity depends on theirs. We have the opportunity to nurture and to destroy. This is an indication of our power, and our powerlessness.

But are we able to live in harmony with each other and our environment? Our future hangs on this question as by a slender silken thread. ∎

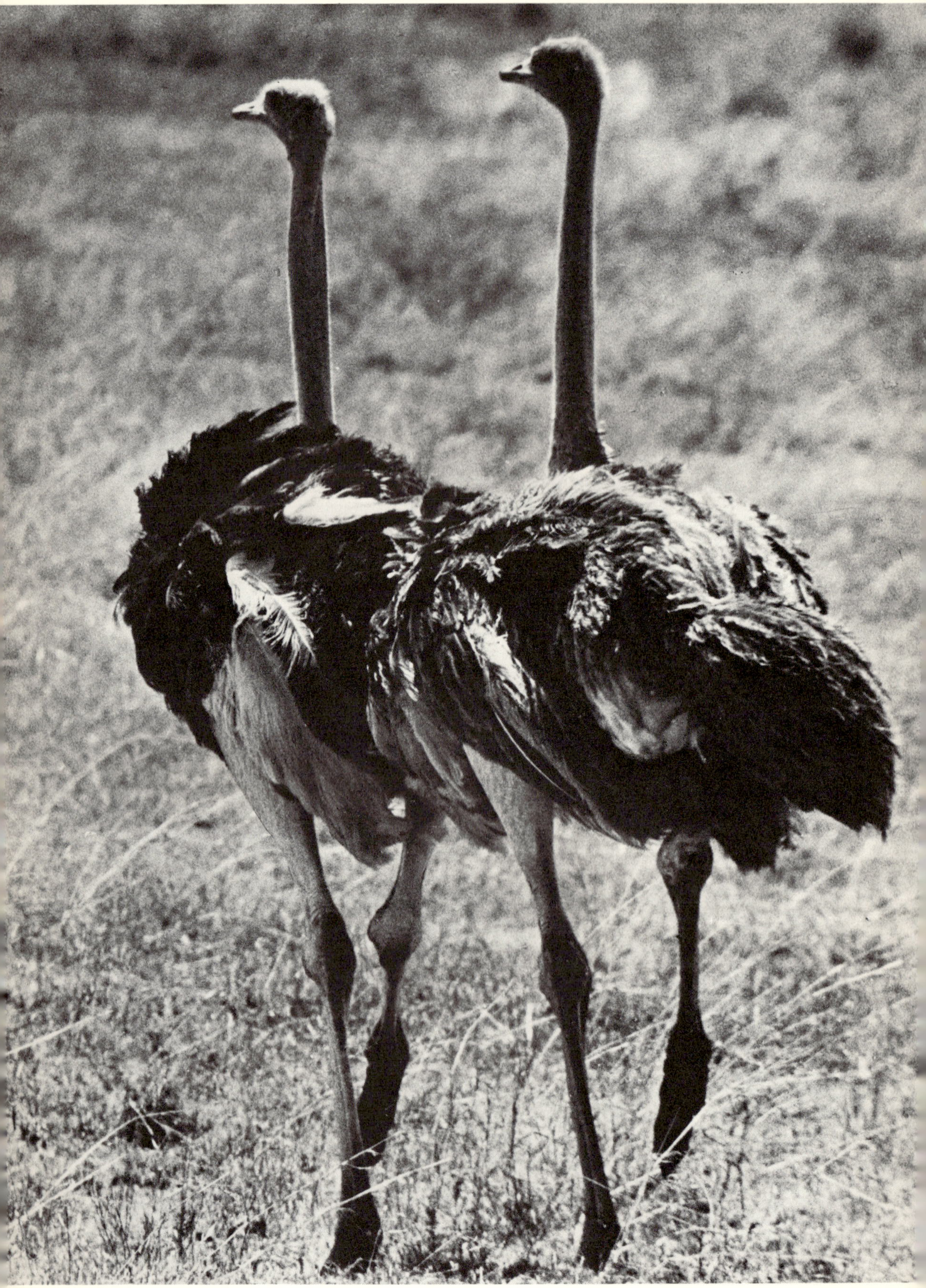

BIBLIOGRAPHY

Africana. Official quarterly handbook of the East African Wildlife Society. Nairobi. (Periodical.)

Bell, R. H. V. "The Use of the Herb Layer by Grazing Ungulates in the Serengeti," Watson, A. (ed.). *Animal Populations in Relation to Their Food Resources*. British Ecological Society Symposia, No. 10. Edinburgh: Blackwell, 1970.

Black, J. *The Dominion of Man*. Edinburgh: Edinburgh University Press, 1970.

Cloudsley-Thompson, J. L. *Animal Twilight, Man and Game in Eastern Africa*. Chester Springs, Pennsylvania: Dufour, 1967.

———. *The Zoology of Tropical Africa*. New York: Norton, 1969.

Cott, H. B. "The Nile Crocodile in Uganda and Northern Rhodesia," *Transactions of the Zoological Society of London* Vol. 29, Part 4, 1961.

Dale, I. R. and Greenway, P. J. *Kenya Trees and Shrubs*. Nairobi: Buchanan's Kenya Estates, Ltd., 1961.

Davies, W. and Skidmore, C. L. (eds.). *Tropical Pastures*. London: Faber and Faber, Ltd., 1966.

Ostriches are not at all rare in East Africa. You see them running along at a fine trot— well-adapted, strong, quick birds. They have a perfect view of their surroundings from their large, shaded eyes which are two and a half meters above the ground.

Delwiche, C. C. "The Nitrogen Cycle," *Scientific American* Vol. 223, No. 3, 1970.

Dorst, J. and Dandelot, P. *A Field Guide to the Larger Mammals of Africa*. London: Collins, 1969; Peterson Field Guide Series, 1970.

Ecologist, The. Wadebridge, Cornwall. (Monthly periodical.)

Elliot, H. F. L. (ed.). *Ecology of Man in the Tropical Environment*. IUCN Publication. New series, No. 4, 1964.

Estes, R. D. "The Comparative Behaviour of Grant's and Thomson's Gazelles," *Journal of Mammalogy* Vol. 48, 1967.

Fisher, J., Simon, N., and Vincent, J. *Wildlife in Danger*. New York: Viking, 1969.

Foster, J. B. and Dagg, A. I. "Notes on the Biology of the Giraffe," *East African Wildlife Journal* Vol. 10, 1972.

Golley, F. B. and Misra, R. (eds.). *Tropical Ecology with an Emphasis on Organic Productivity*. Athens, Georgia: University of Georgia Press, 1972.

Innis, A. C. "The Behaviour of the Giraffe in Eastern Transvaal," *Proceedings of the Zoological Society of London* No. 131, 1958.

Kenya. *National Report on the Human Environment in Kenya*. Nairobi, 1971.

Kingdon, J. *East African Mammals*. Vol. 1: *An Atlas of Evolution in Africa*. London and New York: Academic Press, 1971.

Klopfer, P. H. *Behavioral Aspects of Ecology*. Englewood Cliffs, N.J.: Prentice-Hall, 1972.

Laws, R. M. "Elephants as Agents of Habitat and Landscape Change in East Africa," *Oikos* 21. Copenhagen, 1970.

Laws, R. M. and Parker, I. S. C. "Recent Studies of Elephant Populations in East Africa," *Symposia of the Zoological Society of London* No. 21, 1968.

Lundholm, B. (ed.). "Ecology and the Less Developed Countries," *Ecological Research Committee Bulletin* No. 13, 1971.

McIlroy, R. J. *An Introduction to Tropical Grassland Husbandry.* Oxford: Oxford University Press, 1972.

"Man in the Living Environment," *Report of the Workshop on Global Ecological Problems 1971.* Madison, Wisconsin, 1972.

Owen, D. F. *Animal Ecology in Tropical Africa.* Edinburgh and London: Oliver and Boyd, 1966.

Pratt, D. J. and Knight, J. "Bush-control Studies in the Drier Areas of Kenya," *Journal of Applied Ecology* Vol. 8, 1971.

Richards, P. W. *The Tropical Rain Forest.* Cambridge: Cambridge University Press, 1952.

Russell, W. M. S. *Man, Nature and History.* London: Aldus, 1967.

Sanderson, I. T. *Ivan Sanderson's Book of Great Jungles.* New York: Simon and Schuster, 1965.

Schaller, G. B. "Life of the King of Beasts," *National Geographic* No. 1, 1969.

Schenkel, R. and Schenkel-Hulliger, L. *Ecology and Behaviour of the Black Rhinosceros.* Hamburg: Verlag Paul Parey, 1969.

Smith, R. L. (ed.). *The Ecology of Man.* New York: Harper and Row, 1972.

Spinage, C. A. *The Book of the Giraffe.* Boston: Houghton Mifflin, 1968.

Thomas, M. F. and Whittington, G. W. (eds.). *Environment and Land Use in Africa.* London: Eyre Methuen, Ltd., 1969.

Uganda National Parks. Handbook. Kampala, 1971.

United Nations. *Report of the United Nations Conference on the Human Environment.* Stockholm, June 5–16, 1972. New York: United Nations, 1973.

Vesey-Fitzgerald, D. F. "Grazing Succession Among East African Game Animals," *Journal of Mammalogy* Vol. 41, 1960.

Watson, R. M. and Bell, R. H. V. "The Distribution, Abundance and Status of Elephant in the Serengeti Region of Northern Tanzania," *Journal of Applied Ecology* Vol. 6, No. 2, 1969.

Western, D. and Sindiyo, D. M. "The Status of the Amboseli Rhino Population," *East African Wildlife Journal* Vol. 10, 1972.

Williams, J. G. A. *A Field Guide to the Birds of East and Central Africa.* Boston: Houghton Mifflin, 1964.

———. *A Field Guide to the National Parks of East Africa.* Boston: Houghton Mifflin, 1968.

Wing, L. D. and Buss, I. O. *Elephants and Forests.* Wildlife Monographs No. 19, 1970.

INDEX

Aberdare Mountains (Kenya), 118
Africa, 27, 39, 55, 160; East, 27, 47, 59, 68, 76, 138, 139, 160, 161, 167, 192, 196; North, 67; tropical, 68; West, 172. *See also* names of countries
Albert, Lake (Uganda), 122, 128
Amboseli National Park (Kenya), viii, 142; rhinos of, 12, 13; lions of, 76–78
Antelope, 14, 39, 54, 58, 59, 66, 122, 139, 148, 156; impalas, 47, 58, 81, 167; kob, 48, 50, 52; kudu, 133; oribi, 46, 53
Ants, stinging, 34–35
Asia, 67, 160. *See also* Japan
Australia, 27

Baboons, 107
Bangladesh, 70
Birds, 28, 47, 128, 174, 188–205, 206
Budongo Forest (Uganda), 118, 120–21
Buffalo, 6, 9, 59, 68, 76, 81, 106, 112, 122, 150, 158, 160
Buffalo weaverbirds, 18
Bush pigs, 76

Carolinas, North and South, 73
Cattle, 40, 41, 53, 55, 58, 66, 138, 139, 143, 156, 160, 161–63, 203
Cattle egrets, 117, 118, 128
Central America, 183
Cobra, Egyptian, 122
Coke's hartebeest, 148
Colobus monkey (guereza), 118, 175
Cormorants, 203
Crakes, 107
Crocodiles, 96, 98–99, 100, 102, 104, 106–107

Deer, 99
Dung beetles, 124

Eagles, 192, 201
East Africa, 27, 47, 68, 138, 139, 160, 161, 167, 192, 196; national parks, 59, 76. *See also* names of countries
Edward, Lake, viii
Egrets *see* Cattle egrets
Egypt, 67
Egyptian cobra, 122
Eland, 56, 58, 160

Elephants, xii, 5, 6, 29, 34, 39, 106, 112, 117–35, 120–121, 123, 128, 130, 134, 143, 158, 186, 188, 199
Elk, 27–29
Euphrates River, 67
Europe, 47, 67, 183, 201. *See also* Sweden

Fish, 192–205
Fish eagles, 192, 200
Flamingos, 190, 192, 193, 194, 196, 198

Gazelles, xii, 59, 66, 80–81, 99, 156; gerenuk (giraffe), 132; Grant's, 138, 140, 160, 161; Thomson's, 66, 81, 136, 138, 149, 151, 158, 161
Gerenuk (giraffe gazelle), 132
Giraffes, xii, xiv, 2, 4, 5, 6, 7, 11, 12, 13, 14, 20, 22, 24, 27, 29, 34–35, 58, 66, 70, 81, 107, 122, 188
Gnus, 7–9, 59, 80, 81, 93, 139, 141, 142, 147, 150, 151, 167
Goats *see* Cattle
Grant's gazelle, 138, 140, 160, 161
Grebes, 192, 199
Guerezas (colobus monkeys), 118, 175

Hartebeests, 38, 146, 148
Herbivores, 58, 59, 66, 68, 81, 139, 151, 158
Herons, 29, 48, 117, 122, 192, 199
Hippopotamus, 5, 76, 96, 106, 110, 112, 114, 158, 160, 188, 199
Hornbills, 118
Hyena, 76, 93

Iceland, 144
Impalas, 47, 58, 81, 167
India, 70
Indian Ocean, 40, 125

Jackal, 199
Jackson's hartebeest, 38
Japan, 179

Kabalega National Park (Uganda), viii, 47, 99, 103, 119, 121–22, 126–27, 131
Kakamega (Kenya), 182–84, 185
Karamoja (Uganda), 54
Kenya, 47, 55, 67, 119, 138, 144, 161; Aberdare Mountains, 118; Amboseli National Park, viii, 12, 13, 76–78, 142; elephants in, 120; Kakamega, 182, 183, 184; Lake Nakuru National Park, viii, 187–205; Lake Rudolf, 125; Masailand, 39–41;

209

Kenya (*continued*)
  Nairobi National Park, viii, 196; Tsavo National Park, viii, 25, 34, 118
Kenya, Mount, 127
Kibale Forest Reserve (Uganda), 119
Kilimanjaro, Mount (Tanzania), viii, 76, 180
Kob, 48, 50, 52
Kudu, 133

Lake Manyara National Park (Tanzania), viii, 139
Lake Nakuru National Park (Kenya), viii, 187–205
Leopards, 122, 199
Lions, 39, 59, 68, 74, 75–96

Marabou stork, 194
Martins, 48, 122
Masailand (Kenya), 39–41
Mombasa, 53, 125
Monitor lizards, 107
Monkeys, 174; colobus, 118, 175
Mosquitoes, 192, 199
Murchison Park *see* Kabalega National Park

Nairobi National Park (Kenya), viii, 196
Naivasha, Lake, 201
Ngorongoro crater (Tanzania), 142
Ngorongoro National Park (Tanzania), viii, 92
Nile River *see* Victoria Nile
Njoro River, 203

Olduvai Gorge (Tanzania), 12
Oribi, 46, 53
Ostrich, 81, 202, 204, 206
Oxpeckers, 28

Pelicans, 190, 192, 198, 199
Piapiacs, 28

Queen Elizabeth Park, *see* Ruwenzori National Park

Rhinoceros, 5, 7, 12, 16, 18, 25, 27, 28, 30, 32, 34, 41, 66, 96, 122; black (hook-lipped), 9, 18; white (square-lipped), 10
Rhodesia, 107, 163
Rudolf, Lake (Kenya), 125
Rukwa, Lake (Tanzania), 158–60
Ruwenzori National Park (Uganda), viii, 47, 110
Rwindi-Rutshuru plain (Zaire), 125

Sand martin, 48, 122
Seronera Valley, 125–26

Serengeti National Park (Tanzania), viii, 2–5, 6–12, 14, 66, 68, 72–73, 125, 139, 146, 149, 151; lions in, 76, 78, 80–94
Sierra Leone, 179
Snails, 188, 199
Somalia, 125
South Africa, 163
Soviet Union, 160
Squirrels, 47
Stork, 192, 199; Marabou, 194; open-bill, 188, 189
Suswa, Mount (Kenya), 39
Sweden, 26, 47, 55, 99, 139, 170, 201

Tanganyika, 6
Tanzania, viii, 7, 41, 47, 59–66, 67, 73, 120, 138; Lake Manyara National Park, viii, 139; Lake Rukwa, 158–60; Mount Kilimanjaro, viii, 76, 180; Ngorongoro National Park, viii, 92; Serengeti National Park, viii, 2–5, 6–12, 14, 66, 68, 72–73, 76, 78, 80–94, 125, 139, 146, 149, 151
Terns, 192
Thomson's gazelle, 66, 81, 136, 138, 149, 151–58, 161
Tigris River, 67
Topis, 146, 147, 149, 150, 151, 160, 167
Trinidad, 174
Tsavo National Park (Kenya), viii, 25, 34, 118, 126
Tsetse flies, 99, 139

Uganda, 47, 138, 161, 171; Budongo Forest, 118, 120–21; elephants in, 117–23, 126; Kabalega National Park, viii, 47, 99, 103, 119, 121–22, 126–27; Karamoja, 54; Kibale Forest Reserve, 119; Lake Albert, 122, 129; Ruwenzori National Park, viii, 47, 110

Victoria Nile, 99, 106–7

Warthogs, 39, 76, 78, 80, 85–88, 146
Weaverbirds, 18, 96
West Indies, 174
Wood ibis, 196

Yellow wagtails, 29
Yemen, 68

Zaire, viii, 121; Parc des Virunga, 125
Zebras, xii, 5, 9, 14, 54, 66, 68, 70, 72, 73, 80, 81, 139, 141, 142, 147, 149, 150, 151, 152, 156, 157, 158, 167
Zebus, 145, 160. *See also* Cattle